the AMAZING SPIDER-MAN
DANGER ZONE

AMAZING SPIDER-MAN #692-694
Writer: **DAN SLOTT**
Penciler: **HUMBERTO RAMOS**
Inker: **VICTOR OLAZABA**
Colorist: **EDGAR DELGADO**
Letterer: **VC'S CHRIS ELIOPOULOS**

AVENGING SPIDER-MAN #11
Writer: **ZEB WELLS**
Artist: **STEVE DILLON**
Colorist: **FRANK MARTIN JR.**
Letterer: **VC'S CHRIS ELIOPOULOS**

AMAZING SPIDER-MAN #695-697
Writer: **DAN SLOTT** & **CHRISTOS GAGE**
Penciler: **GIUSEPPE CAMUNCOLI**
Inker: **DAN GREEN**
Colorist: **ANTONIO FABELA**
Letterer: **VC'S CHRIS ELIOPOULOS**

Assistant Editor: **ELLIE PYLE** • Associate Editor: **SANA AMANAT**
Editor: **STEPHEN WACKER** • Executive Editor: **TOM BREVOORT**

Dedicated to Steve, Stan, John, Gil, Roy, Gerry, Ross and everyone who paved the way.

Collection Editor: **JENNIFER GRÜNWALD** • Assistant Editors: **ALEX STARBUCK** & **NELSON RIBEIRO**
Editor, Special Projects: **MARK D. BEAZLEY** • Senior Editor, Special Projects: **JEFF YOUNGQUIST**
Senior Vice President of Sales: **DAVID GABRIEL** • SVP of Brand Planning & Communications: **MICHAEL PASCIULLO**

Editor in Chief: **AXEL ALONSO** • Chief Creative Officer: **JOE QUESADA** • Publisher: **DAN BUCKLEY** • Executive Producer: **ALAN FINE**

SPIDER-MAN: DANGER ZONE. Contains material originally published in magazine form as AMAZING SPIDER-MAN #692-697 and AVENGING SPIDER-MAN #11. First printing 2012. Hardcover ISBN# 978-0-7851-6009-0. Softcover ISBN# 978-0-7851-6010-6. Published by MARVEL WORLDWIDE, INC., a subsidiary of MARVEL ENTERTAINMENT, LLC. OFFICE OF PUBLICATION: 135 West 50th Street, New York, NY 10020. Copyright © 2012 and 2013 Marvel Characters, Inc. All rights reserved. Hardcover: $24.99 per copy in the U.S. and $27.99 in Canada (GST #R127032852). Softcover: $19.99 per copy in the U.S. and $21.99 in Canada (GST #R127032852). Canadian Agreement #40668537. All characters featured in this issue and the distinctive names and likenesses thereof, and all related indicia are trademarks of Marvel Characters, Inc. No similarity between any of the names, characters, persons, and/or institutions in this magazine with those of any living or dead person or institution is intended, and any such similarity which may exist is purely coincidental. **Printed in the U.S.A.** ALAN FINE, EVP - Office of the President, Marvel Worldwide, Inc. and EVP & CMO Marvel Characters B.V.; DAN BUCKLEY, Publisher & President - Print, Animation & Digital Divisions; JOE QUESADA, Chief Creative Officer; TOM BREVOORT, SVP of Publishing; DAVID BOGART, SVP of Operations & Procurement, Publishing; RUWAN JAYATILLEKE, SVP & Associate Publisher, Publishing; C.B. CEBULSKI, SVP of Creator & Content Development; DAVID GABRIEL, SVP of Publishing Sales & Circulation; MICHAEL PASCIULLO, SVP of Brand Planning & Communications; JIM O'KEEFE, VP of Operations & Logistics; DAN CARR, Executive Director of Publishing Technology; SUSAN CRESPI, Editorial Operations Manager; ALEX MORALES, Publishing Operations Manager; STAN LEE, Chairman Emeritus. For information regarding advertising in Marvel Comics or on Marvel.com, please contact Niza Disla,

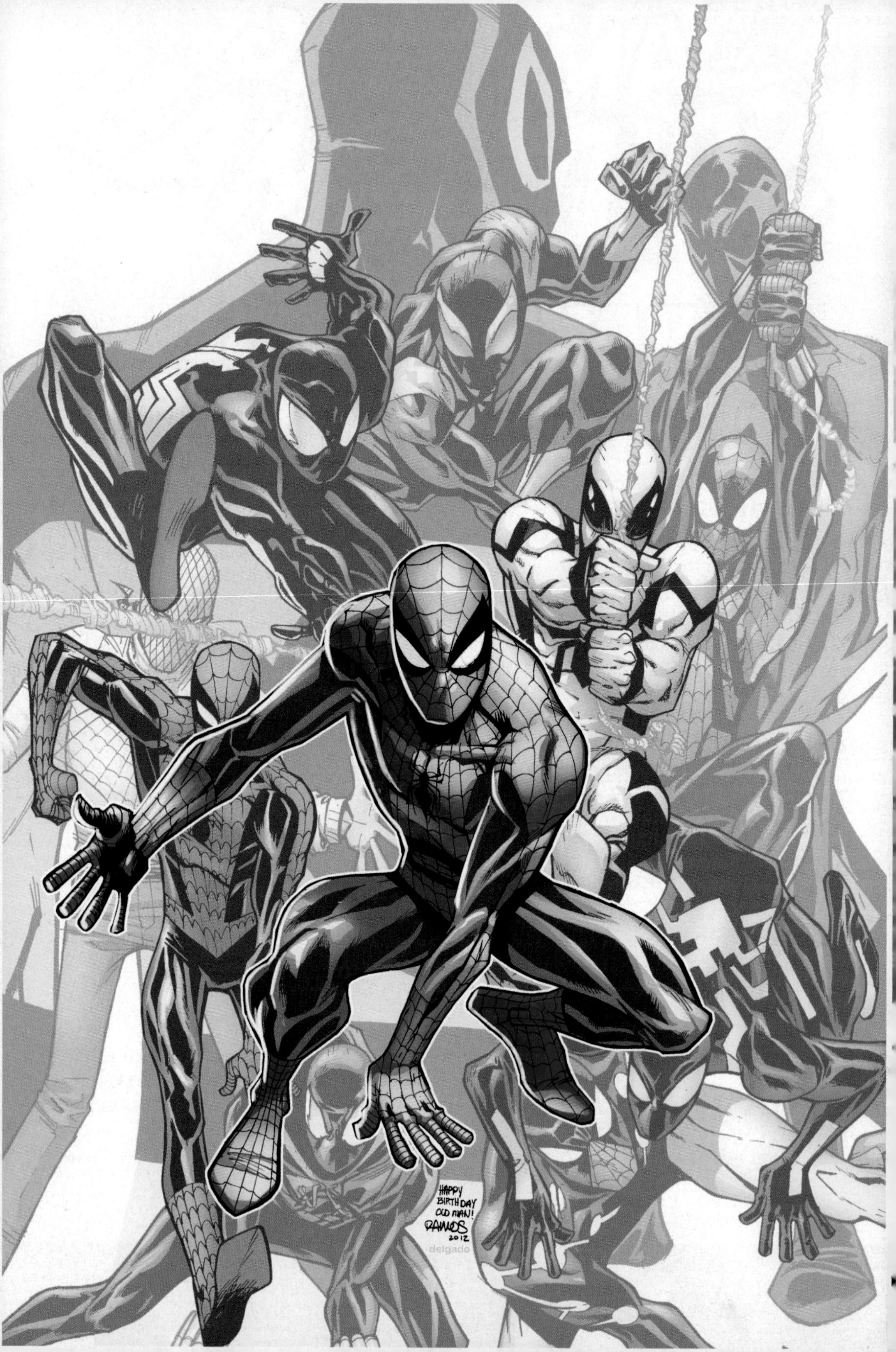
HAPPY BIRTHDAY OLD MAN!
RAMOS 2012
delgado

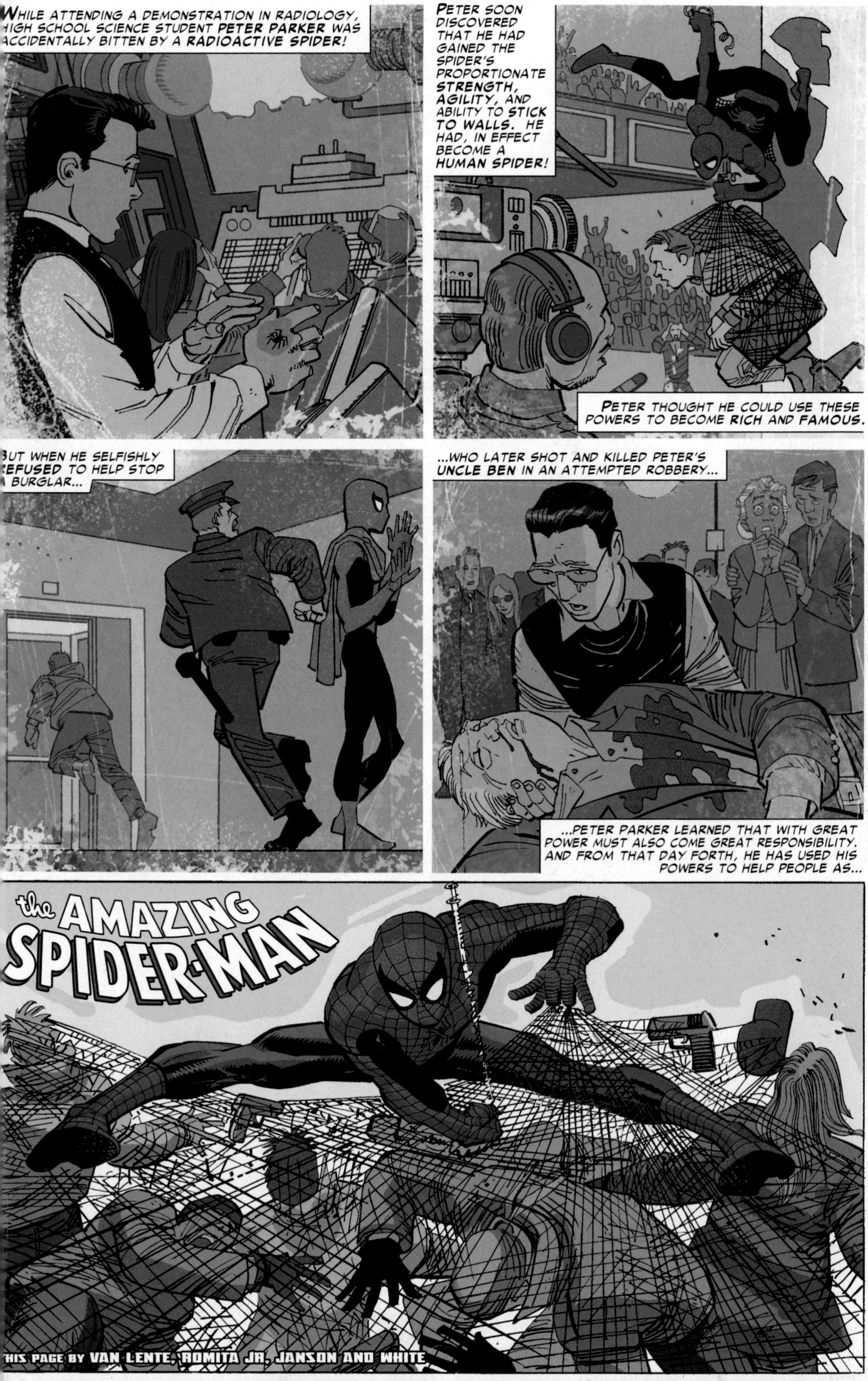
WHILE ATTENDING A DEMONSTRATION IN RADIOLOGY, HIGH SCHOOL SCIENCE STUDENT PETER PARKER WAS ACCIDENTALLY BITTEN BY A RADIOACTIVE SPIDER!
PETER SOON DISCOVERED THAT HE HAD GAINED THE SPIDER'S PROPORTIONATE STRENGTH, AGILITY, AND ABILITY TO STICK TO WALLS. HE HAD, IN EFFECT BECOME A HUMAN SPIDER!
PETER THOUGHT HE COULD USE THESE POWERS TO BECOME RICH AND FAMOUS.
BUT WHEN HE SELFISHLY REFUSED TO HELP STOP A BURGLAR...
...WHO LATER SHOT AND KILLED PETER'S UNCLE BEN IN AN ATTEMPTED ROBBERY...
...PETER PARKER LEARNED THAT WITH GREAT POWER MUST ALSO COME GREAT RESPONSIBILITY. AND FROM THAT DAY FORTH, HE HAS USED HIS POWERS TO HELP PEOPLE AS...
the AMAZING SPIDER-MAN
THIS PAGE BY VAN LENTE, ROMITA JR, JANSON AND WHITE

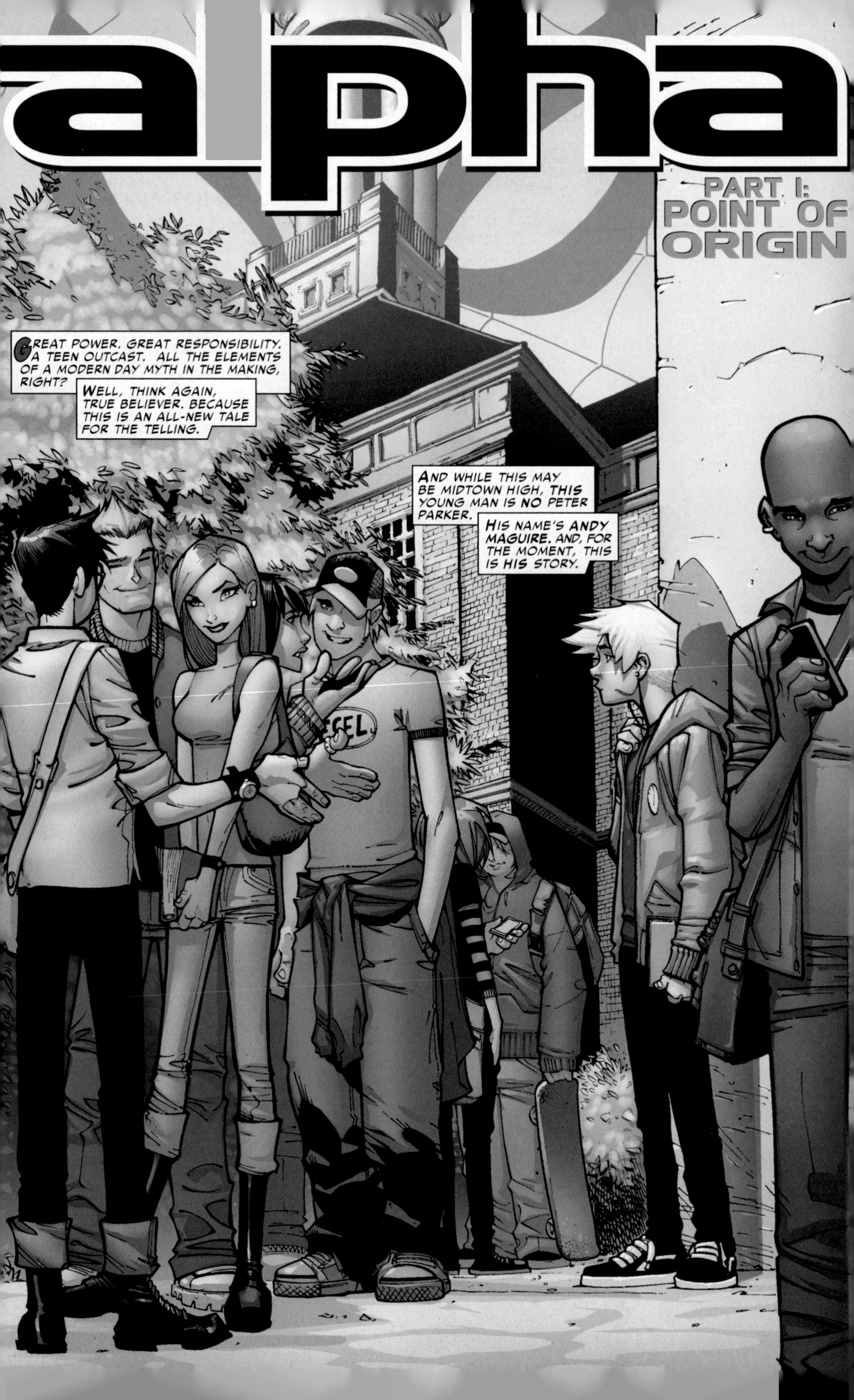
alpha
PART I: POINT OF ORIGIN
GREAT POWER. GREAT RESPONSIBILITY. A TEEN OUTCAST. ALL THE ELEMENTS OF A MODERN DAY MYTH IN THE MAKING, RIGHT?
WELL, THINK AGAIN, TRUE BELIEVER. BECAUSE THIS IS AN ALL-NEW TALE FOR THE TELLING.
AND WHILE THIS MAY BE MIDTOWN HIGH, THIS YOUNG MAN IS NO PETER PARKER.
HIS NAME'S ANDY MAGUIRE. AND, FOR THE MOMENT, THIS IS HIS STORY.

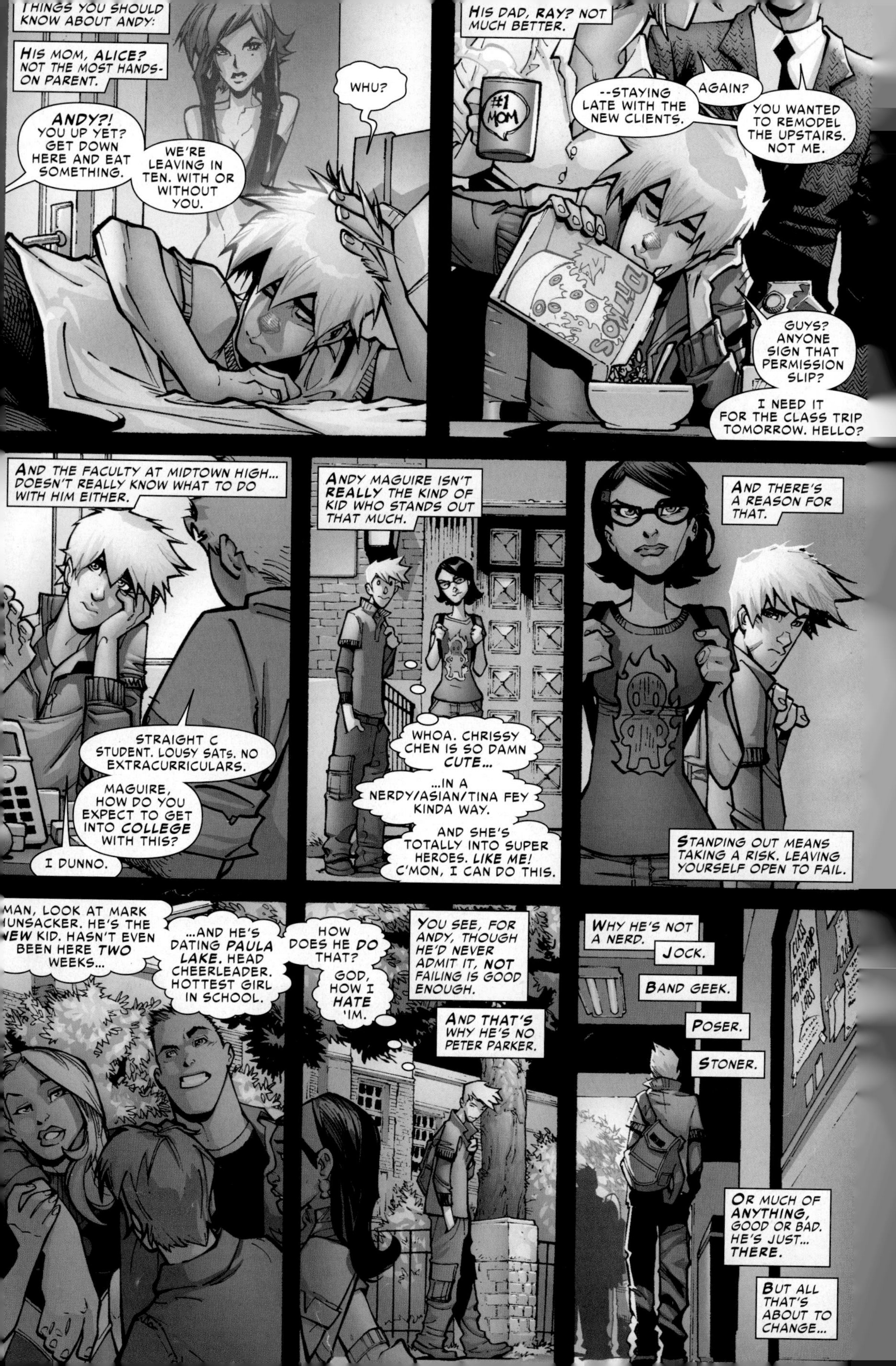

THINGS YOU SHOULD KNOW ABOUT ANDY:
HIS MOM, ALICE? NOT THE MOST HANDS-ON PARENT.
ANDY?! YOU UP YET? GET DOWN HERE AND EAT SOMETHING.
WE'RE LEAVING IN TEN. WITH OR WITHOUT YOU.
WHU?
HIS DAD, RAY? NOT MUCH BETTER.
#1 MOM
--STAYING LATE WITH THE NEW CLIENTS.
AGAIN?
YOU WANTED TO REMODEL THE UPSTAIRS. NOT ME.
GUYS? ANYONE SIGN THAT PERMISSION SLIP?
I NEED IT FOR THE CLASS TRIP TOMORROW. HELLO?
AND THE FACULTY AT MIDTOWN HIGH... DOESN'T REALLY KNOW WHAT TO DO WITH HIM EITHER.
STRAIGHT C STUDENT. LOUSY SATS. NO EXTRACURRICULARS.
MAGUIRE, HOW DO YOU EXPECT TO GET INTO COLLEGE WITH THIS?
I DUNNO.
ANDY MAGUIRE ISN'T REALLY THE KIND OF KID WHO STANDS OUT THAT MUCH.
WHOA. CHRISSY CHEN IS SO DAMN CUTE...
...IN A NERDY/ASIAN/TINA FEY KINDA WAY.
AND SHE'S TOTALLY INTO SUPER HEROES. LIKE ME! C'MON, I CAN DO THIS.
AND THERE'S A REASON FOR THAT.
STANDING OUT MEANS TAKING A RISK. LEAVING YOURSELF OPEN TO FAIL.
MAN, LOOK AT MARK HUNSACKER. HE'S THE NEW KID. HASN'T EVEN BEEN HERE TWO WEEKS...
...AND HE'S DATING PAULA LAKE. HEAD CHEERLEADER. HOTTEST GIRL IN SCHOOL.
HOW DOES HE DO THAT?
GOD, HOW I HATE 'IM.
YOU SEE, FOR ANDY, THOUGH HE'D NEVER ADMIT IT, NOT FAILING IS GOOD ENOUGH.
AND THAT'S WHY HE'S NO PETER PARKER.
WHY HE'S NOT A NERD.
JOCK.
BAND GEEK.
POSER.
STONER.
OR MUCH OF ANYTHING, GOOD OR BAD. HE'S JUST... THERE.
BUT ALL THAT'S ABOUT TO CHANGE...

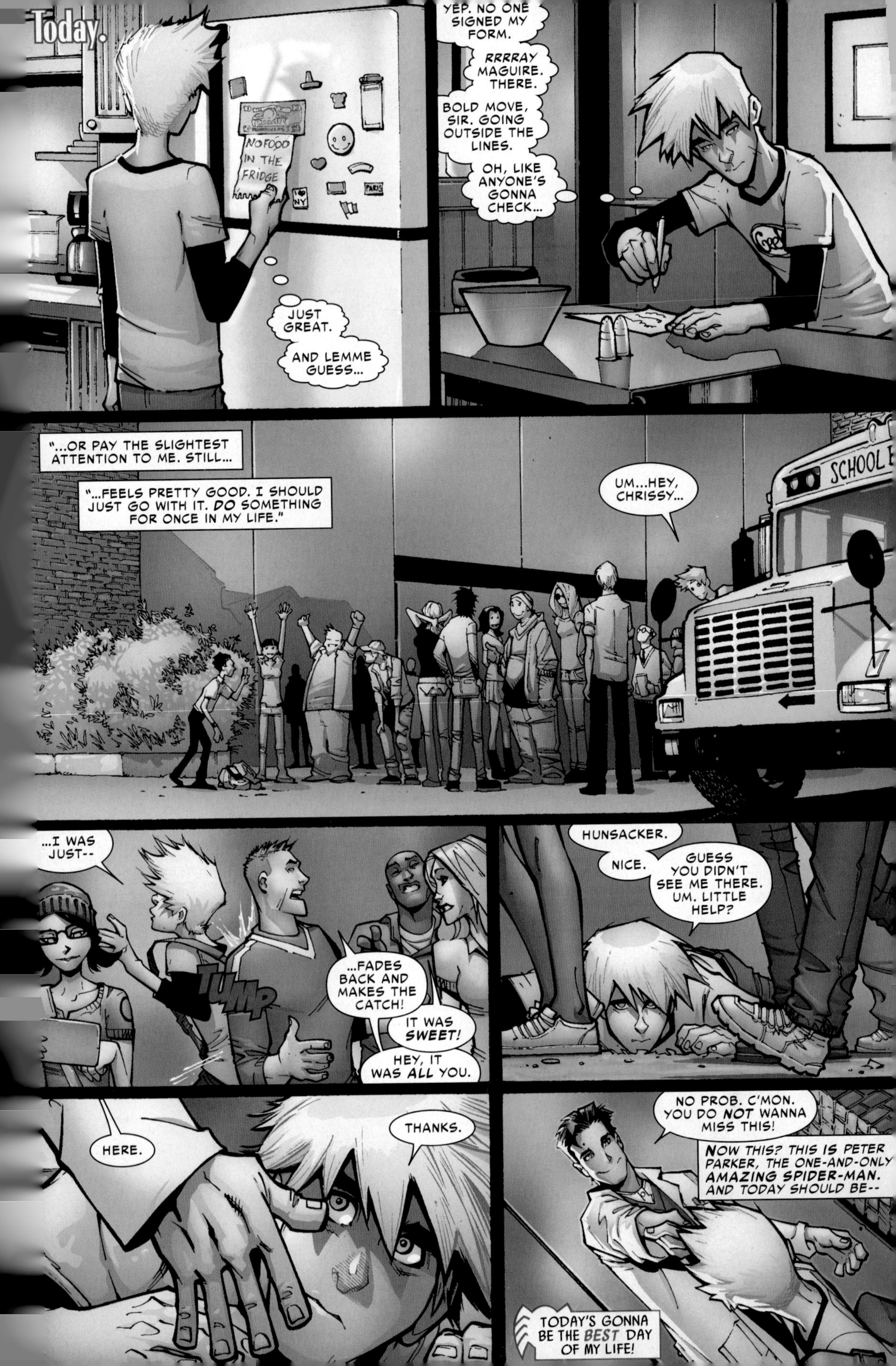
Today.
NO FOOD IN THE FRIDGE
PARIS
I ♥ NY
JUST GREAT.
AND LEMME GUESS...
YEP. NO ONE SIGNED MY FORM.
RRRRAY MAGUIRE. THERE.
BOLD MOVE, SIR. GOING OUTSIDE THE LINES.
OH, LIKE ANYONE'S GONNA CHECK...
"...OR PAY THE SLIGHTEST ATTENTION TO ME. STILL...
"...FEELS PRETTY GOOD. I SHOULD JUST GO WITH IT. DO SOMETHING FOR ONCE IN MY LIFE."
UM...HEY, CHRISSY...
SCHOOL B
...I WAS JUST--
THUMP
...FADES BACK AND MAKES THE CATCH!
IT WAS SWEET!
HEY, IT WAS ALL YOU.
HUNSACKER.
NICE.
GUESS YOU DIDN'T SEE ME THERE. UM. LITTLE HELP?
HERE.
THANKS.
NO PROB. C'MON. YOU DO NOT WANNA MISS THIS!
NOW THIS? THIS IS PETER PARKER, THE ONE-AND-ONLY AMAZING SPIDER-MAN. AND TODAY SHOULD BE--
TODAY'S GONNA BE THE BEST DAY OF MY LIFE!

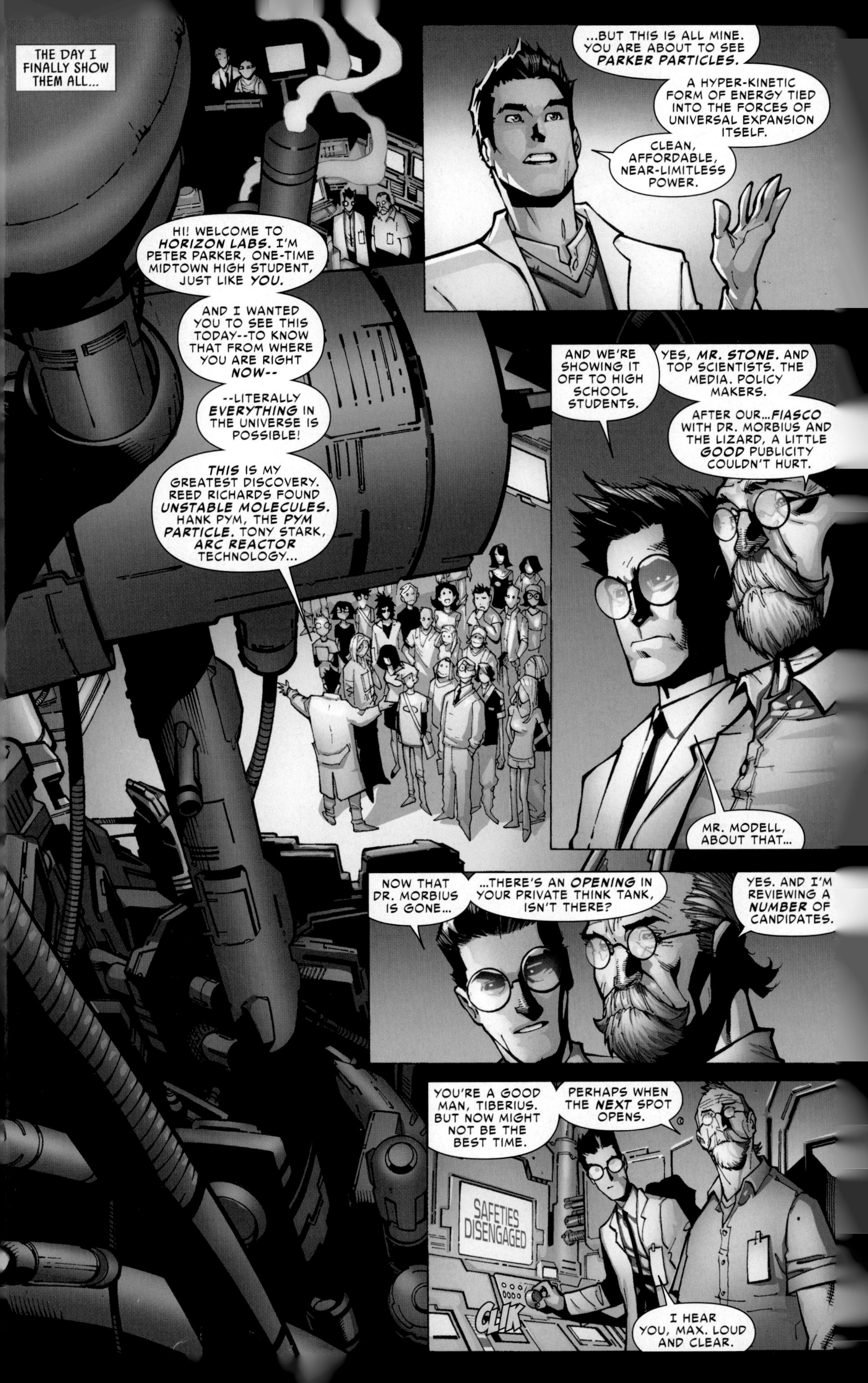
THE DAY I FINALLY SHOW THEM ALL...
HI! WELCOME TO HORIZON LABS. I'M PETER PARKER, ONE-TIME MIDTOWN HIGH STUDENT, JUST LIKE YOU.
AND I WANTED YOU TO SEE THIS TODAY--TO KNOW THAT FROM WHERE YOU ARE RIGHT NOW--
--LITERALLY EVERYTHING IN THE UNIVERSE IS POSSIBLE!
THIS IS MY GREATEST DISCOVERY. REED RICHARDS FOUND UNSTABLE MOLECULES. HANK PYM, THE PYM PARTICLE. TONY STARK, ARC REACTOR TECHNOLOGY...
...BUT THIS IS ALL MINE. YOU ARE ABOUT TO SEE PARKER PARTICLES.
A HYPER-KINETIC FORM OF ENERGY TIED INTO THE FORCES OF UNIVERSAL EXPANSION ITSELF.
CLEAN, AFFORDABLE, NEAR-LIMITLESS POWER.
AND WE'RE SHOWING IT OFF TO HIGH SCHOOL STUDENTS.
YES, MR. STONE. AND TOP SCIENTISTS. THE MEDIA. POLICY MAKERS.
AFTER OUR...FIASCO WITH DR. MORBIUS AND THE LIZARD, A LITTLE GOOD PUBLICITY COULDN'T HURT.
MR. MODELL, ABOUT THAT...
NOW THAT DR. MORBIUS IS GONE...
...THERE'S AN OPENING IN YOUR PRIVATE THINK TANK, ISN'T THERE?
YES. AND I'M REVIEWING A NUMBER OF CANDIDATES.
YOU'RE A GOOD MAN, TIBERIUS. BUT NOW MIGHT NOT BE THE BEST TIME.
PERHAPS WHEN THE NEXT SPOT OPENS.
SAFETIES DISENGAGED
CLIK
I HEAR YOU, MAX. LOUD AND CLEAR.

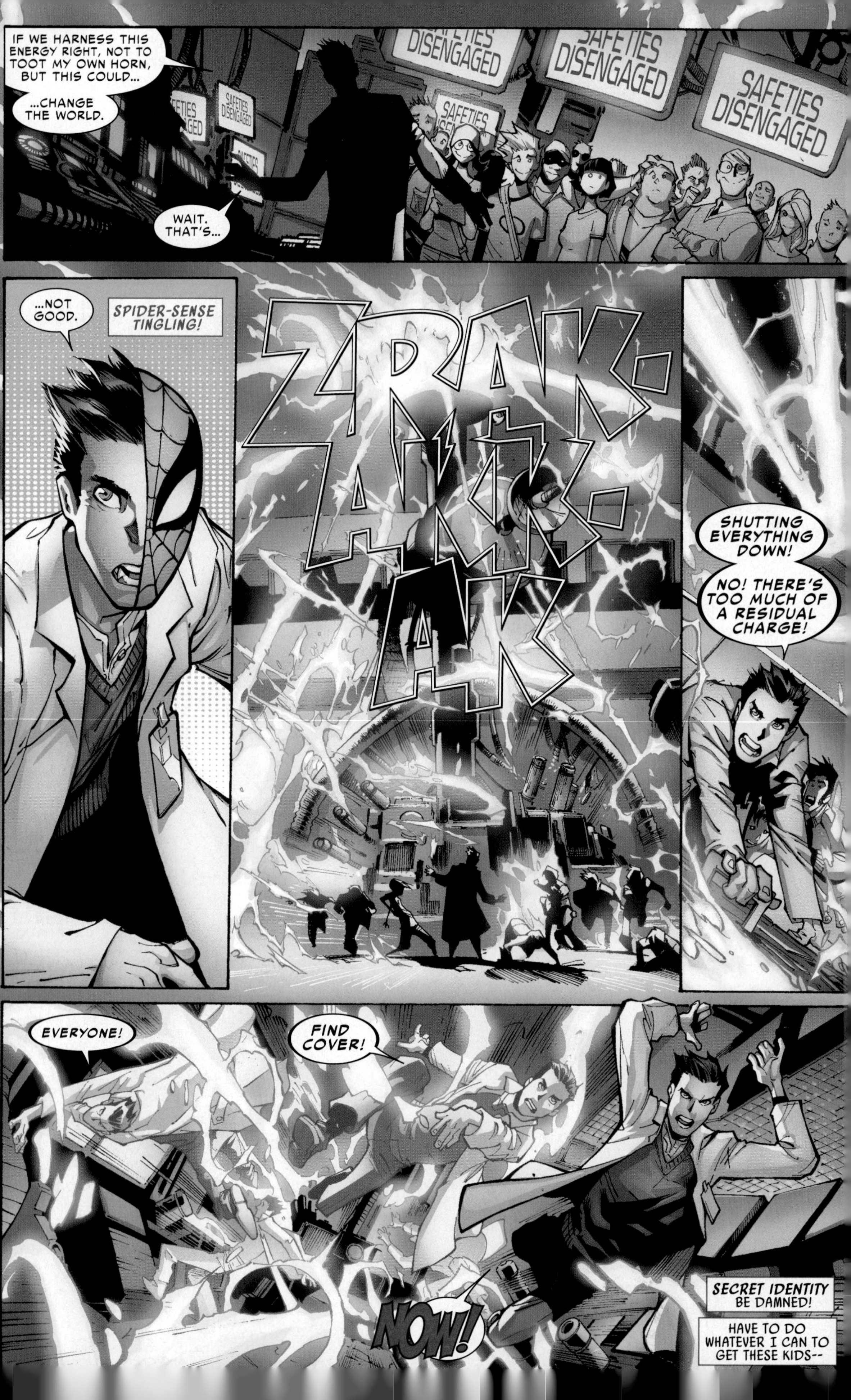
IF WE HARNESS THIS ENERGY RIGHT, NOT TO TOOT MY OWN HORN, BUT THIS COULD...
...CHANGE THE WORLD.
SAFETIES DISENGAGED
WAIT. THAT'S...
...NOT GOOD.
SPIDER-SENSE TINGLING!
ZRAK-AKK-AK
SHUTTING EVERYTHING DOWN!
NO! THERE'S TOO MUCH OF A RESIDUAL CHARGE!
EVERYONE!
FIND COVER!
NOW!
SECRET IDENTITY BE DAMNED!
HAVE TO DO WHATEVER I CAN TO GET THESE KIDS--

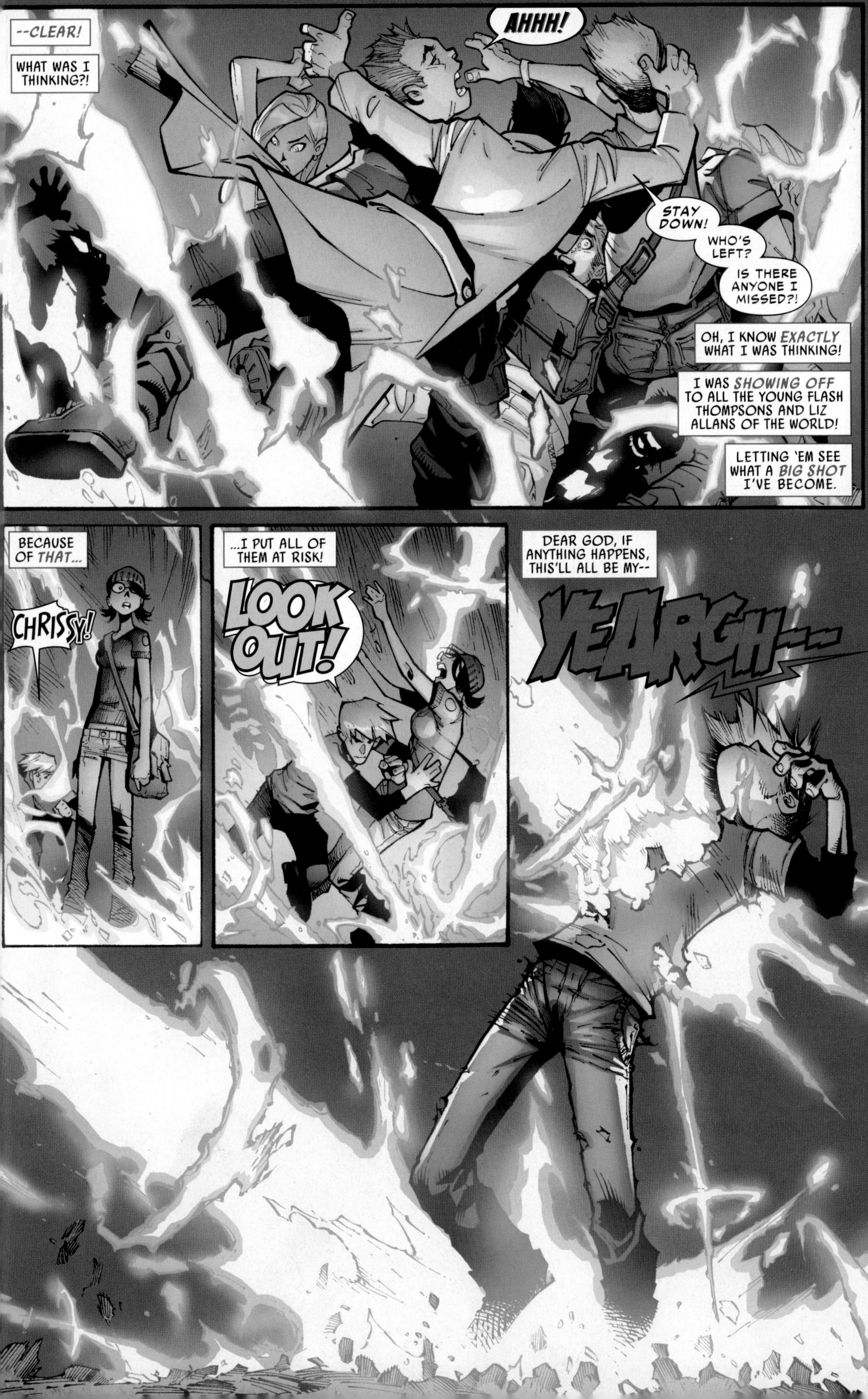
--CLEAR!
WHAT WAS I THINKING?!
AHHH!
STAY DOWN!
WHO'S LEFT?
IS THERE ANYONE I MISSED?!
OH, I KNOW EXACTLY WHAT I WAS THINKING!
I WAS SHOWING OFF TO ALL THE YOUNG FLASH THOMPSONS AND LIZ ALLANS OF THE WORLD!
LETTING 'EM SEE WHAT A BIG SHOT I'VE BECOME.
BECAUSE OF THAT...
CHRISSY!
...I PUT ALL OF THEM AT RISK!
LOOK OUT!
DEAR GOD, IF ANYTHING HAPPENS, THIS'LL ALL BE MY--
YEARGH--

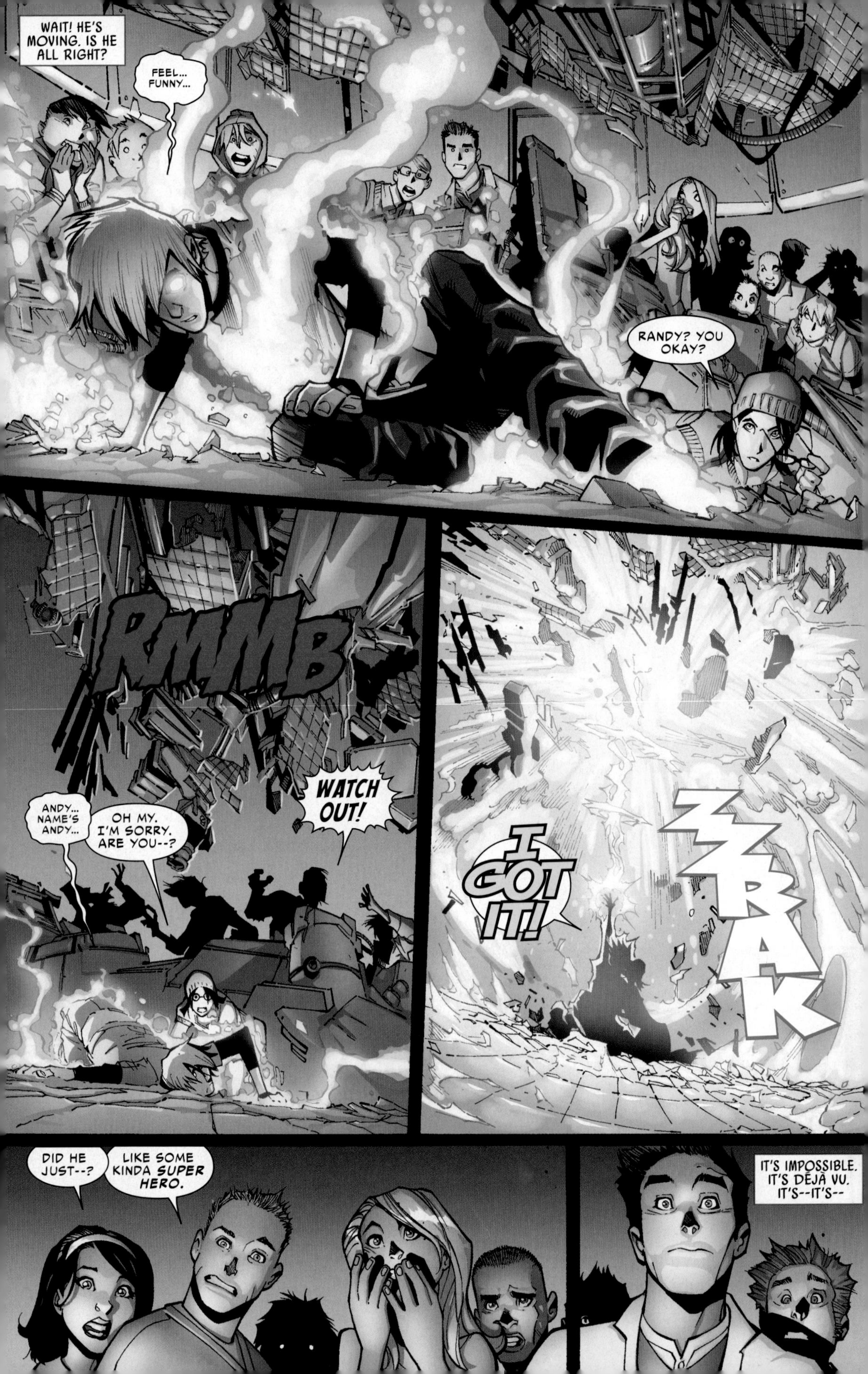
WAIT! HE'S MOVING. IS HE ALL RIGHT?
FEEL... FUNNY...
RANDY? YOU OKAY?
RMMB
ANDY... NAME'S ANDY...
OH MY. I'M SORRY. ARE YOU--?
WATCH OUT!
I GOT IT!
ZZRAK
DID HE JUST--?
LIKE SOME KINDA *SUPER HERO.*
IT'S IMPOSSIBLE. IT'S DÉJÀ VU. IT'S--IT'S--

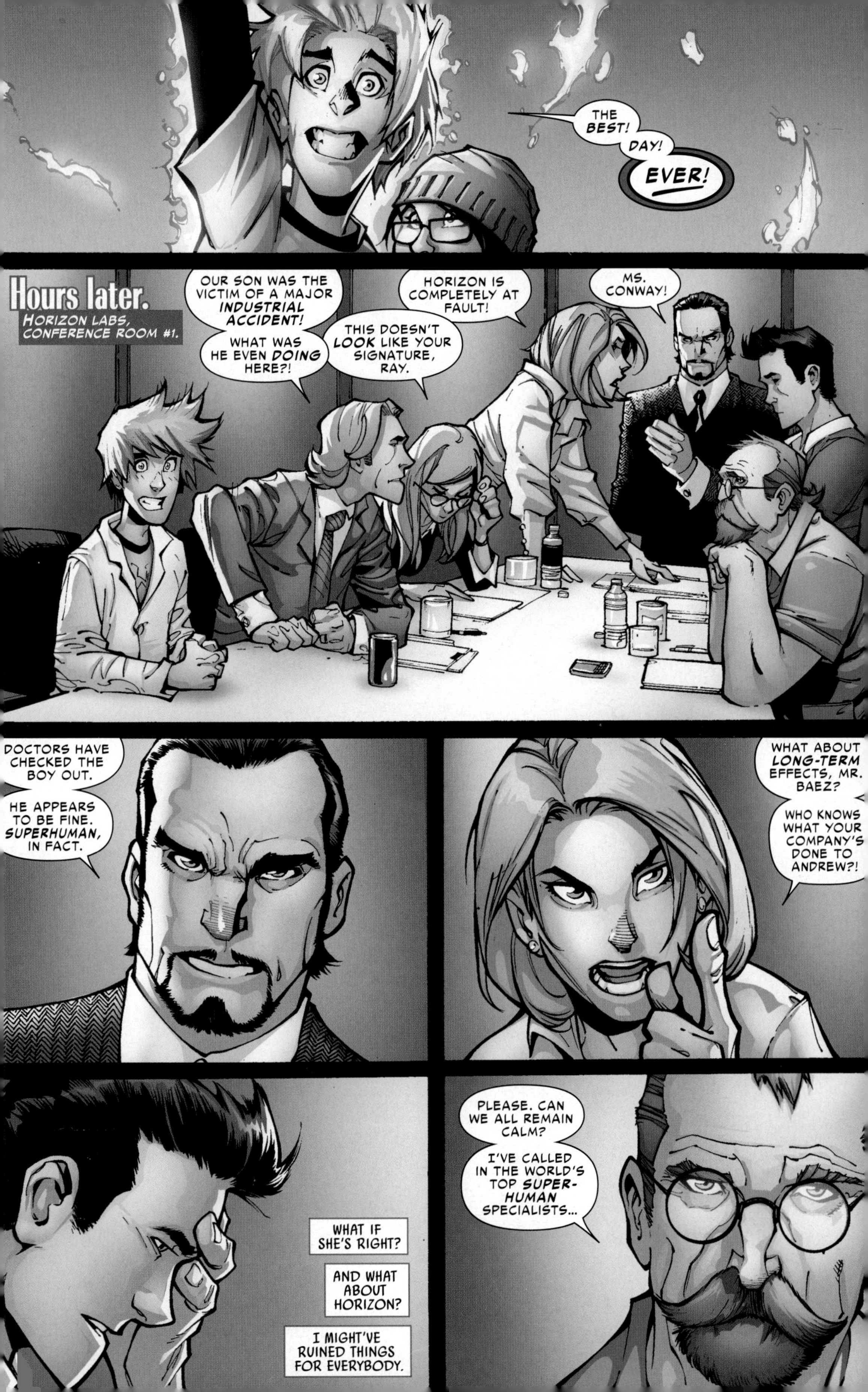
THE BEST! DAY! EVER!
Hours later.
HORIZON LABS, CONFERENCE ROOM #1.
OUR SON WAS THE VICTIM OF A MAJOR INDUSTRIAL ACCIDENT!
WHAT WAS HE EVEN DOING HERE?!
THIS DOESN'T LOOK LIKE YOUR SIGNATURE, RAY.
HORIZON IS COMPLETELY AT FAULT!
MS. CONWAY!
DOCTORS HAVE CHECKED THE BOY OUT.
HE APPEARS TO BE FINE. SUPERHUMAN, IN FACT.
WHAT ABOUT LONG-TERM EFFECTS, MR. BAEZ?
WHO KNOWS WHAT YOUR COMPANY'S DONE TO ANDREW?!
WHAT IF SHE'S RIGHT?
AND WHAT ABOUT HORIZON?
I MIGHT'VE RUINED THINGS FOR EVERYBODY.
PLEASE. CAN WE ALL REMAIN CALM?
I'VE CALLED IN THE WORLD'S TOP SUPER-HUMAN SPECIALISTS...

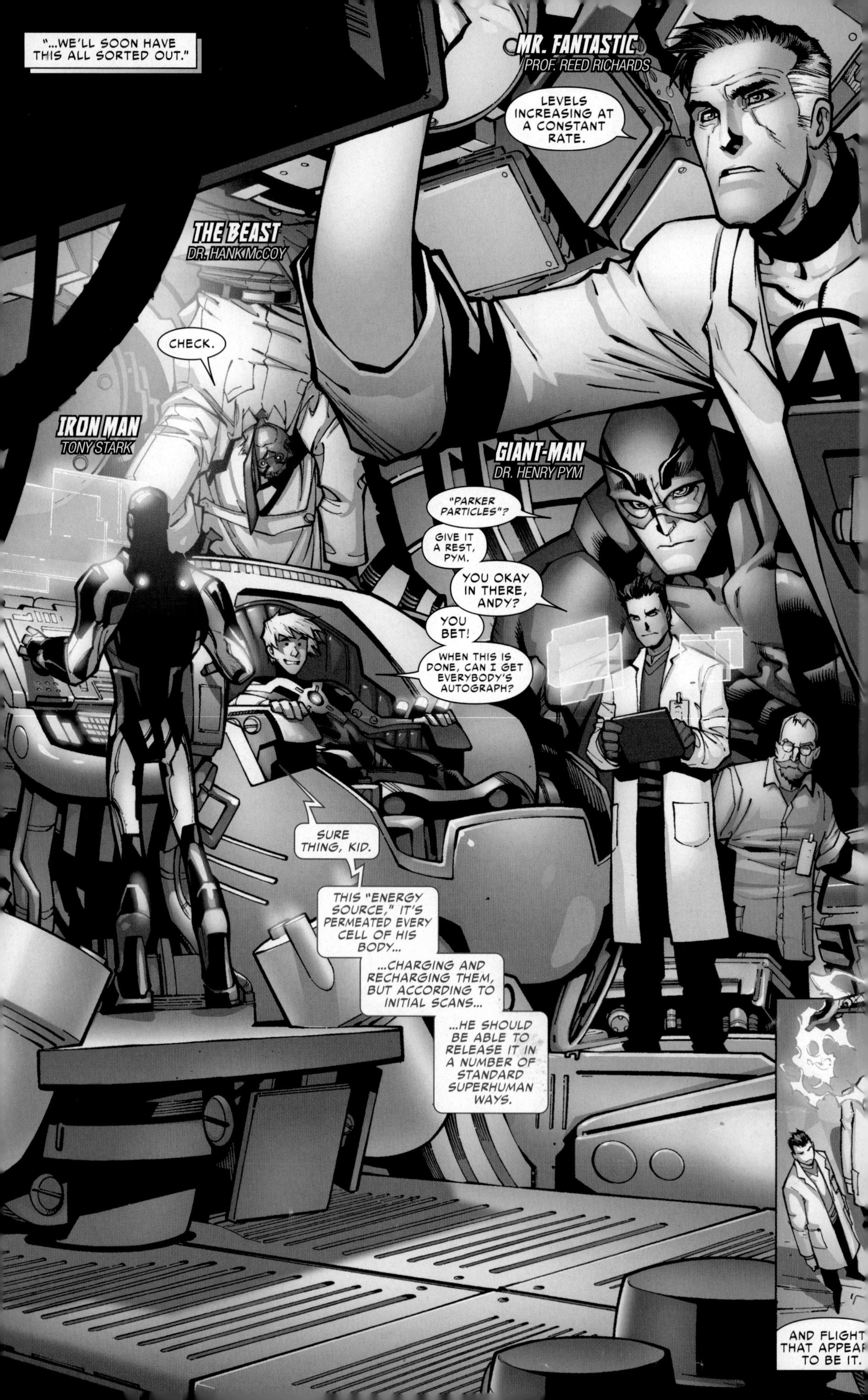
"...WE'LL SOON HAVE THIS ALL SORTED OUT."
MR. FANTASTIC
PROF. REED RICHARDS
LEVELS INCREASING AT A CONSTANT RATE.
THE BEAST
DR. HANK McCOY
CHECK.
IRON MAN
TONY STARK
GIANT-MAN
DR. HENRY PYM
"PARKER PARTICLES"?
GIVE IT A REST, PYM.
YOU OKAY IN THERE, ANDY?
YOU BET!
WHEN THIS IS DONE, CAN I GET EVERYBODY'S AUTOGRAPH?
SURE THING, KID.
THIS "ENERGY SOURCE," IT'S PERMEATED EVERY CELL OF HIS BODY...
...CHARGING AND RECHARGING THEM, BUT ACCORDING TO INITIAL SCANS...
...HE SHOULD BE ABLE TO RELEASE IT IN A NUMBER OF STANDARD SUPERHUMAN WAYS.
AND FLIGHT THAT APPEAR TO BE IT.

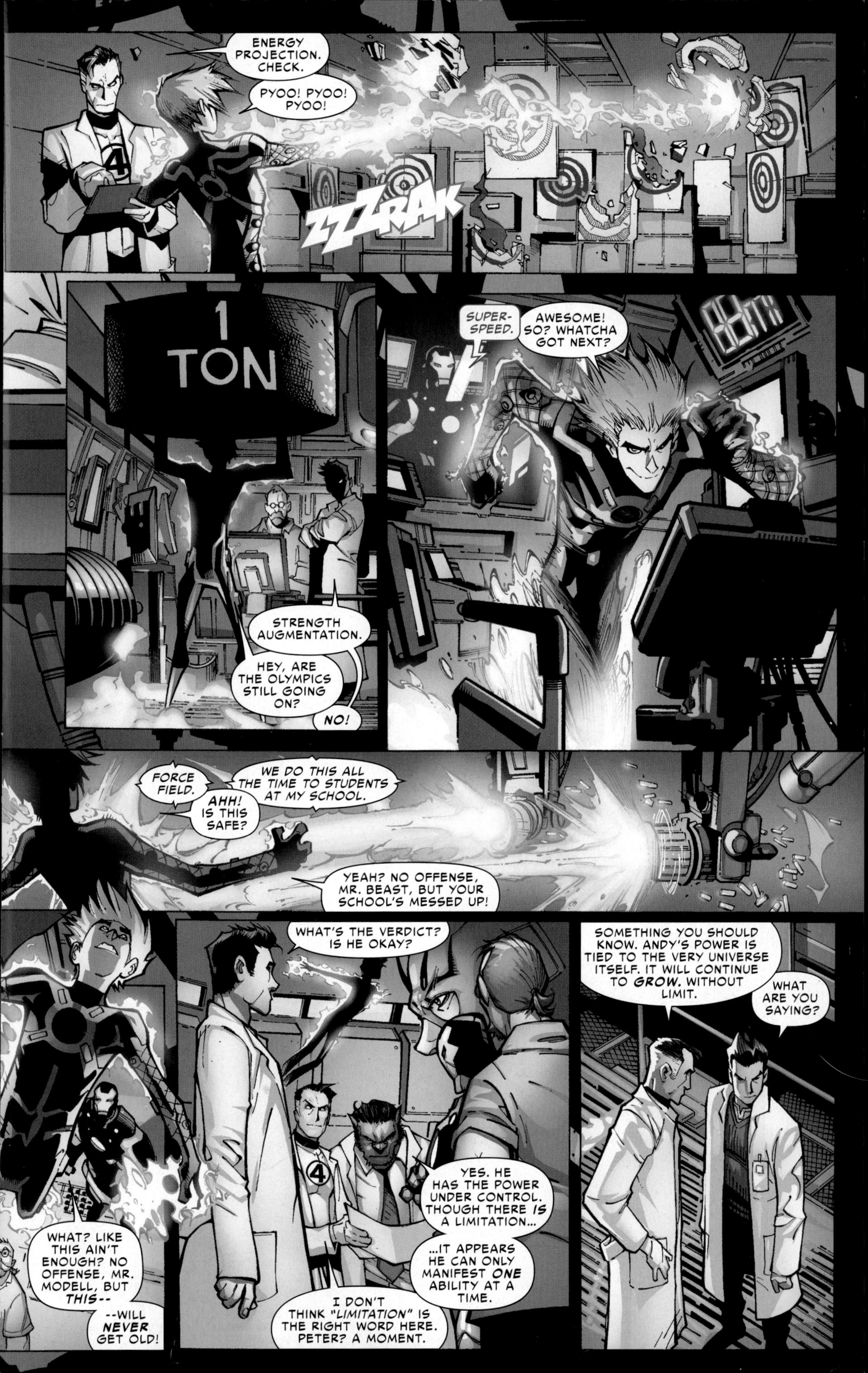
ENERGY PROJECTION. CHECK.
PYOO! PYOO! PYOO!
ZZZRAK
1 TON
STRENGTH AUGMENTATION.
HEY, ARE THE OLYMPICS STILL GOING ON?
NO!
SUPER-SPEED.
AWESOME! SO? WHATCHA GOT NEXT?
FORCE FIELD.
AHH! IS THIS SAFE?
WE DO THIS ALL THE TIME TO STUDENTS AT MY SCHOOL.
YEAH? NO OFFENSE, MR. BEAST, BUT YOUR SCHOOL'S MESSED UP!
WHAT? LIKE THIS AIN'T ENOUGH? NO OFFENSE, MR. MODELL, BUT THIS--
--WILL NEVER GET OLD!
WHAT'S THE VERDICT? IS HE OKAY?
YES. HE HAS THE POWER UNDER CONTROL. THOUGH THERE IS A LIMITATION...
...IT APPEARS HE CAN ONLY MANIFEST ONE ABILITY AT A TIME.
I DON'T THINK "LIMITATION" IS THE RIGHT WORD HERE. PETER? A MOMENT.
SOMETHING YOU SHOULD KNOW. ANDY'S POWER IS TIED TO THE VERY UNIVERSE ITSELF. IT WILL CONTINUE TO GROW. WITHOUT LIMIT.
WHAT ARE YOU SAYING?

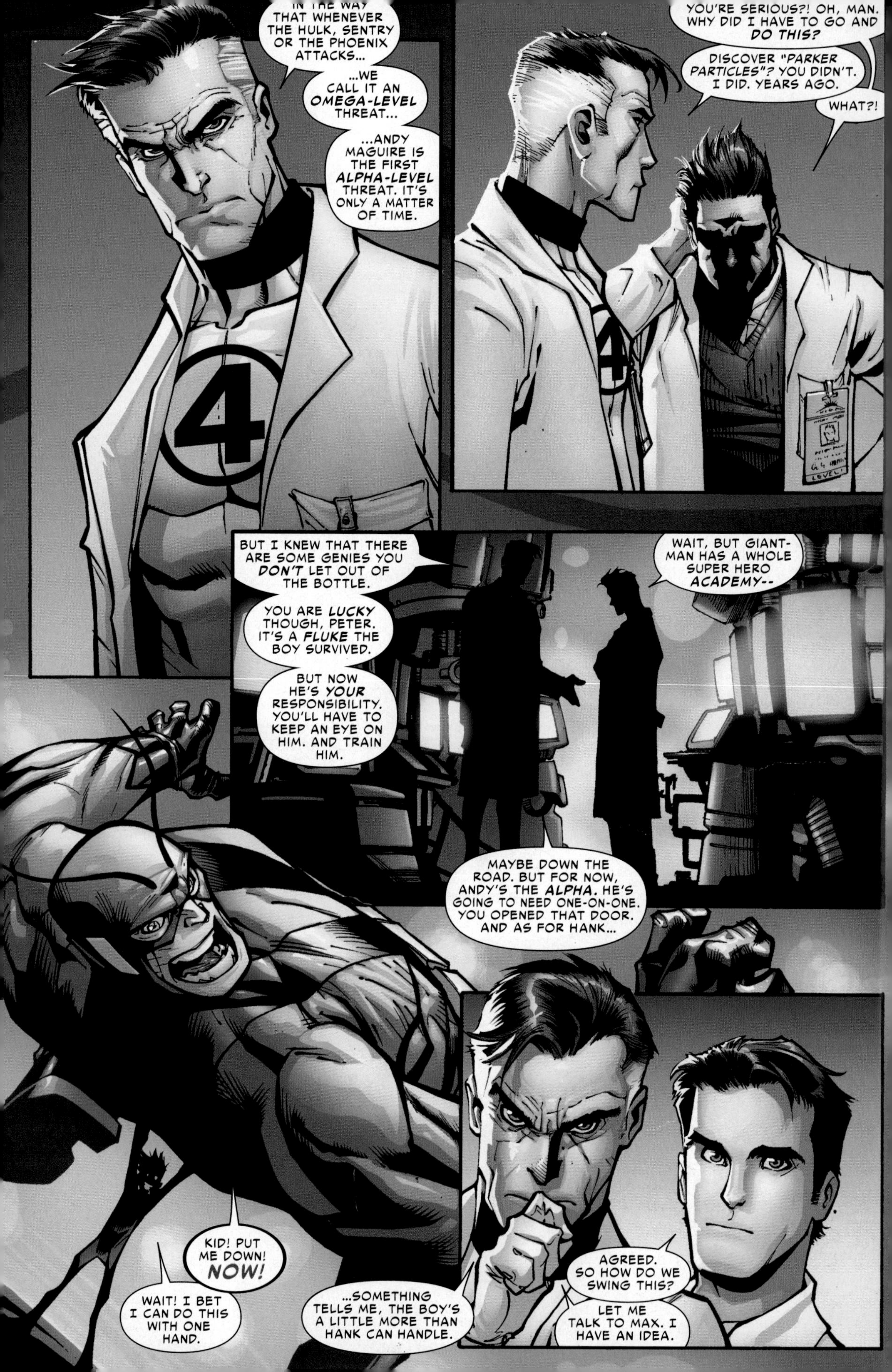
IN THE WAY THAT WHENEVER THE HULK, SENTRY OR THE PHOENIX ATTACKS...
...WE CALL IT AN OMEGA-LEVEL THREAT...
...ANDY MAGUIRE IS THE FIRST ALPHA-LEVEL THREAT. IT'S ONLY A MATTER OF TIME.
YOU'RE SERIOUS?! OH, MAN. WHY DID I HAVE TO GO AND DO THIS?
DISCOVER "PARKER PARTICLES"? YOU DIDN'T. I DID. YEARS AGO.
WHAT?!
BUT I KNEW THAT THERE ARE SOME GENIES YOU DON'T LET OUT OF THE BOTTLE.
YOU ARE LUCKY THOUGH, PETER. IT'S A FLUKE THE BOY SURVIVED.
BUT NOW HE'S YOUR RESPONSIBILITY. YOU'LL HAVE TO KEEP AN EYE ON HIM. AND TRAIN HIM.
WAIT, BUT GIANT-MAN HAS A WHOLE SUPER HERO ACADEMY--
MAYBE DOWN THE ROAD. BUT FOR NOW, ANDY'S THE ALPHA. HE'S GOING TO NEED ONE-ON-ONE. YOU OPENED THAT DOOR. AND AS FOR HANK...
KID! PUT ME DOWN! NOW!
WAIT! I BET I CAN DO THIS WITH ONE HAND.
...SOMETHING TELLS ME, THE BOY'S A LITTLE MORE THAN HANK CAN HANDLE.
AGREED. SO HOW DO WE SWING THIS?
LET ME TALK TO MAX. I HAVE AN IDEA.

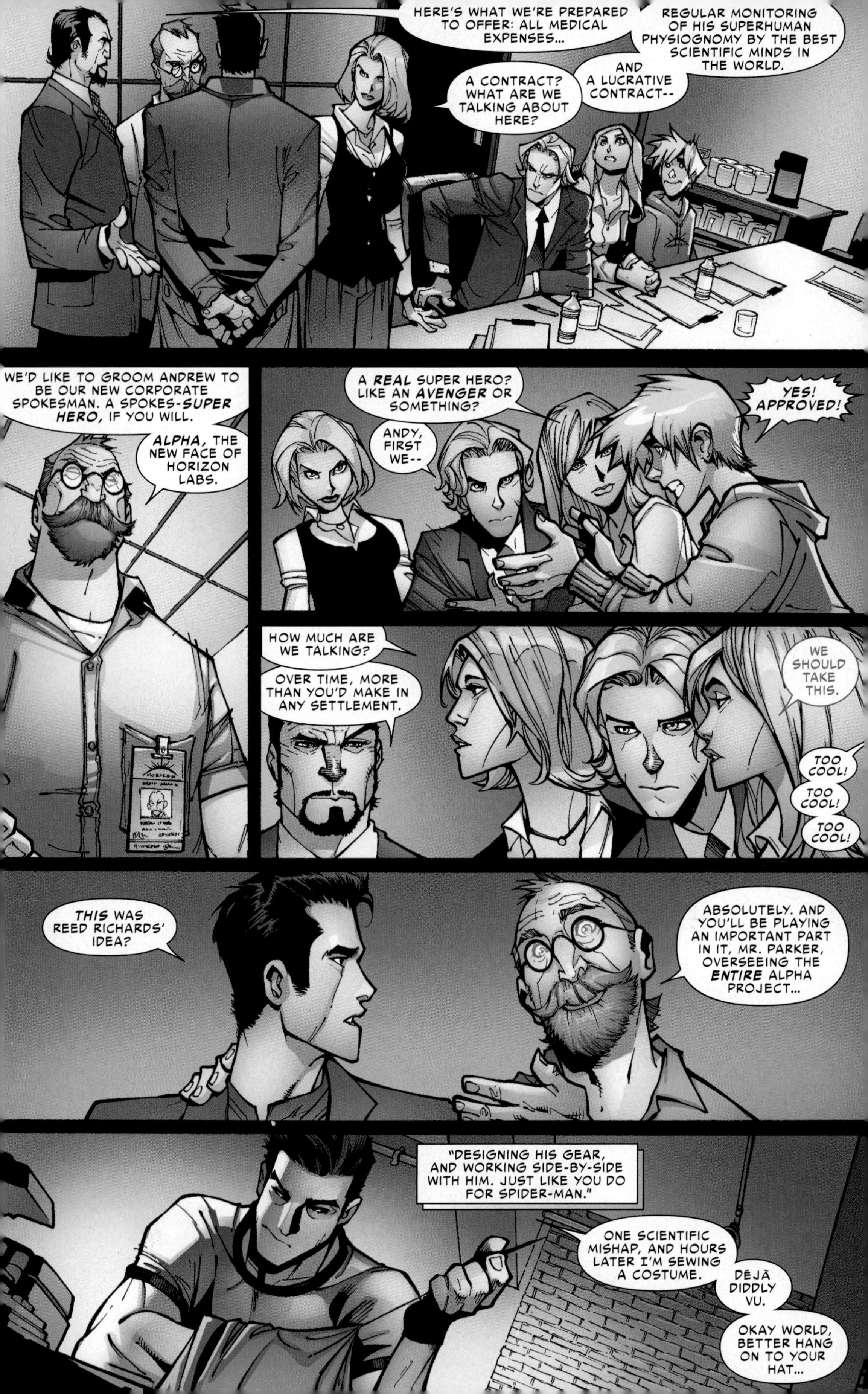

HERE'S WHAT WE'RE PREPARED TO OFFER: ALL MEDICAL EXPENSES...
REGULAR MONITORING OF HIS SUPERHUMAN PHYSIOGNOMY BY THE BEST SCIENTIFIC MINDS IN THE WORLD.
AND A LUCRATIVE CONTRACT--
A CONTRACT? WHAT ARE WE TALKING ABOUT HERE?
WE'D LIKE TO GROOM ANDREW TO BE OUR NEW CORPORATE SPOKESMAN. A SPOKES-SUPER HERO, IF YOU WILL.
ALPHA, THE NEW FACE OF HORIZON LABS.
A REAL SUPER HERO? LIKE AN AVENGER OR SOMETHING?
ANDY, FIRST WE--
YES! APPROVED!
HOW MUCH ARE WE TALKING?
OVER TIME, MORE THAN YOU'D MAKE IN ANY SETTLEMENT.
WE SHOULD TAKE THIS.
TOO COOL!
TOO COOL!
TOO COOL!
THIS WAS REED RICHARDS' IDEA?
ABSOLUTELY. AND YOU'LL BE PLAYING AN IMPORTANT PART IN IT, MR. PARKER, OVERSEEING THE ENTIRE ALPHA PROJECT...
"DESIGNING HIS GEAR, AND WORKING SIDE-BY-SIDE WITH HIM. JUST LIKE YOU DO FOR SPIDER-MAN."
ONE SCIENTIFIC MISHAP, AND HOURS LATER I'M SEWING A COSTUME.
DÉJÀ DIDDLY VU.
OKAY WORLD, BETTER HANG ON TO YOUR HAT...

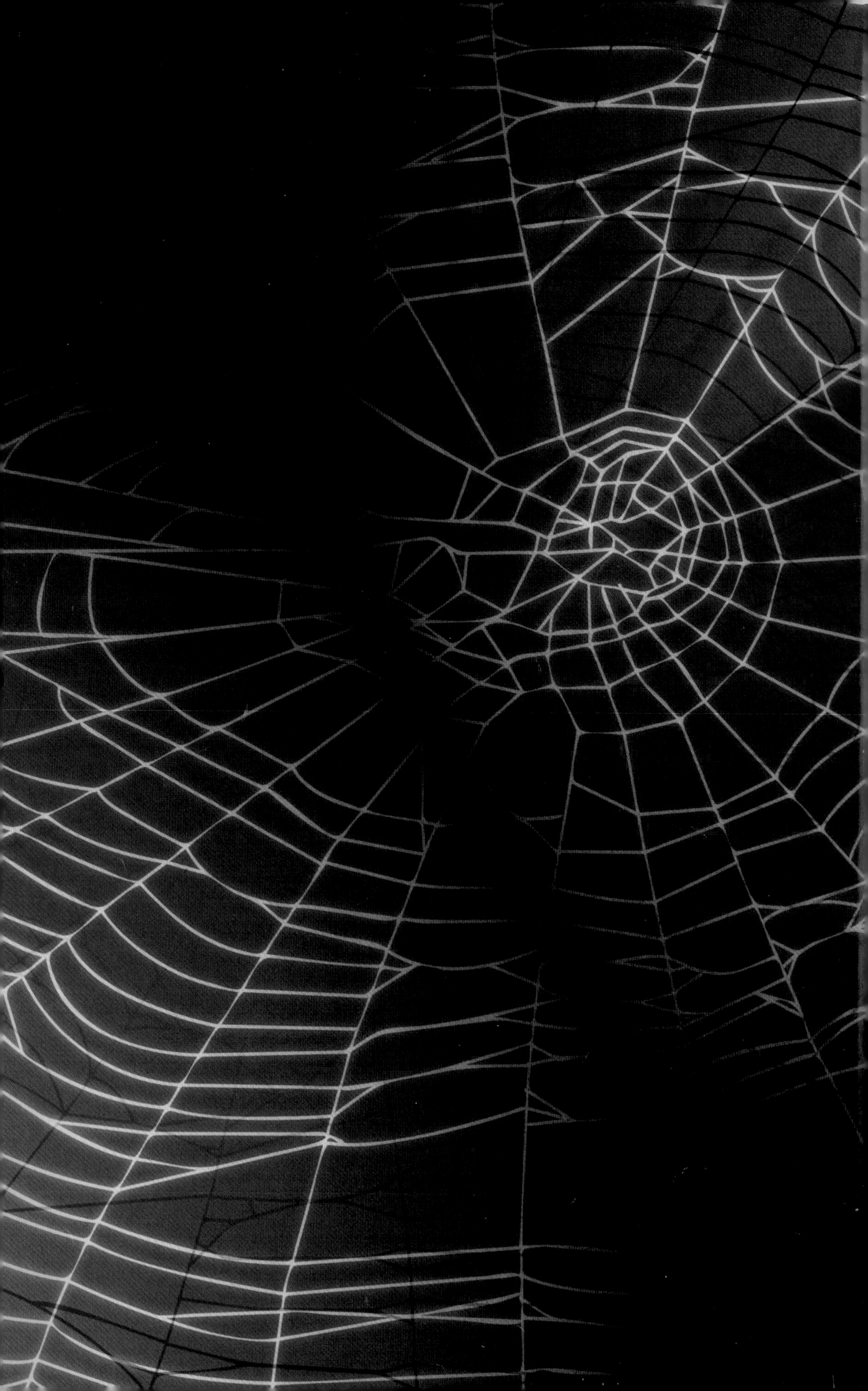

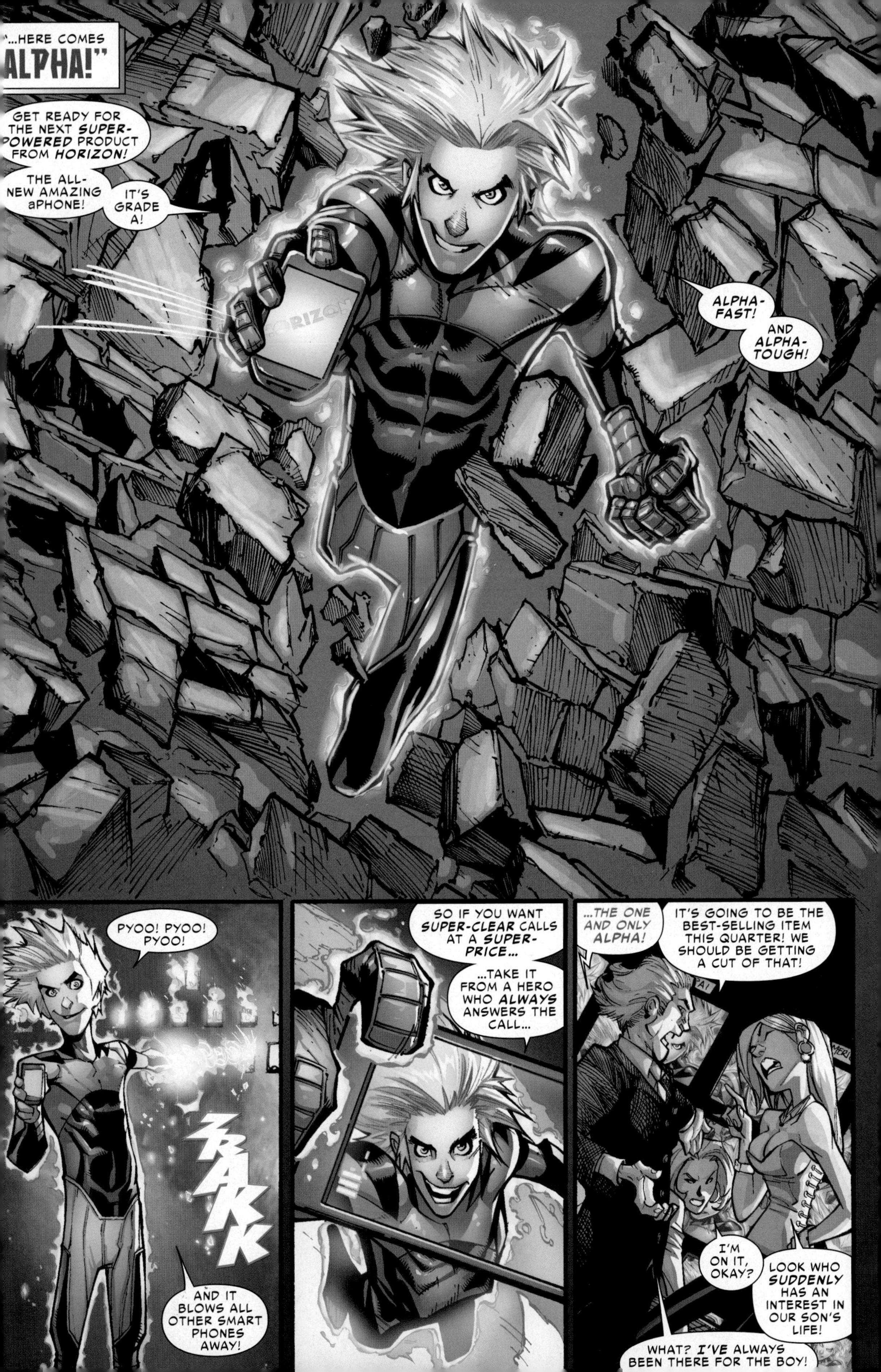
"...HERE COMES ALPHA!"
GET READY FOR THE NEXT SUPER-POWERED PRODUCT FROM HORIZON!
THE ALL-NEW AMAZING aPHONE!
IT'S GRADE A!
ALPHA-FAST!
AND ALPHA-TOUGH!
PYOO! PYOO! PYOO!
ZRAKK
AND IT BLOWS ALL OTHER SMART PHONES AWAY!
SO IF YOU WANT SUPER-CLEAR CALLS AT A SUPER-PRICE...
...TAKE IT FROM A HERO WHO ALWAYS ANSWERS THE CALL...
...THE ONE AND ONLY ALPHA!
IT'S GOING TO BE THE BEST-SELLING ITEM THIS QUARTER! WE SHOULD BE GETTING A CUT OF THAT!
I'M ON IT, OKAY?
LOOK WHO SUDDENLY HAS AN INTEREST IN OUR SON'S LIFE!
WHAT? I'VE ALWAYS BEEN THERE FOR THE BOY!

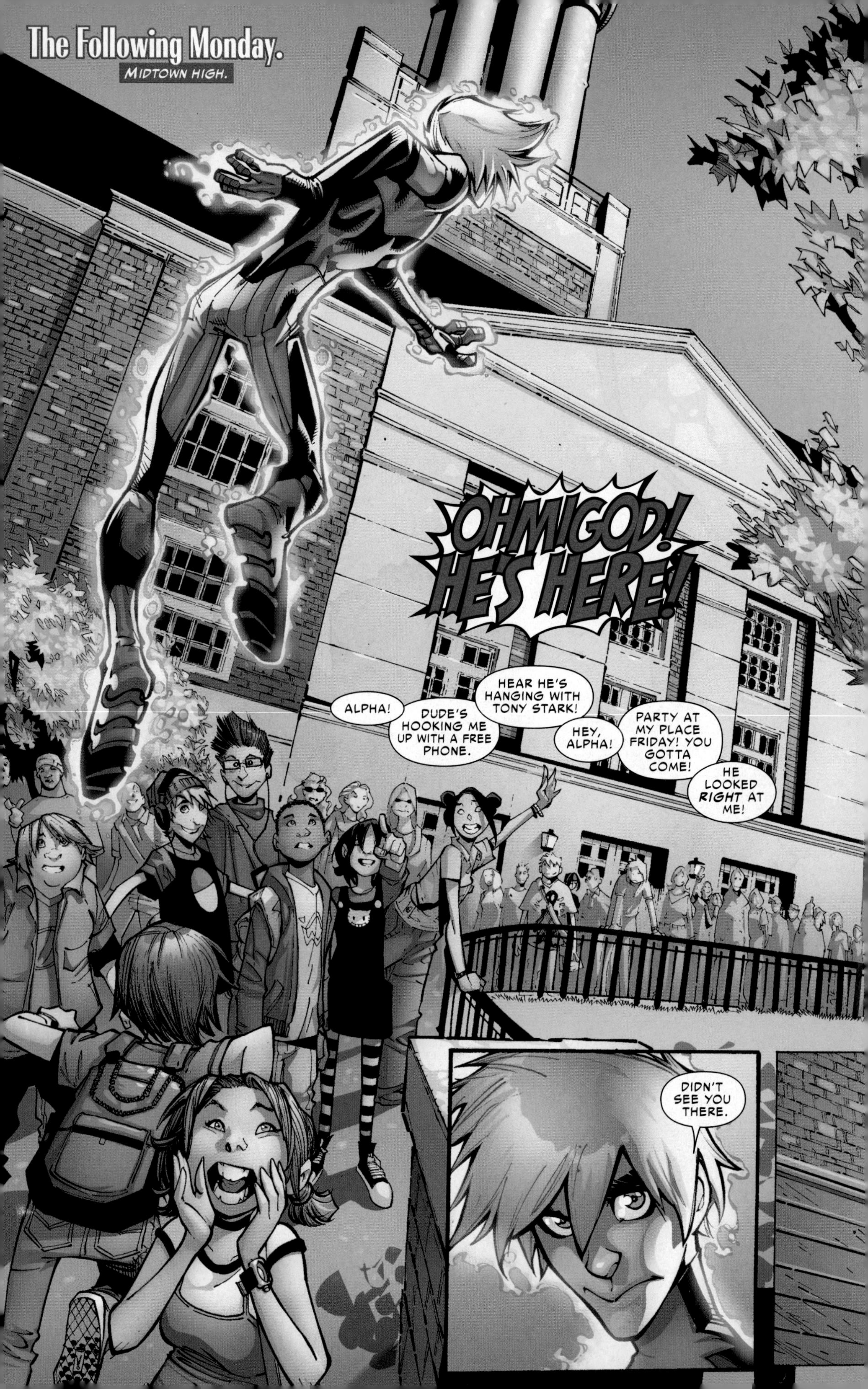

The Following Monday.
MIDTOWN HIGH.
OHMIGOD! HE'S HERE!
ALPHA!
DUDE'S HOOKING ME UP WITH A FREE PHONE.
HEAR HE'S HANGING WITH TONY STARK!
HEY, ALPHA!
PARTY AT MY PLACE FRIDAY! YOU GOTTA COME!
HE LOOKED RIGHT AT ME!
DIDN'T SEE YOU THERE.

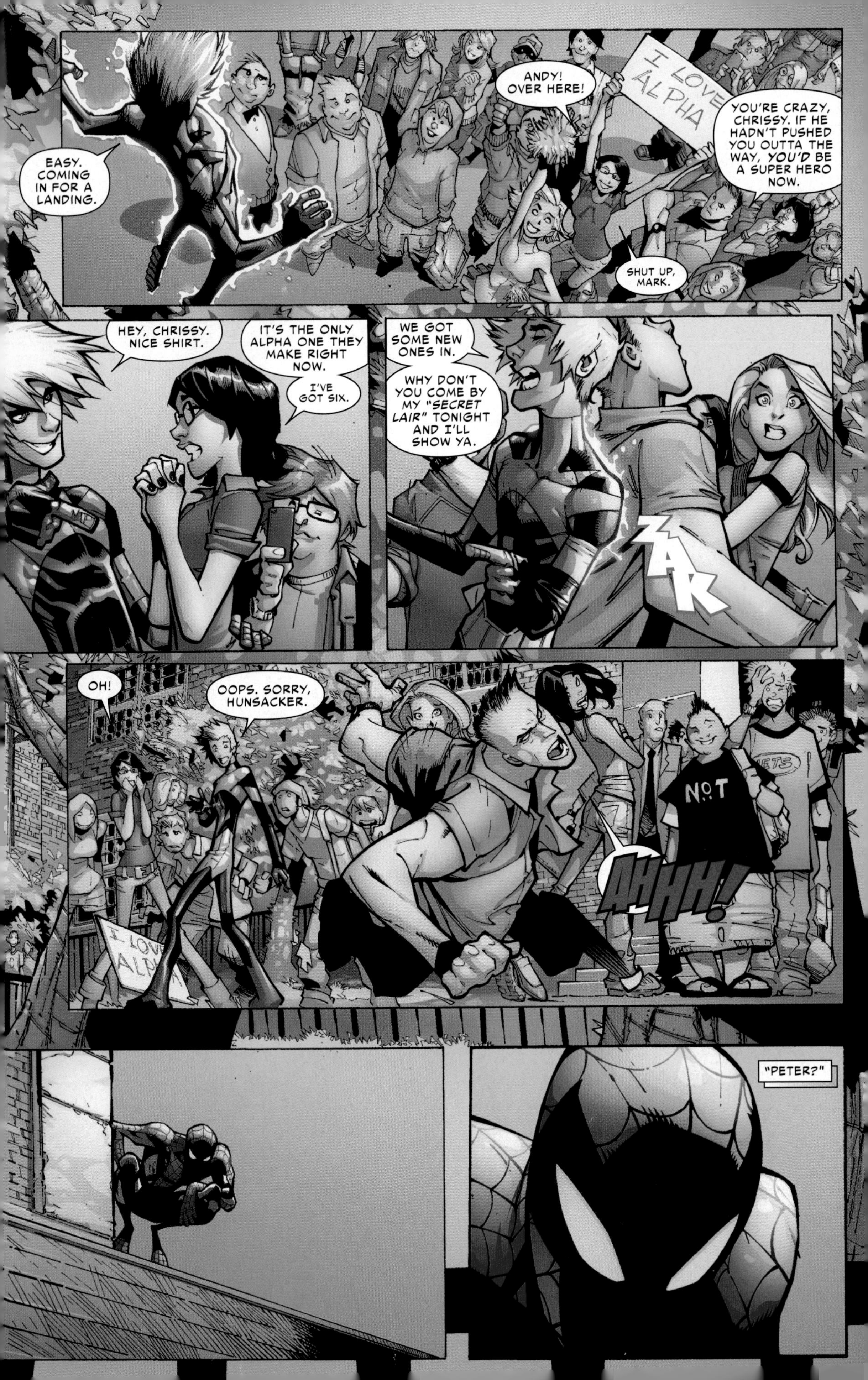

EASY. COMING IN FOR A LANDING.
ANDY! OVER HERE!
I LOVE ALPHA
YOU'RE CRAZY, CHRISSY. IF HE HADN'T PUSHED YOU OUTTA THE WAY, YOU'D BE A SUPER HERO NOW.
SHUT UP, MARK.
HEY, CHRISSY. NICE SHIRT.
IT'S THE ONLY ALPHA ONE THEY MAKE RIGHT NOW.
I'VE GOT SIX.
WE GOT SOME NEW ONES IN.
WHY DON'T YOU COME BY MY "SECRET LAIR" TONIGHT AND I'LL SHOW YA.
ZAK
OH!
OOPS. SORRY, HUNSACKER.
AHHH!
"PETER?"

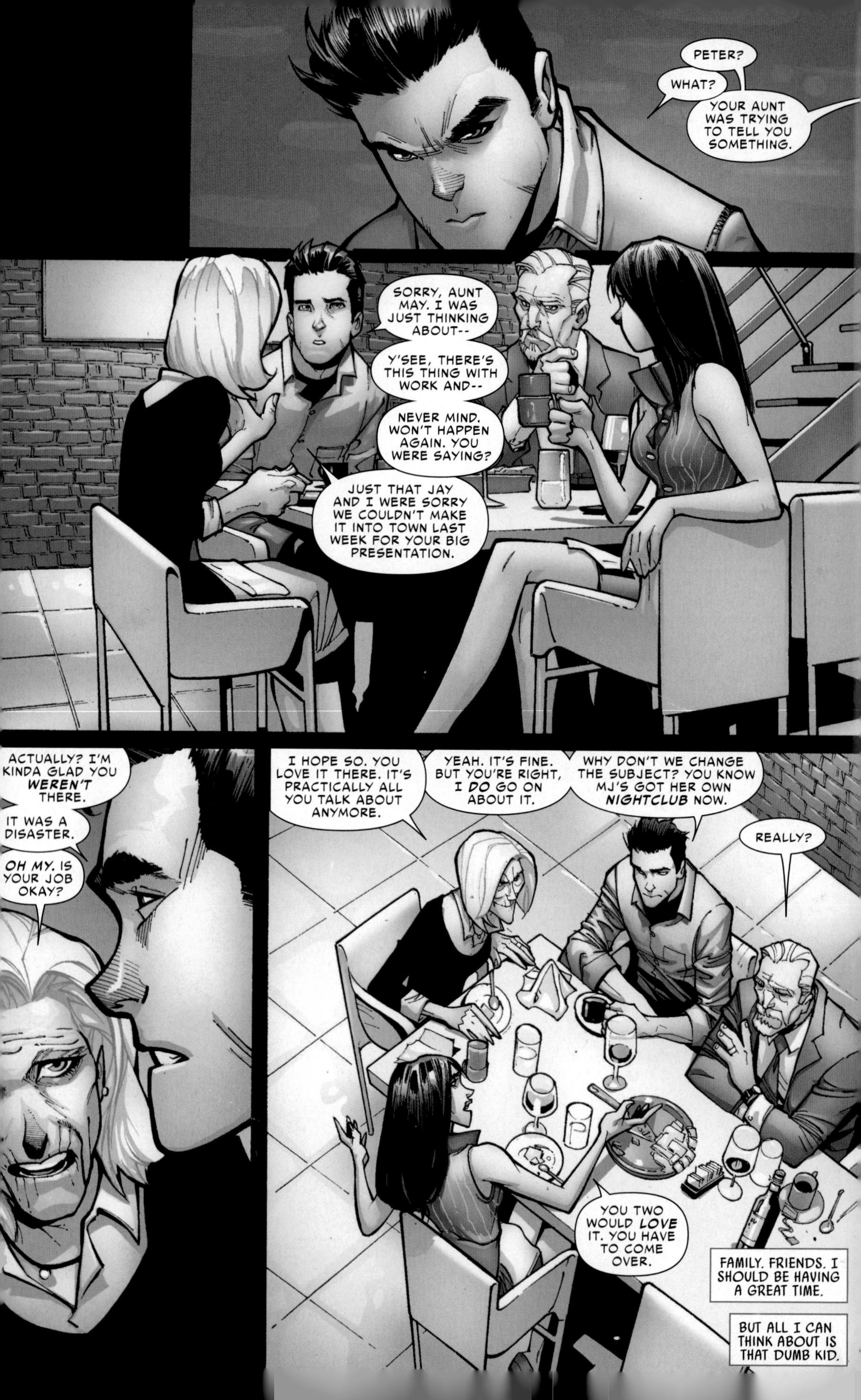
PETER?
WHAT?
YOUR AUNT WAS TRYING TO TELL YOU SOMETHING.
SORRY, AUNT MAY. I WAS JUST THINKING ABOUT--
Y'SEE, THERE'S THIS THING WITH WORK AND--
NEVER MIND. WON'T HAPPEN AGAIN. YOU WERE SAYING?
JUST THAT JAY AND I WERE SORRY WE COULDN'T MAKE IT INTO TOWN LAST WEEK FOR YOUR BIG PRESENTATION.
ACTUALLY? I'M KINDA GLAD YOU *WEREN'T* THERE.
IT WAS A DISASTER.
OH MY. IS YOUR JOB OKAY?
I HOPE SO. YOU LOVE IT THERE. IT'S PRACTICALLY ALL YOU TALK ABOUT ANYMORE.
YEAH. IT'S FINE. BUT YOU'RE RIGHT, *I DO* GO ON ABOUT IT.
WHY DON'T WE CHANGE THE SUBJECT? YOU KNOW MJ'S GOT HER OWN *NIGHTCLUB* NOW.
REALLY?
YOU TWO WOULD *LOVE* IT. YOU HAVE TO COME OVER.
FAMILY. FRIENDS. I SHOULD BE HAVING A GREAT TIME.
BUT ALL I CAN THINK ABOUT IS THAT DUMB KID.

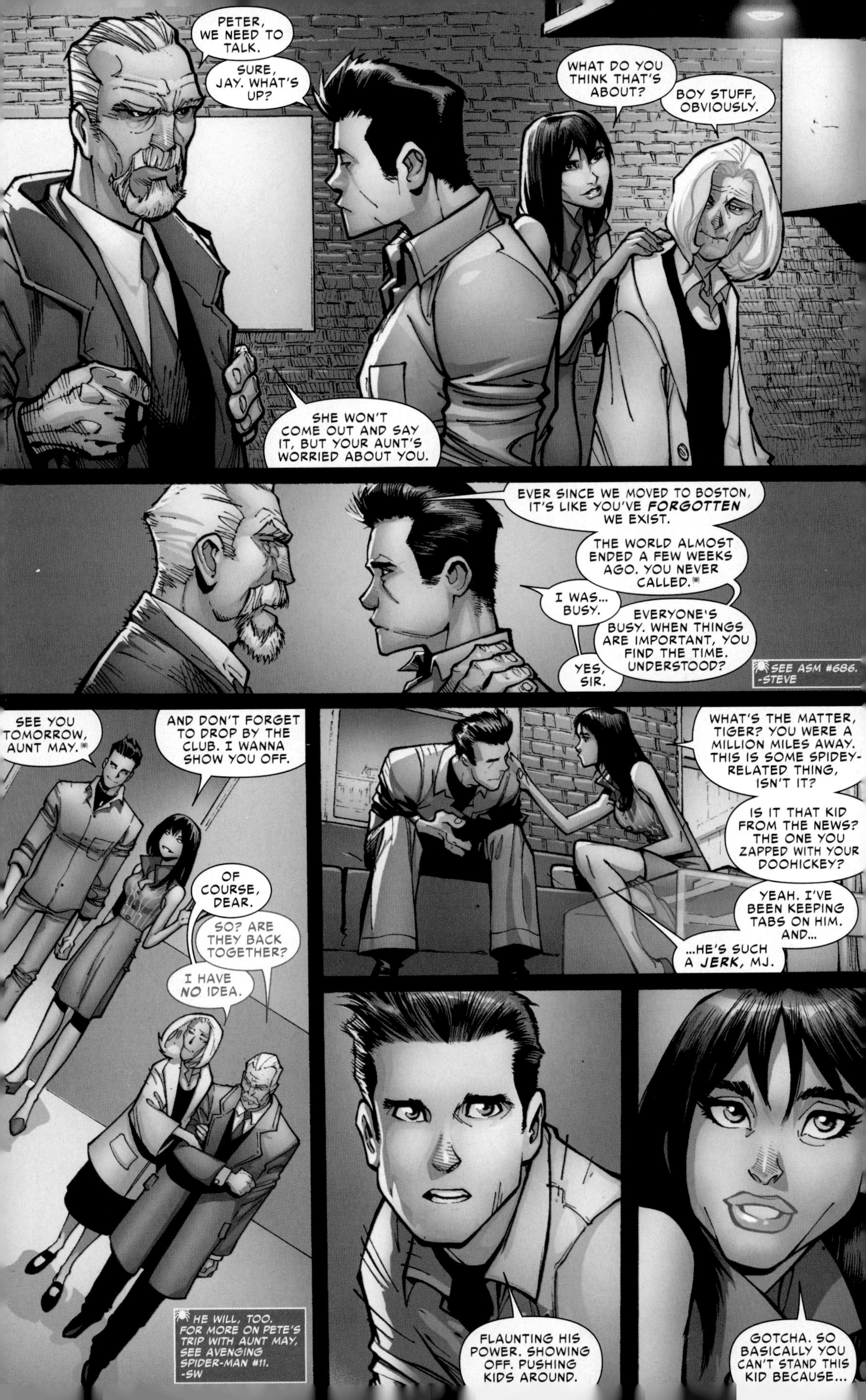

PETER, WE NEED TO TALK.
SURE, JAY. WHAT'S UP?
WHAT DO YOU THINK THAT'S ABOUT?
BOY STUFF, OBVIOUSLY.
SHE WON'T COME OUT AND SAY IT, BUT YOUR AUNT'S WORRIED ABOUT YOU.
EVER SINCE WE MOVED TO BOSTON, IT'S LIKE YOU'VE FORGOTTEN WE EXIST.
THE WORLD ALMOST ENDED A FEW WEEKS AGO. YOU NEVER CALLED.
I WAS... BUSY.
EVERYONE'S BUSY. WHEN THINGS ARE IMPORTANT, YOU FIND THE TIME. UNDERSTOOD?
YES, SIR.
SEE ASM #686. -STEVE
SEE YOU TOMORROW, AUNT MAY.
AND DON'T FORGET TO DROP BY THE CLUB. I WANNA SHOW YOU OFF.
OF COURSE, DEAR.
SO? ARE THEY BACK TOGETHER?
I HAVE NO IDEA.
HE WILL, TOO. FOR MORE ON PETE'S TRIP WITH AUNT MAY, SEE AVENGING SPIDER-MAN #11. -SW
WHAT'S THE MATTER, TIGER? YOU WERE A MILLION MILES AWAY. THIS IS SOME SPIDEY-RELATED THING, ISN'T IT?
IS IT THAT KID FROM THE NEWS? THE ONE YOU ZAPPED WITH YOUR DOOHICKEY?
YEAH. I'VE BEEN KEEPING TABS ON HIM. AND...
...HE'S SUCH A JERK, MJ.
FLAUNTING HIS POWER. SHOWING OFF. PUSHING KIDS AROUND.
GOTCHA. SO BASICALLY YOU CAN'T STAND THIS KID BECAUSE...

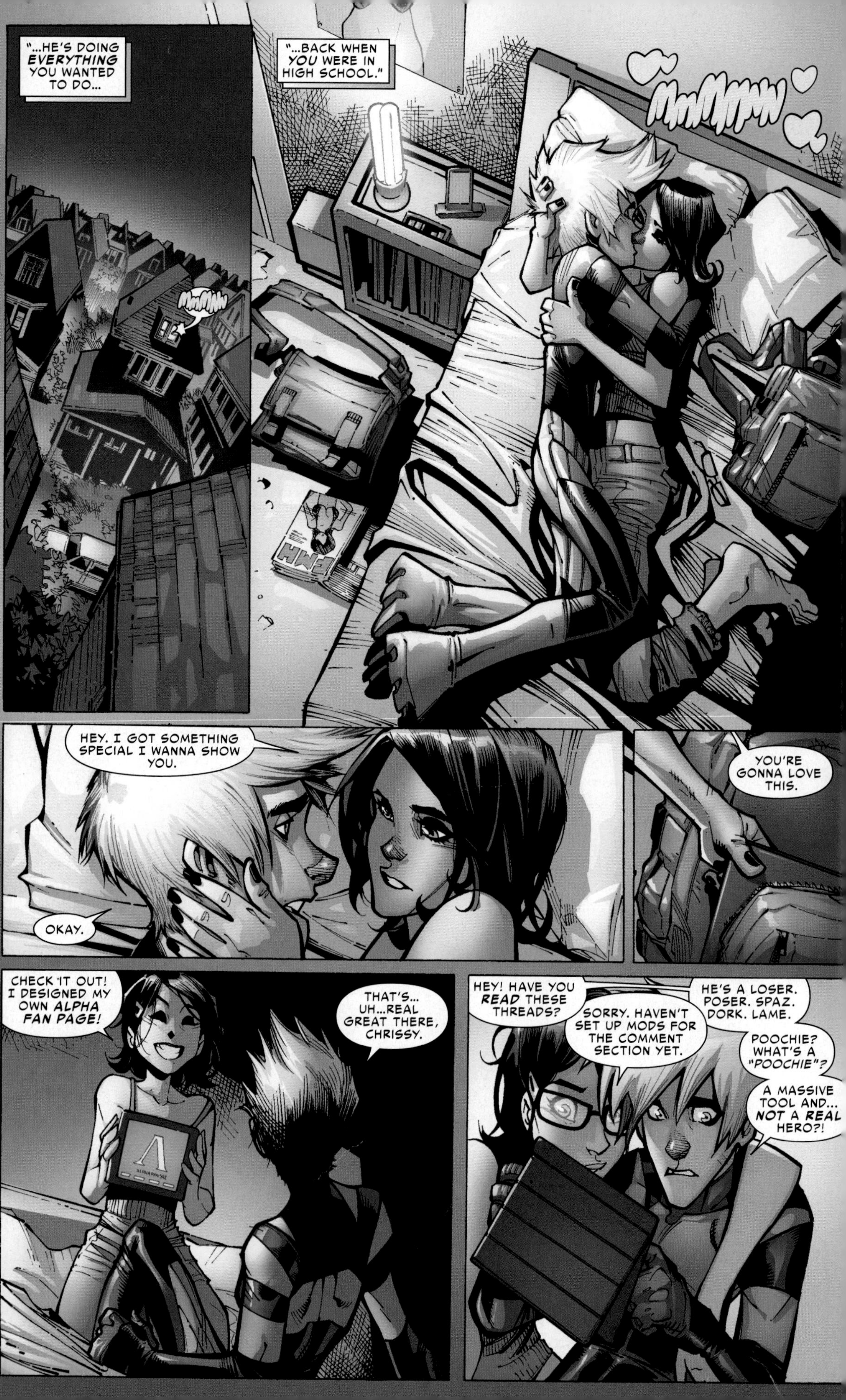
"...HE'S DOING EVERYTHING YOU WANTED TO DO...
"...BACK WHEN YOU WERE IN HIGH SCHOOL."
MMMMMW
MMMMW
HEY. I GOT SOMETHING SPECIAL I WANNA SHOW YOU.
OKAY.
YOU'RE GONNA LOVE THIS.
CHECK IT OUT! I DESIGNED MY OWN ALPHA FAN PAGE!
THAT'S... UH...REAL GREAT THERE, CHRISSY.
HEY! HAVE YOU READ THESE THREADS?
SORRY. HAVEN'T SET UP MODS FOR THE COMMENT SECTION YET.
HE'S A LOSER. POSER. SPAZ. DORK. LAME.
POOCHIE? WHAT'S A "POOCHIE"?
A MASSIVE TOOL AND... NOT A REAL HERO?!

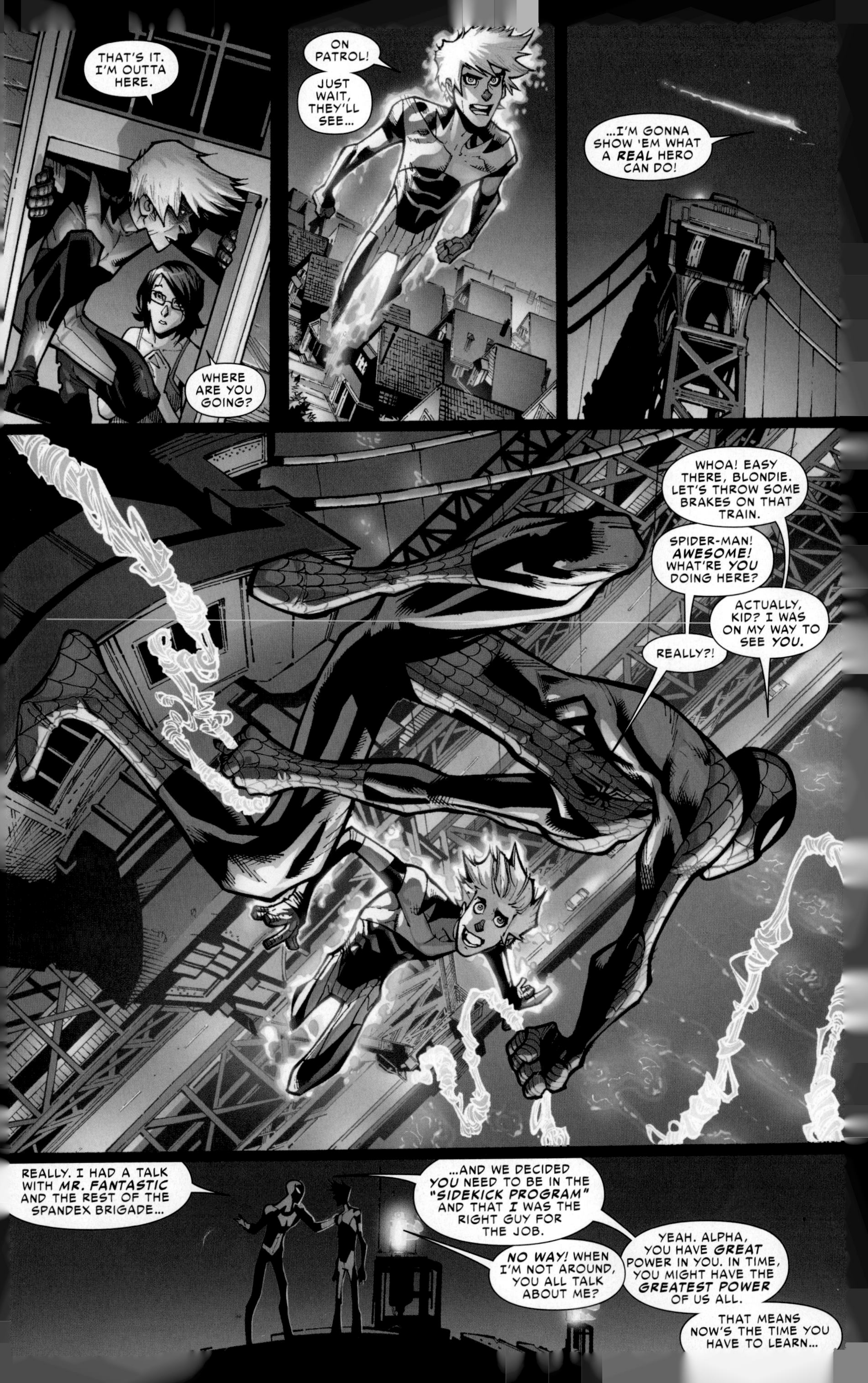
THAT'S IT. I'M OUTTA HERE.
WHERE ARE YOU GOING?
ON PATROL!
JUST WAIT, THEY'LL SEE...
...I'M GONNA SHOW 'EM WHAT A *REAL* HERO CAN DO!
WHOA! EASY THERE, BLONDIE. LET'S THROW SOME BRAKES ON THAT TRAIN.
SPIDER-MAN! ***AWESOME!*** WHAT'RE ***YOU*** DOING HERE?
ACTUALLY, KID? I WAS ON MY WAY TO SEE ***YOU.***
REALLY?!
REALLY. I HAD A TALK WITH ***MR. FANTASTIC*** AND THE REST OF THE SPANDEX BRIGADE...
...AND WE DECIDED ***YOU*** NEED TO BE IN THE ***"SIDEKICK PROGRAM"*** AND THAT ***I*** WAS THE RIGHT GUY FOR THE JOB.
NO WAY! WHEN I'M NOT AROUND, YOU ALL TALK ABOUT ME?
YEAH. ALPHA, YOU HAVE ***GREAT*** POWER IN YOU. IN TIME, YOU MIGHT HAVE THE ***GREATEST POWER*** OF US ALL.
THAT MEANS NOW'S THE TIME YOU HAVE TO LEARN...

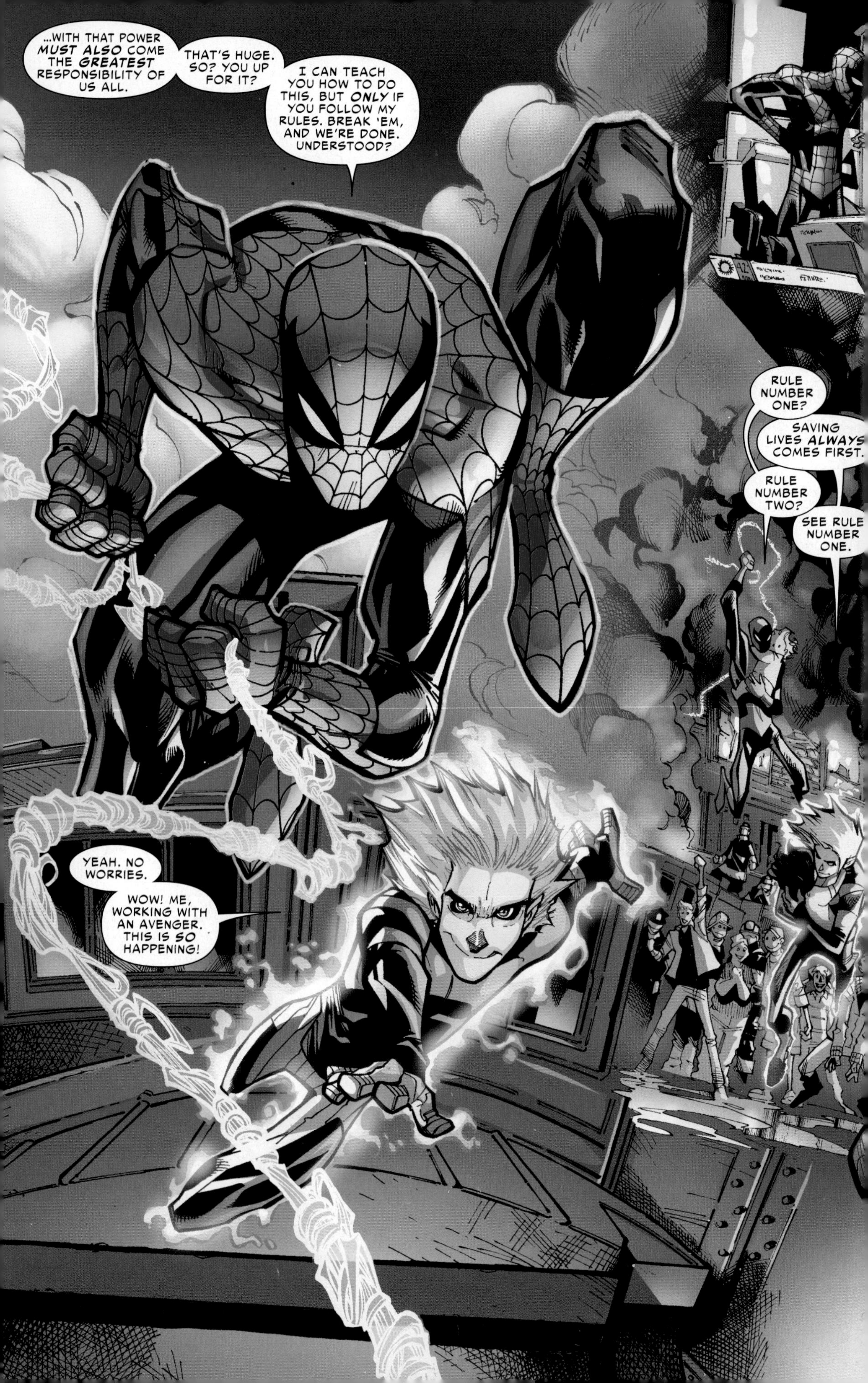
...WITH THAT POWER MUST ALSO COME THE GREATEST RESPONSIBILITY OF US ALL.
THAT'S HUGE. SO? YOU UP FOR IT?
I CAN TEACH YOU HOW TO DO THIS, BUT ONLY IF YOU FOLLOW MY RULES. BREAK 'EM, AND WE'RE DONE. UNDERSTOOD?
RULE NUMBER ONE?
SAVING LIVES ALWAYS COMES FIRST.
RULE NUMBER TWO?
SEE RULE NUMBER ONE.
YEAH. NO WORRIES.
WOW! ME, WORKING WITH AN AVENGER. THIS IS SO HAPPENING!

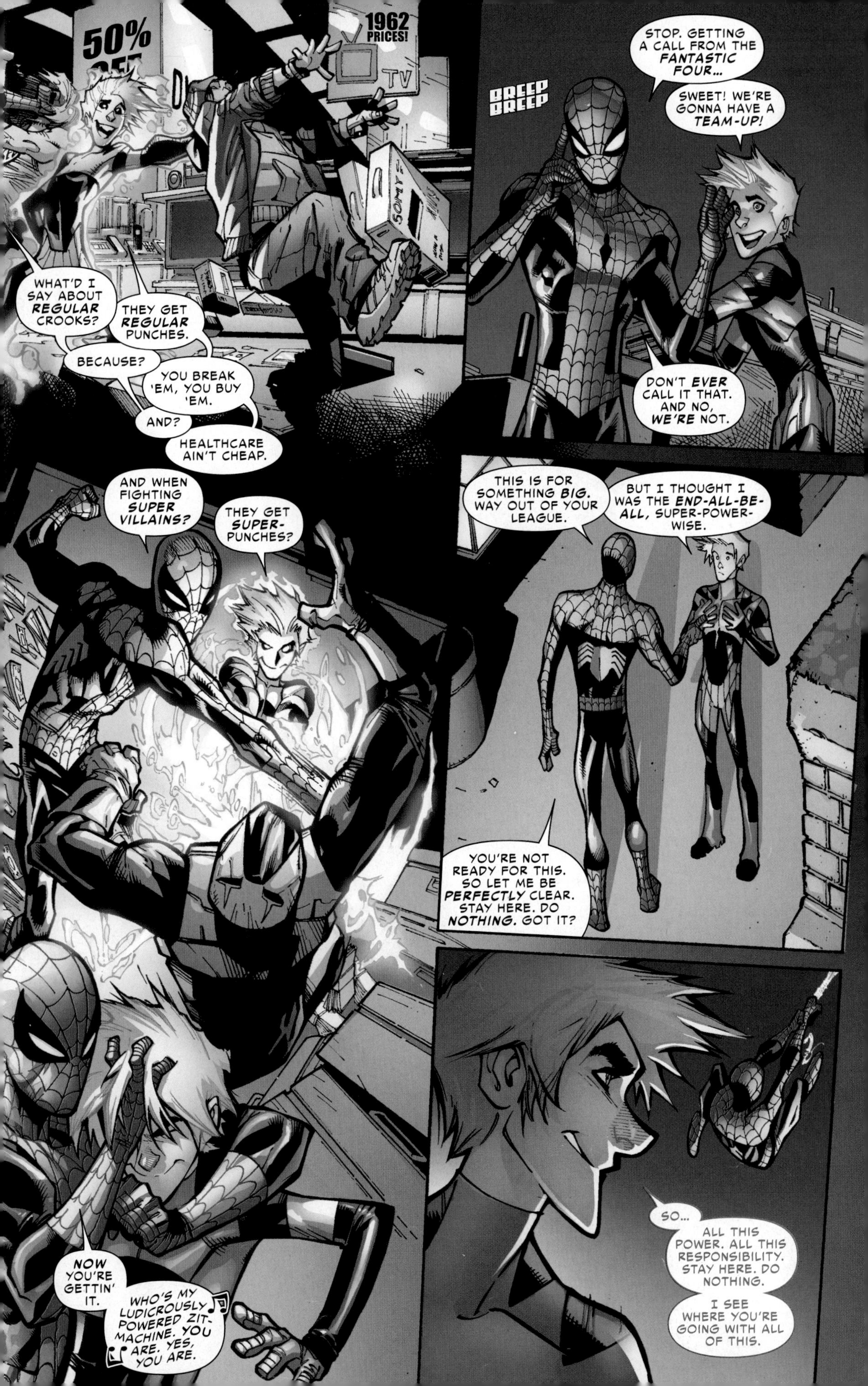
50% OFF
1962 PRICES!
TV
SOMY
WHAT'D I SAY ABOUT REGULAR CROOKS?
THEY GET REGULAR PUNCHES.
BECAUSE?
YOU BREAK 'EM, YOU BUY 'EM.
AND?
HEALTHCARE AIN'T CHEAP.
BREEP BREEP
STOP. GETTING A CALL FROM THE FANTASTIC FOUR...
SWEET! WE'RE GONNA HAVE A TEAM-UP!
DON'T EVER CALL IT THAT. AND NO, WE'RE NOT.
AND WHEN FIGHTING SUPER VILLAINS?
THEY GET SUPER-PUNCHES?
NOW YOU'RE GETTIN' IT.
WHO'S MY LUDICROUSLY POWERED ZIT-MACHINE. YOU ARE. YES, YOU ARE.
THIS IS FOR SOMETHING BIG. WAY OUT OF YOUR LEAGUE.
BUT I THOUGHT I WAS THE END-ALL-BE-ALL, SUPER-POWER-WISE.
YOU'RE NOT READY FOR THIS. SO LET ME BE PERFECTLY CLEAR. STAY HERE. DO NOTHING. GOT IT?
SO...
ALL THIS POWER. ALL THIS RESPONSIBILITY. STAY HERE. DO NOTHING.
I SEE WHERE YOU'RE GOING WITH ALL OF THIS.

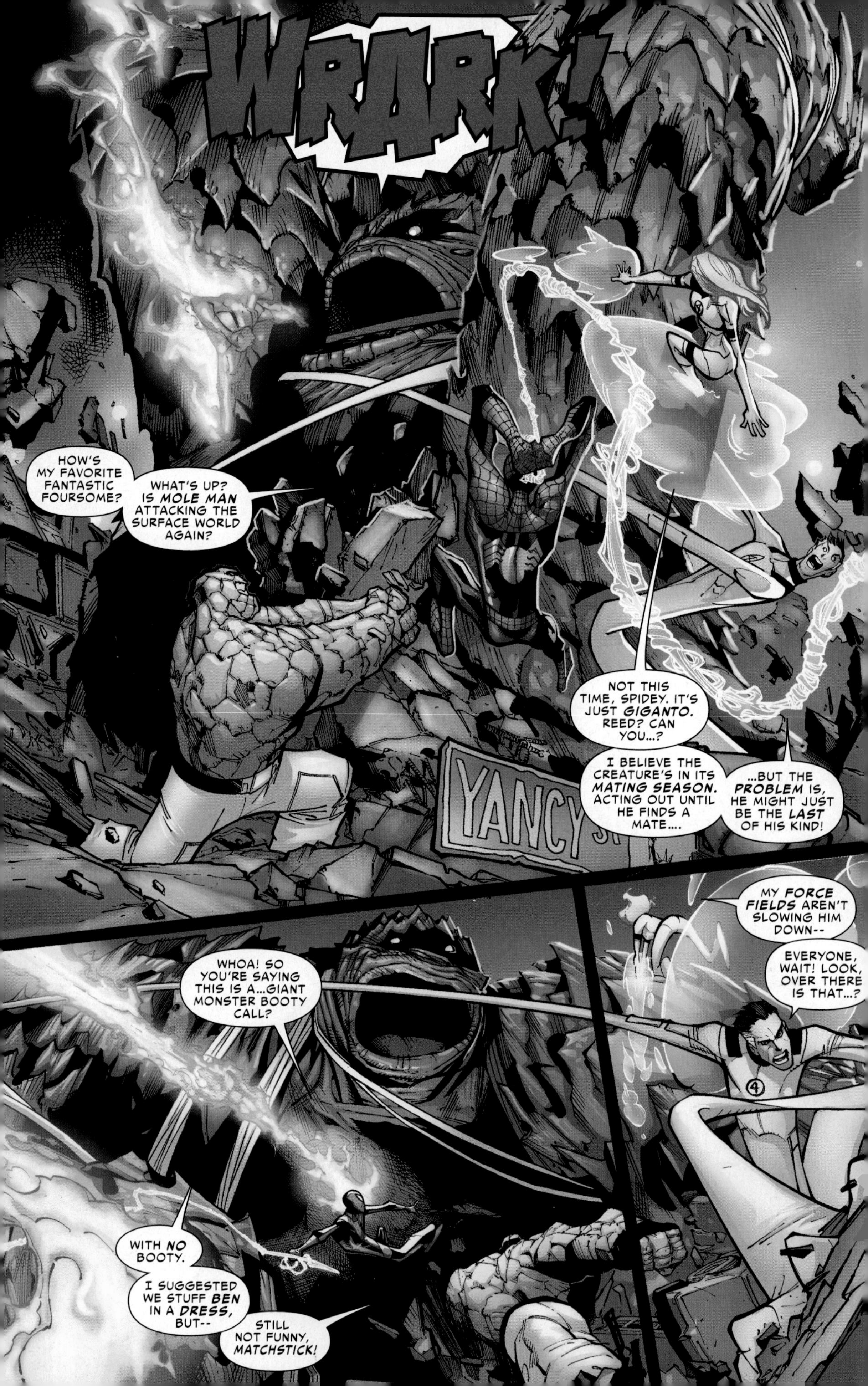
WRARK!
HOW'S MY FAVORITE FANTASTIC FOURSOME?
WHAT'S UP? IS MOLE MAN ATTACKING THE SURFACE WORLD AGAIN?
NOT THIS TIME, SPIDEY. IT'S JUST GIGANTO. REED? CAN YOU...?
I BELIEVE THE CREATURE'S IN ITS MATING SEASON. ACTING OUT UNTIL HE FINDS A MATE....
...BUT THE PROBLEM IS, HE MIGHT JUST BE THE LAST OF HIS KIND!
YANCY ST
WHOA! SO YOU'RE SAYING THIS IS A...GIANT MONSTER BOOTY CALL?
WITH NO BOOTY.
I SUGGESTED WE STUFF BEN IN A DRESS, BUT--
STILL NOT FUNNY, MATCHSTICK!
MY FORCE FIELDS AREN'T SLOWING HIM DOWN--
EVERYONE, WAIT! LOOK, OVER THERE IS THAT...?

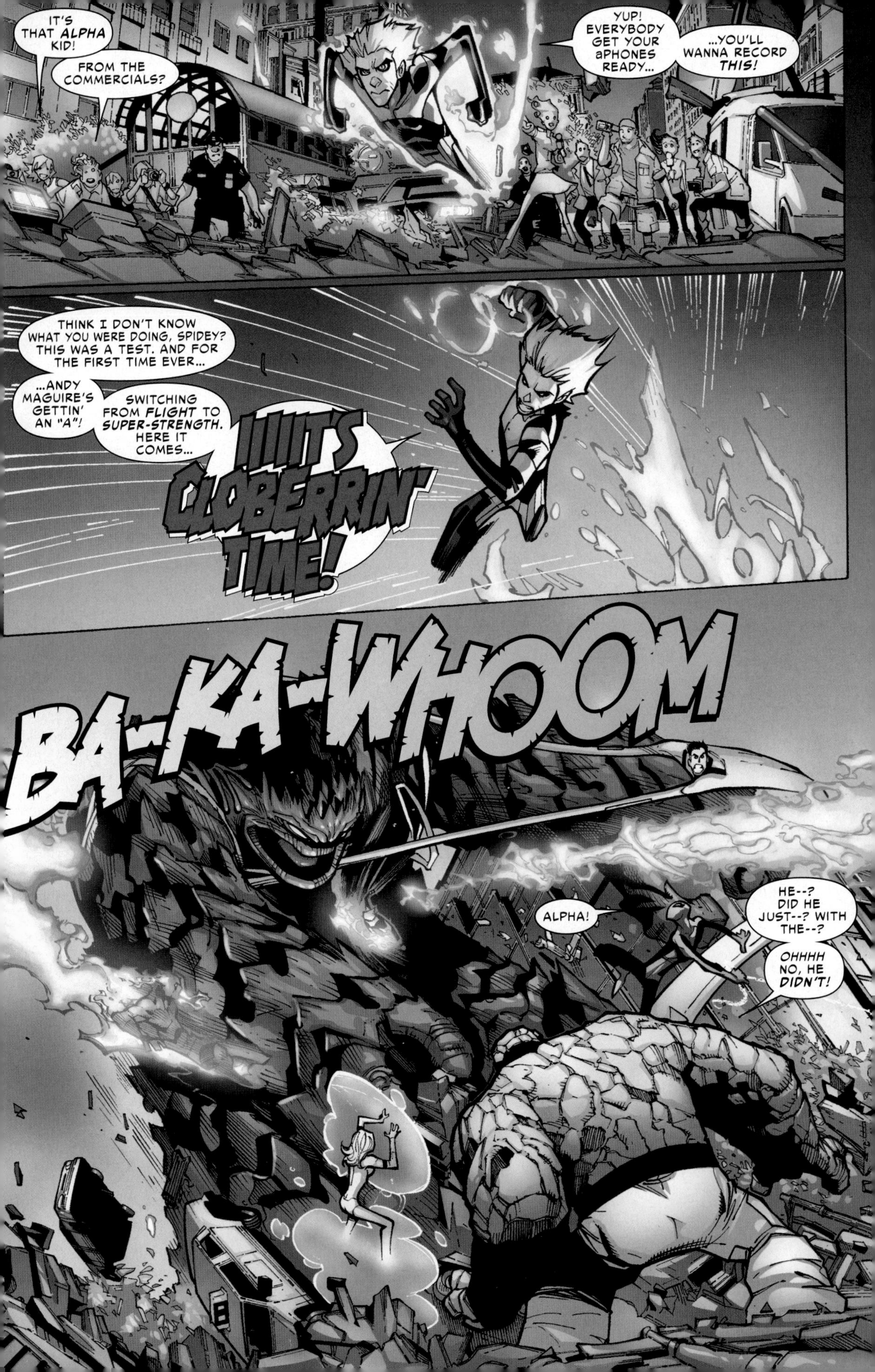
IT'S THAT ALPHA KID!
FROM THE COMMERCIALS?
YUP! EVERYBODY GET YOUR aPHONES READY...
...YOU'LL WANNA RECORD THIS!
THINK I DON'T KNOW WHAT YOU WERE DOING, SPIDEY? THIS WAS A TEST. AND FOR THE FIRST TIME EVER...
...ANDY MAGUIRE'S GETTIN' AN "A"!
SWITCHING FROM FLIGHT TO SUPER-STRENGTH. HERE IT COMES...
IIIIIT'S CLOBERRIN' TIME!
BA-KA-WHOOM
ALPHA!
HE--? DID HE JUST--? WITH THE--?
OHHHH NO, HE DIDN'T!

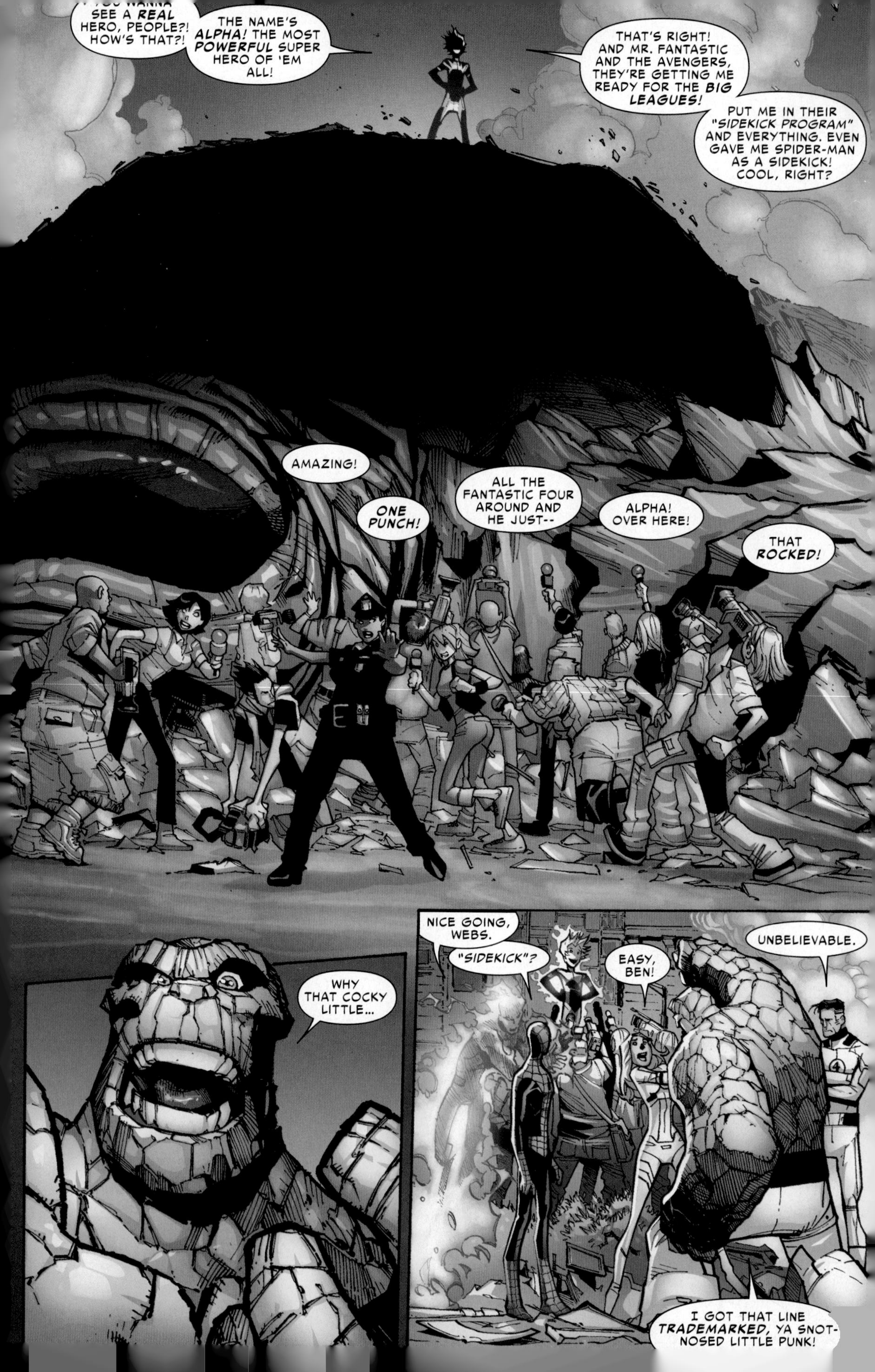
SEE A REAL HERO, PEOPLE?! HOW'S THAT?!
THE NAME'S ALPHA! THE MOST POWERFUL SUPER HERO OF 'EM ALL!
THAT'S RIGHT! AND MR. FANTASTIC AND THE AVENGERS, THEY'RE GETTING ME READY FOR THE BIG LEAGUES!
PUT ME IN THEIR "SIDEKICK PROGRAM" AND EVERYTHING. EVEN GAVE ME SPIDER-MAN AS A SIDEKICK! COOL, RIGHT?
AMAZING!
ONE PUNCH!
ALL THE FANTASTIC FOUR AROUND AND HE JUST--
ALPHA! OVER HERE!
THAT ROCKED!
WHY THAT COCKY LITTLE...
NICE GOING, WEBS.
"SIDEKICK"?
EASY, BEN!
UNBELIEVABLE.
I GOT THAT LINE TRADEMARKED, YA SNOT-NOSED LITTLE PUNK!

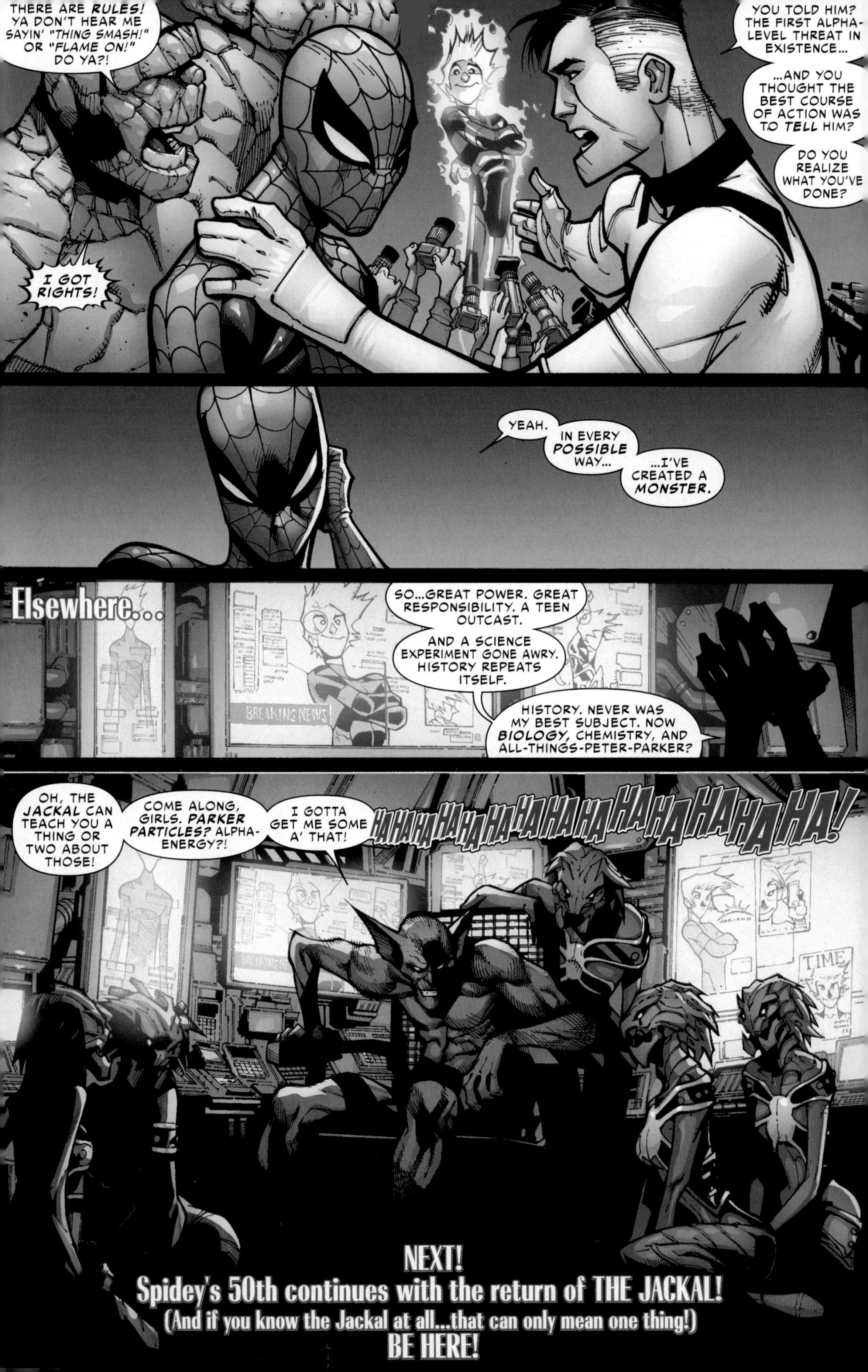
THERE ARE RULES! YA DON'T HEAR ME SAYIN' "THING SMASH!" OR "FLAME ON!" DO YA?!
I GOT RIGHTS!
YOU TOLD HIM? THE FIRST ALPHA-LEVEL THREAT IN EXISTENCE...
...AND YOU THOUGHT THE BEST COURSE OF ACTION WAS TO TELL HIM?
DO YOU REALIZE WHAT YOU'VE DONE?
YEAH.
IN EVERY POSSIBLE WAY...
...I'VE CREATED A MONSTER.
Elsewhere...
SO...GREAT POWER. GREAT RESPONSIBILITY. A TEEN OUTCAST.
AND A SCIENCE EXPERIMENT GONE AWRY. HISTORY REPEATS ITSELF.
HISTORY. NEVER WAS MY BEST SUBJECT. NOW BIOLOGY, CHEMISTRY, AND ALL-THINGS-PETER-PARKER?
OH, THE JACKAL CAN TEACH YOU A THING OR TWO ABOUT THOSE!
COME ALONG, GIRLS. PARKER PARTICLES? ALPHA-ENERGY?!
I GOTTA GET ME SOME A' THAT!
HAHAHAHAHAHAHAHAHAHAHAHAHAHAHAHA!
BREAKING NEWS
TIME
NEXT!
Spidey's 50th continues with the return of THE JACKAL!
(And if you know the Jackal at all...that can only mean one thing!)
BE HERE!

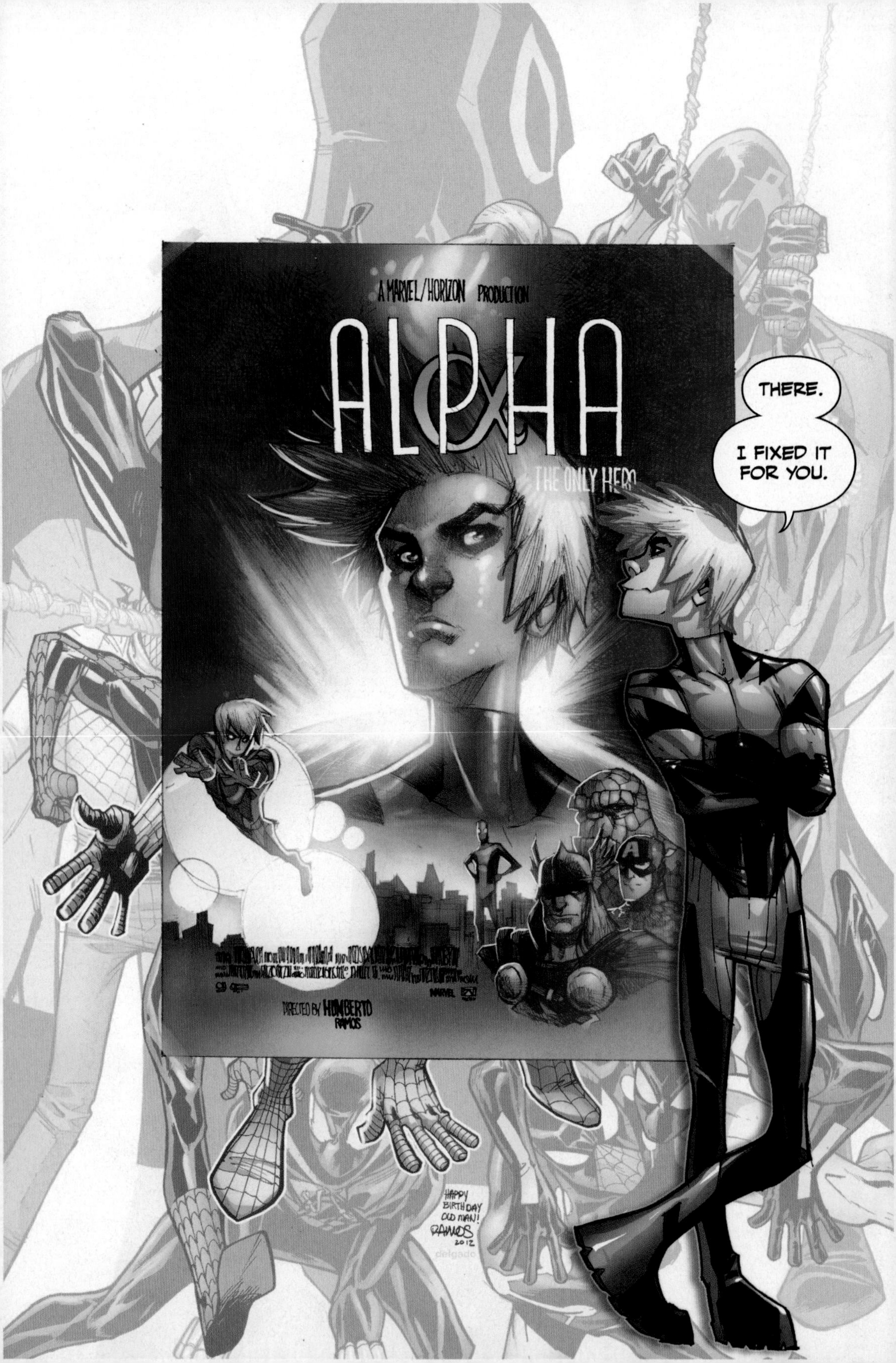
A MARVEL/HORIZON PRODUCTION
ALPHA
THE ONLY HERO
DIRECTED BY HUMBERTO RAMOS
THERE.
I FIXED IT FOR YOU.
HAPPY BIRTHDAY OLD MAN!
RAMOS 2012

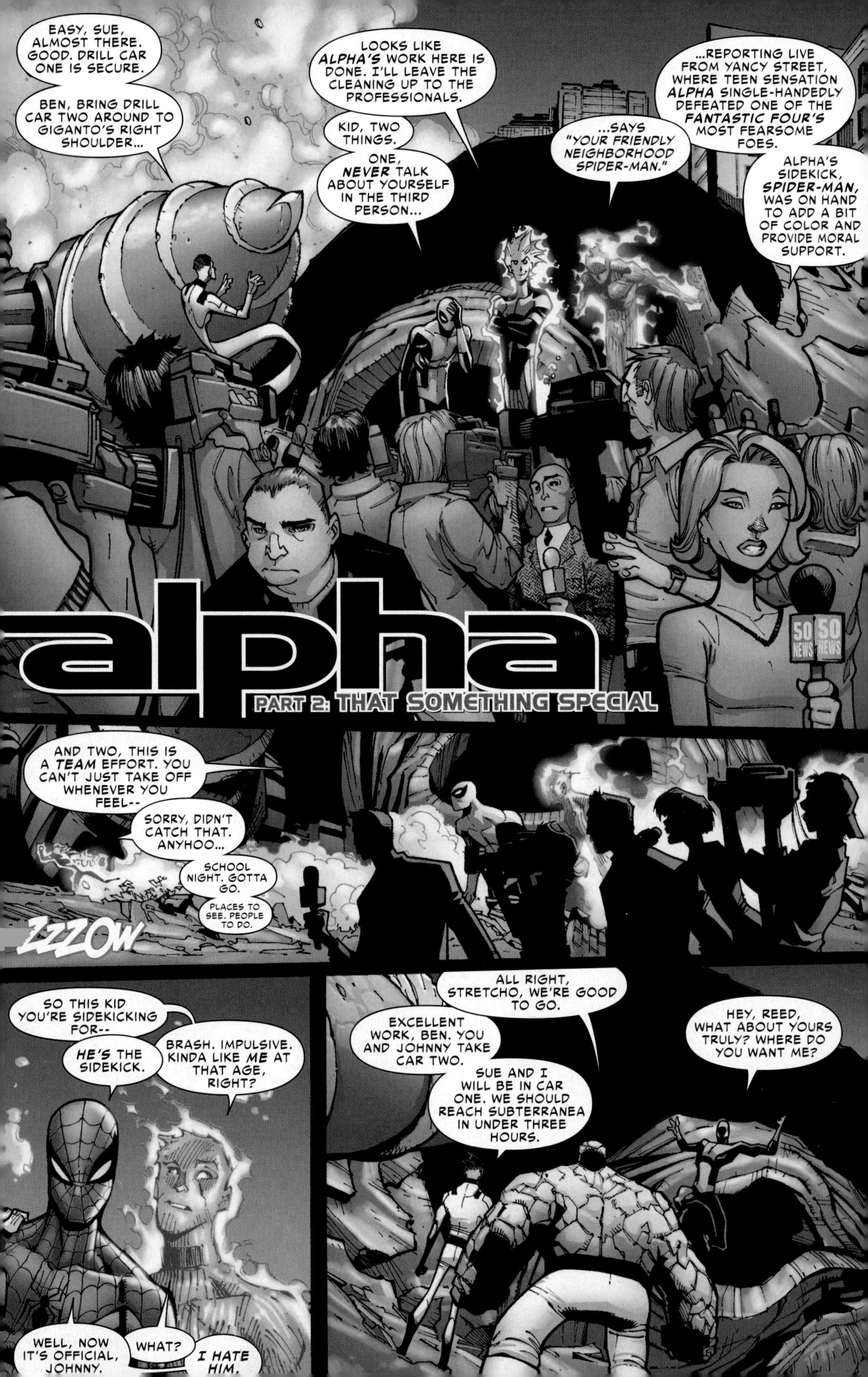
EASY, SUE, ALMOST THERE. GOOD. DRILL CAR ONE IS SECURE.
BEN, BRING DRILL CAR TWO AROUND TO GIGANTO'S RIGHT SHOULDER...
LOOKS LIKE ALPHA'S WORK HERE IS DONE. I'LL LEAVE THE CLEANING UP TO THE PROFESSIONALS.
KID, TWO THINGS.
ONE, NEVER TALK ABOUT YOURSELF IN THE THIRD PERSON...
...SAYS "YOUR FRIENDLY NEIGHBORHOOD SPIDER-MAN."
...REPORTING LIVE FROM YANCY STREET, WHERE TEEN SENSATION ALPHA SINGLE-HANDEDLY DEFEATED ONE OF THE FANTASTIC FOUR'S MOST FEARSOME FOES.
ALPHA'S SIDEKICK, SPIDER-MAN, WAS ON HAND TO ADD A BIT OF COLOR AND PROVIDE MORAL SUPPORT.
50 NEWS
alpha
PART 2: THAT SOMETHING SPECIAL
AND TWO, THIS IS A TEAM EFFORT. YOU CAN'T JUST TAKE OFF WHENEVER YOU FEEL--
SORRY, DIDN'T CATCH THAT. ANYHOO...
SCHOOL NIGHT. GOTTA GO.
PLACES TO SEE. PEOPLE TO DO.
ZZZOW
SO THIS KID YOU'RE SIDEKICKING FOR--
HE'S THE SIDEKICK.
BRASH. IMPULSIVE. KINDA LIKE ME AT THAT AGE, RIGHT?
WELL, NOW IT'S OFFICIAL, JOHNNY.
WHAT?
I HATE HIM.
ALL RIGHT, STRETCHO, WE'RE GOOD TO GO.
EXCELLENT WORK, BEN. YOU AND JOHNNY TAKE CAR TWO.
SUE AND I WILL BE IN CAR ONE. WE SHOULD REACH SUBTERRANEA IN UNDER THREE HOURS.
HEY, REED, WHAT ABOUT YOURS TRULY? WHERE DO YOU WANT ME?

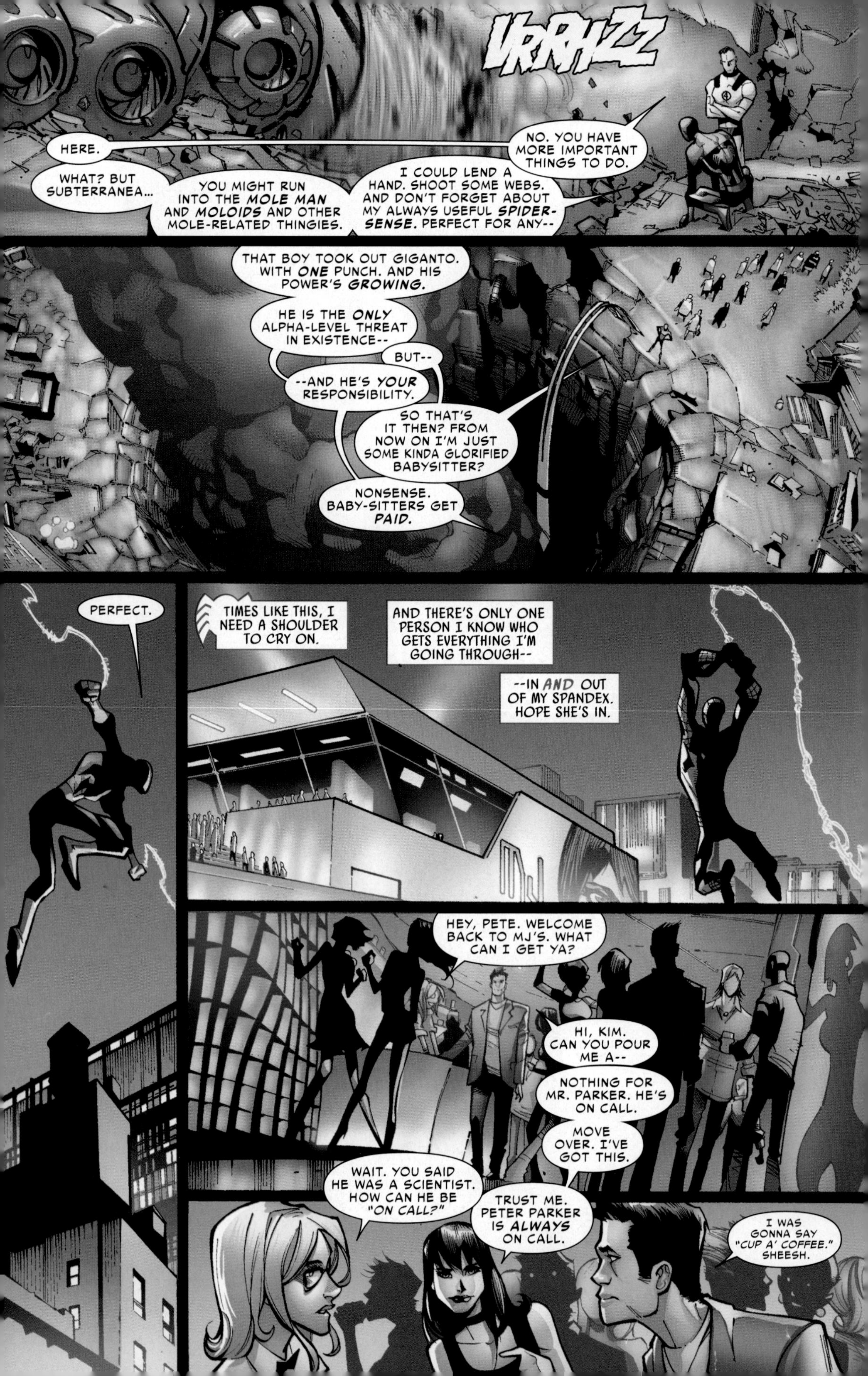
VRRHZZ
HERE.
NO. YOU HAVE MORE IMPORTANT THINGS TO DO.
WHAT? BUT SUBTERRANEA...
YOU MIGHT RUN INTO THE MOLE MAN AND MOLOIDS AND OTHER MOLE-RELATED THINGIES.
I COULD LEND A HAND. SHOOT SOME WEBS. AND DON'T FORGET ABOUT MY ALWAYS USEFUL SPIDER-SENSE. PERFECT FOR ANY--
THAT BOY TOOK OUT GIGANTO. WITH ONE PUNCH. AND HIS POWER'S GROWING.
HE IS THE ONLY ALPHA-LEVEL THREAT IN EXISTENCE--
BUT--
--AND HE'S YOUR RESPONSIBILITY.
SO THAT'S IT THEN? FROM NOW ON I'M JUST SOME KINDA GLORIFIED BABYSITTER?
NONSENSE. BABY-SITTERS GET PAID.
PERFECT.
TIMES LIKE THIS, I NEED A SHOULDER TO CRY ON.
AND THERE'S ONLY ONE PERSON I KNOW WHO GETS EVERYTHING I'M GOING THROUGH--
--IN AND OUT OF MY SPANDEX. HOPE SHE'S IN.
HEY, PETE. WELCOME BACK TO MJ'S. WHAT CAN I GET YA?
HI, KIM. CAN YOU POUR ME A--
NOTHING FOR MR. PARKER. HE'S ON CALL.
MOVE OVER. I'VE GOT THIS.
WAIT. YOU SAID HE WAS A SCIENTIST. HOW CAN HE BE "ON CALL?"
TRUST ME. PETER PARKER IS ALWAYS ON CALL.
I WAS GONNA SAY "CUP A' COFFEE." SHEESH.

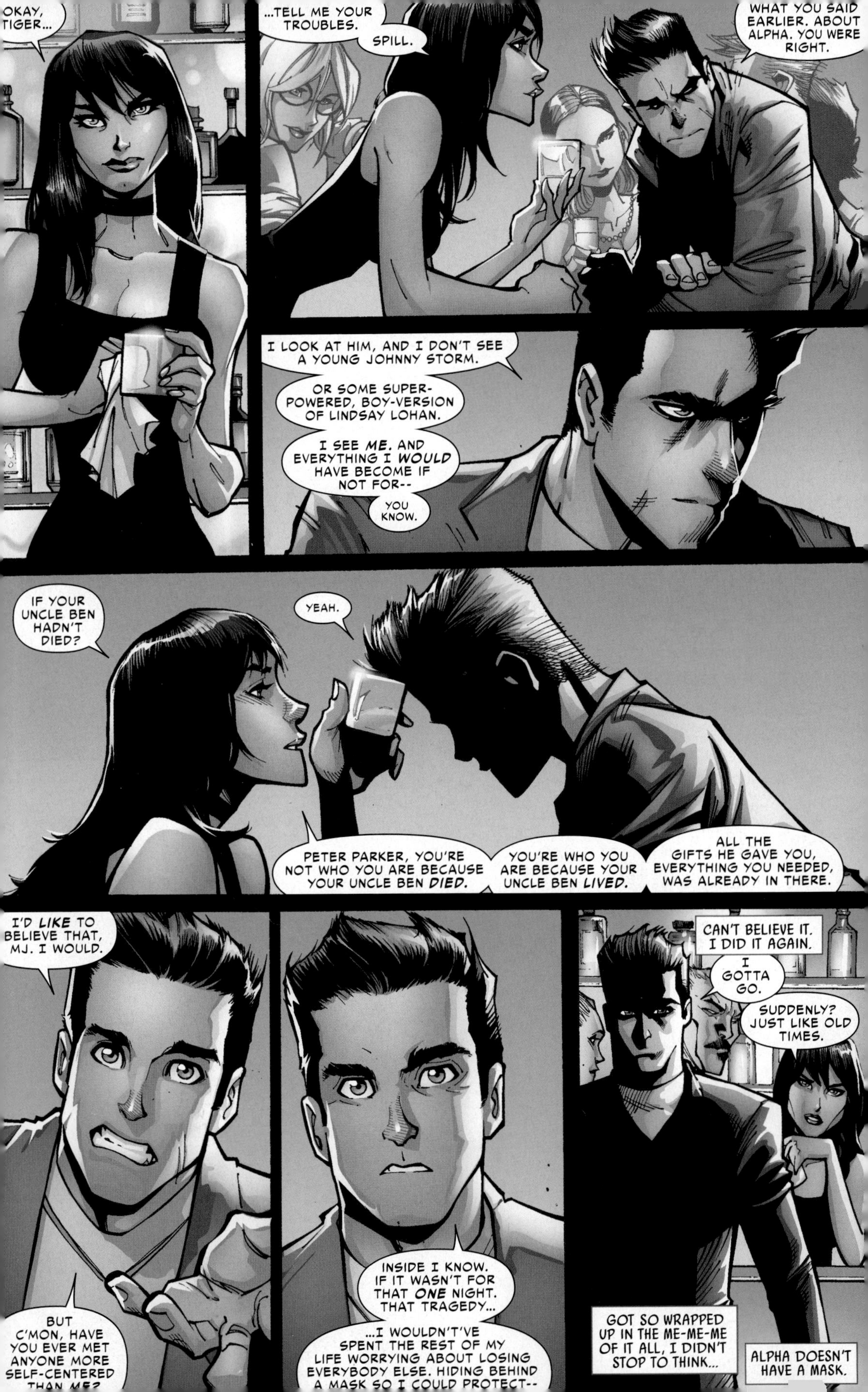
OKAY, TIGER...
...TELL ME YOUR TROUBLES.
SPILL.
WHAT YOU SAID EARLIER. ABOUT ALPHA. YOU WERE RIGHT.
I LOOK AT HIM, AND I DON'T SEE A YOUNG JOHNNY STORM.
OR SOME SUPER-POWERED, BOY-VERSION OF LINDSAY LOHAN.
I SEE *ME*. AND EVERYTHING I *WOULD* HAVE BECOME IF NOT FOR--
YOU KNOW.
IF YOUR UNCLE BEN HADN'T DIED?
YEAH.
PETER PARKER, YOU'RE NOT WHO YOU ARE BECAUSE YOUR UNCLE BEN *DIED*.
YOU'RE WHO YOU ARE BECAUSE YOUR UNCLE BEN *LIVED*.
ALL THE GIFTS HE GAVE YOU, EVERYTHING YOU NEEDED, WAS ALREADY IN THERE.
I'D *LIKE* TO BELIEVE THAT, MJ. I WOULD.
BUT C'MON, HAVE YOU EVER MET ANYONE MORE SELF-CENTERED THAN *ME*?
INSIDE I KNOW. IF IT WASN'T FOR THAT *ONE* NIGHT. THAT TRAGEDY...
...I WOULDN'T'VE SPENT THE REST OF MY LIFE WORRYING ABOUT LOSING EVERYBODY ELSE. HIDING BEHIND A MASK SO I COULD PROTECT--
CAN'T BELIEVE IT. I DID IT AGAIN.
I GOTTA GO.
SUDDENLY? JUST LIKE OLD TIMES.
GOT SO WRAPPED UP IN THE ME-ME-ME OF IT ALL, I DIDN'T STOP TO THINK...
ALPHA DOESN'T HAVE A MASK.

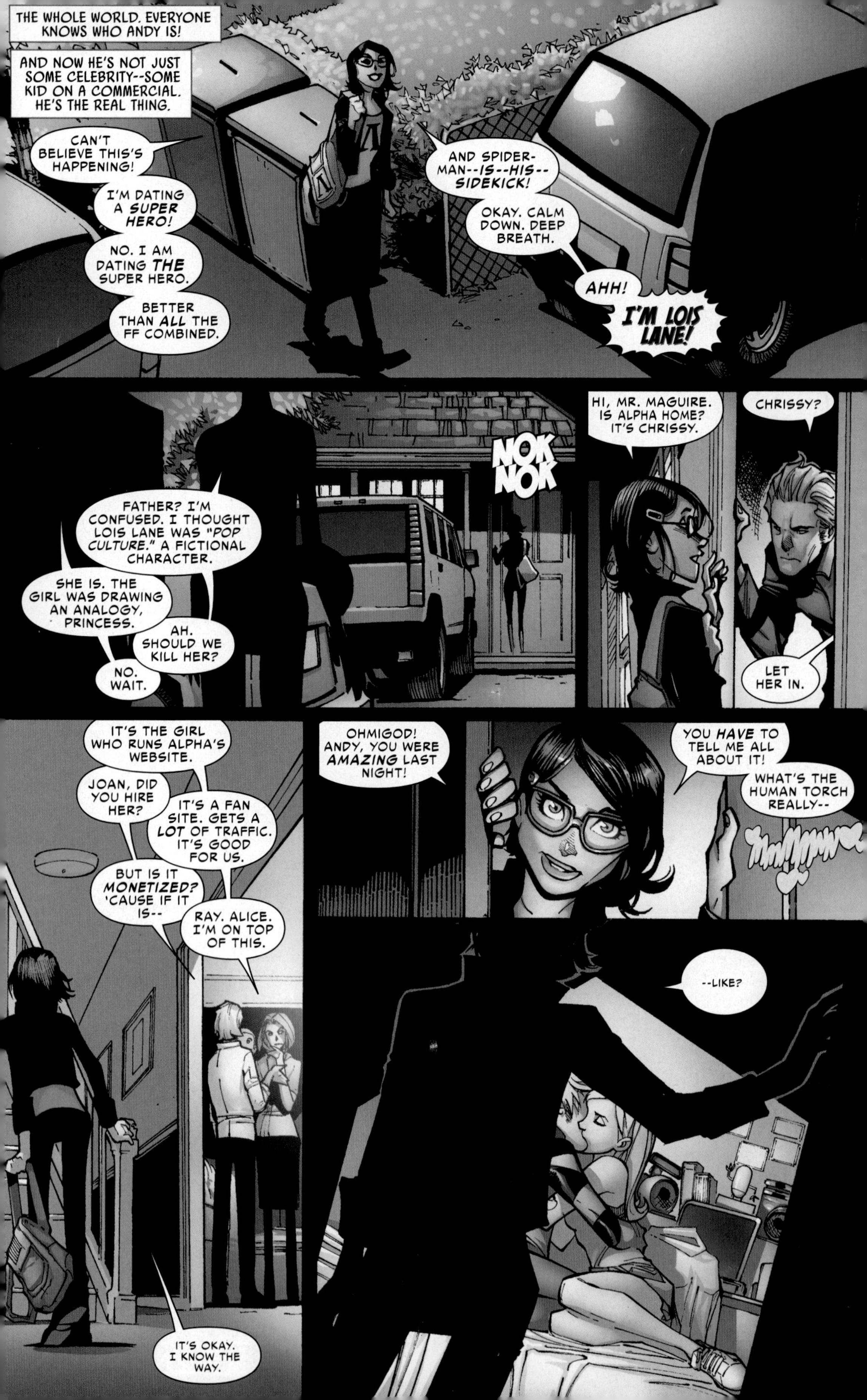
THE WHOLE WORLD. EVERYONE KNOWS WHO ANDY IS!
AND NOW HE'S NOT JUST SOME CELEBRITY--SOME KID ON A COMMERCIAL. HE'S THE REAL THING.
CAN'T BELIEVE THIS'S HAPPENING!
I'M DATING A SUPER HERO!
NO. I AM DATING THE SUPER HERO.
BETTER THAN ALL THE FF COMBINED.
AND SPIDER-MAN--IS--HIS--SIDEKICK!
OKAY. CALM DOWN. DEEP BREATH.
AHH!
I'M LOIS LANE!
FATHER? I'M CONFUSED. I THOUGHT LOIS LANE WAS "POP CULTURE." A FICTIONAL CHARACTER.
SHE IS. THE GIRL WAS DRAWING AN ANALOGY, PRINCESS.
AH. SHOULD WE KILL HER?
NO. WAIT.
NOK NOK
HI, MR. MAGUIRE. IS ALPHA HOME? IT'S CHRISSY.
CHRISSY?
LET HER IN.
IT'S THE GIRL WHO RUNS ALPHA'S WEBSITE.
JOAN, DID YOU HIRE HER?
IT'S A FAN SITE. GETS A LOT OF TRAFFIC. IT'S GOOD FOR US.
BUT IS IT MONETIZED? 'CAUSE IF IT IS--
RAY. ALICE. I'M ON TOP OF THIS.
IT'S OKAY. I KNOW THE WAY.
OHMIGOD! ANDY, YOU WERE AMAZING LAST NIGHT!
YOU HAVE TO TELL ME ALL ABOUT IT!
WHAT'S THE HUMAN TORCH REALLY--
--LIKE?

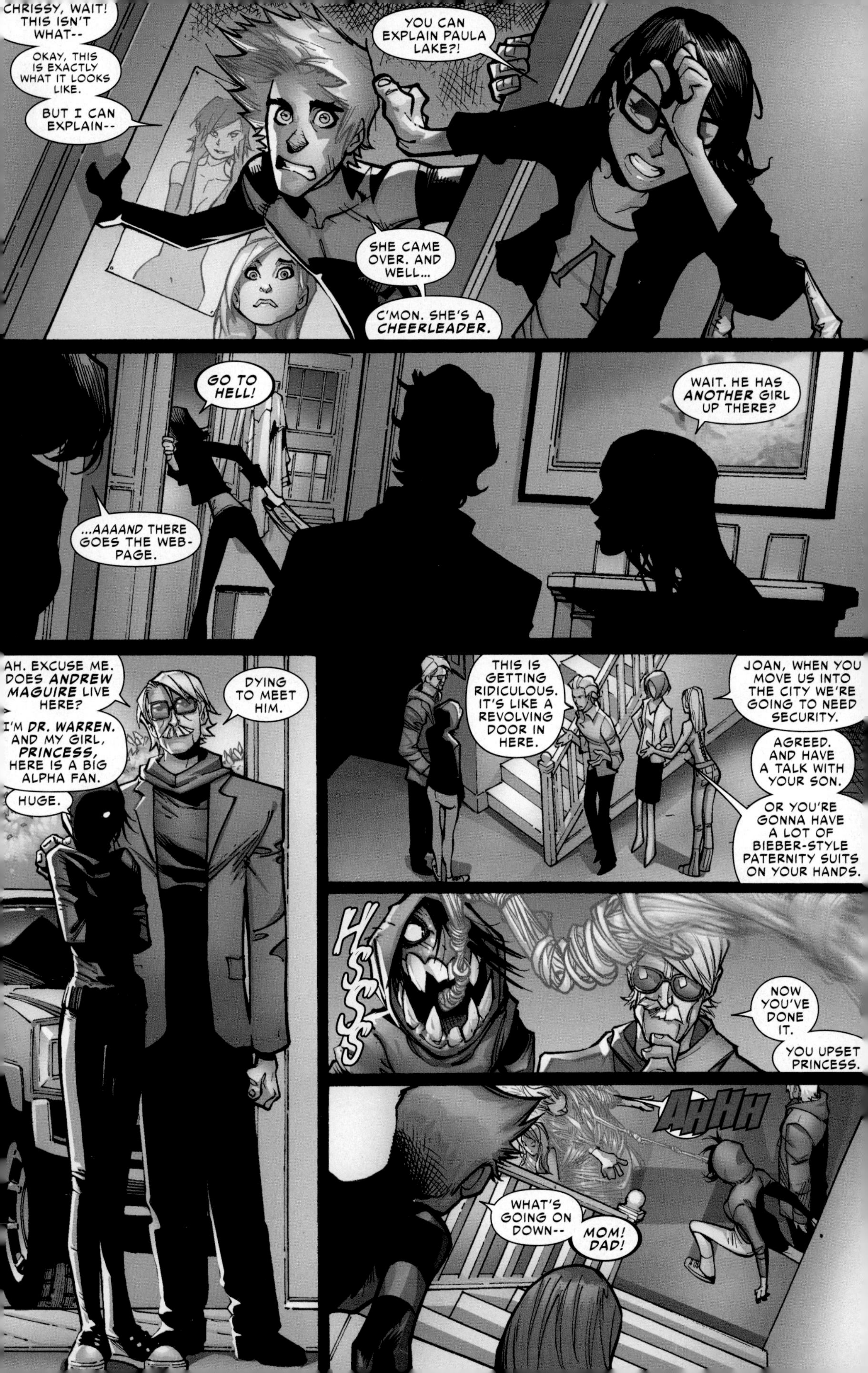

CHRISSY, WAIT! THIS ISN'T WHAT--
OKAY, THIS IS EXACTLY WHAT IT LOOKS LIKE.
BUT I CAN EXPLAIN--
YOU CAN EXPLAIN PAULA LAKE?!
SHE CAME OVER. AND WELL...
C'MON. SHE'S A *CHEERLEADER.*
GO TO *HELL!*
...*AAAAND* THERE GOES THE WEB-PAGE.
WAIT. HE HAS *ANOTHER* GIRL UP THERE?
AH. EXCUSE ME. DOES *ANDREW MAGUIRE* LIVE HERE?
I'M *DR. WARREN.* AND MY GIRL, *PRINCESS,* HERE IS A BIG ALPHA FAN.
HUGE.
DYING TO MEET HIM.
THIS IS GETTING RIDICULOUS. IT'S LIKE A REVOLVING DOOR IN HERE.
JOAN, WHEN YOU MOVE US INTO THE CITY WE'RE GOING TO NEED SECURITY.
AGREED. AND HAVE A TALK WITH YOUR SON.
OR YOU'RE GONNA HAVE A LOT OF BIEBER-STYLE PATERNITY SUITS ON YOUR HANDS.
HSSSS
NOW YOU'VE DONE IT.
YOU UPSET PRINCESS.
AHHH
WHAT'S GOING ON DOWN--
MOM! DAD!

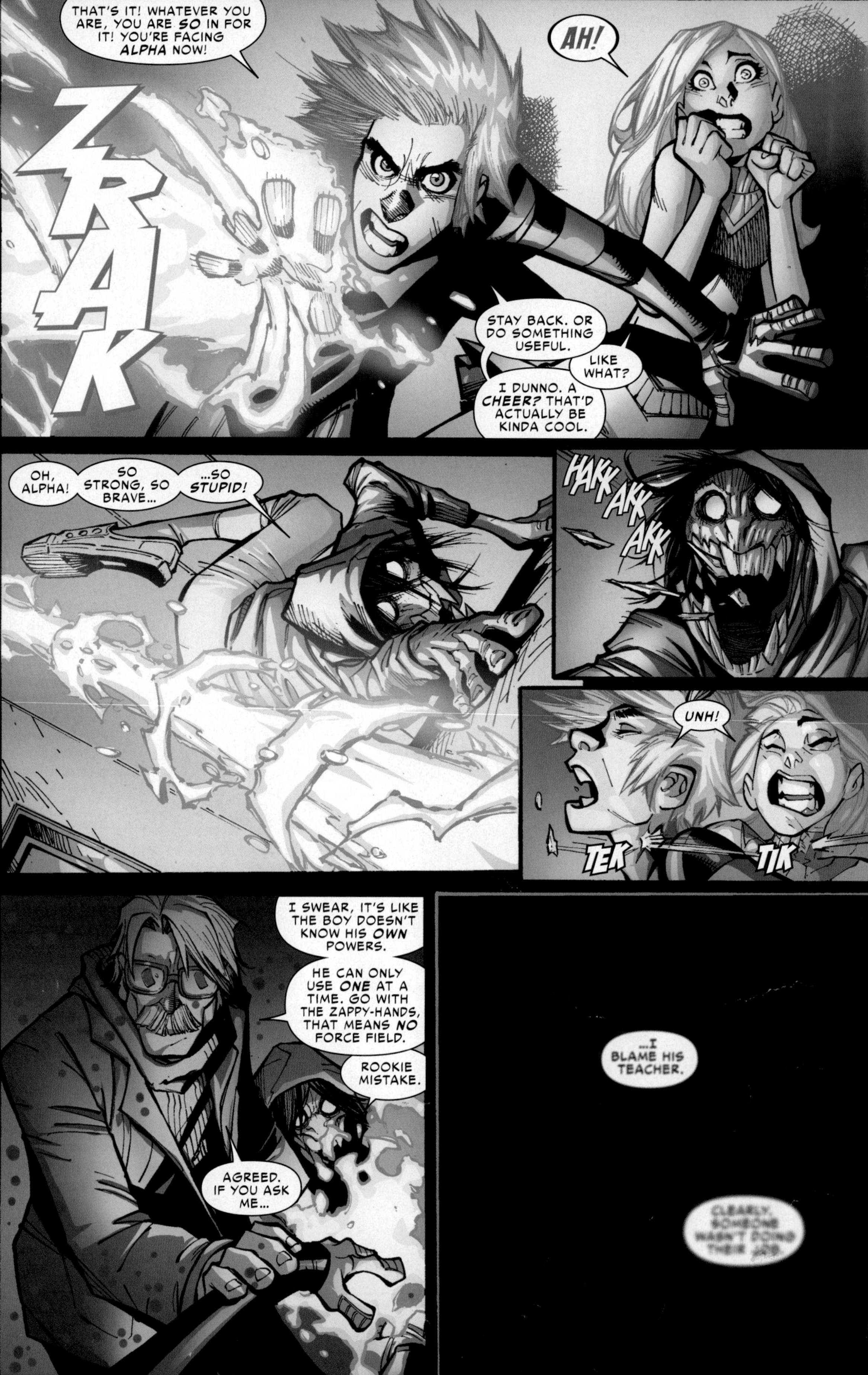
THAT'S IT! WHATEVER YOU ARE, YOU ARE SO IN FOR IT! YOU'RE FACING ALPHA NOW!
ZRAK
AH!
STAY BACK. OR DO SOMETHING USEFUL.
LIKE WHAT?
I DUNNO. A CHEER? THAT'D ACTUALLY BE KINDA COOL.
OH, ALPHA!
SO STRONG, SO BRAVE...
...SO STUPID!
HAKK AKK AKK
UNH!
TEK
TIK
I SWEAR, IT'S LIKE THE BOY DOESN'T KNOW HIS OWN POWERS.
HE CAN ONLY USE ONE AT A TIME. GO WITH THE ZAPPY-HANDS, THAT MEANS NO FORCE FIELD.
ROOKIE MISTAKE.
AGREED. IF YOU ASK ME...
...I BLAME HIS TEACHER.
CLEARLY, SOMEONE WASN'T DOING THEIR JOB.

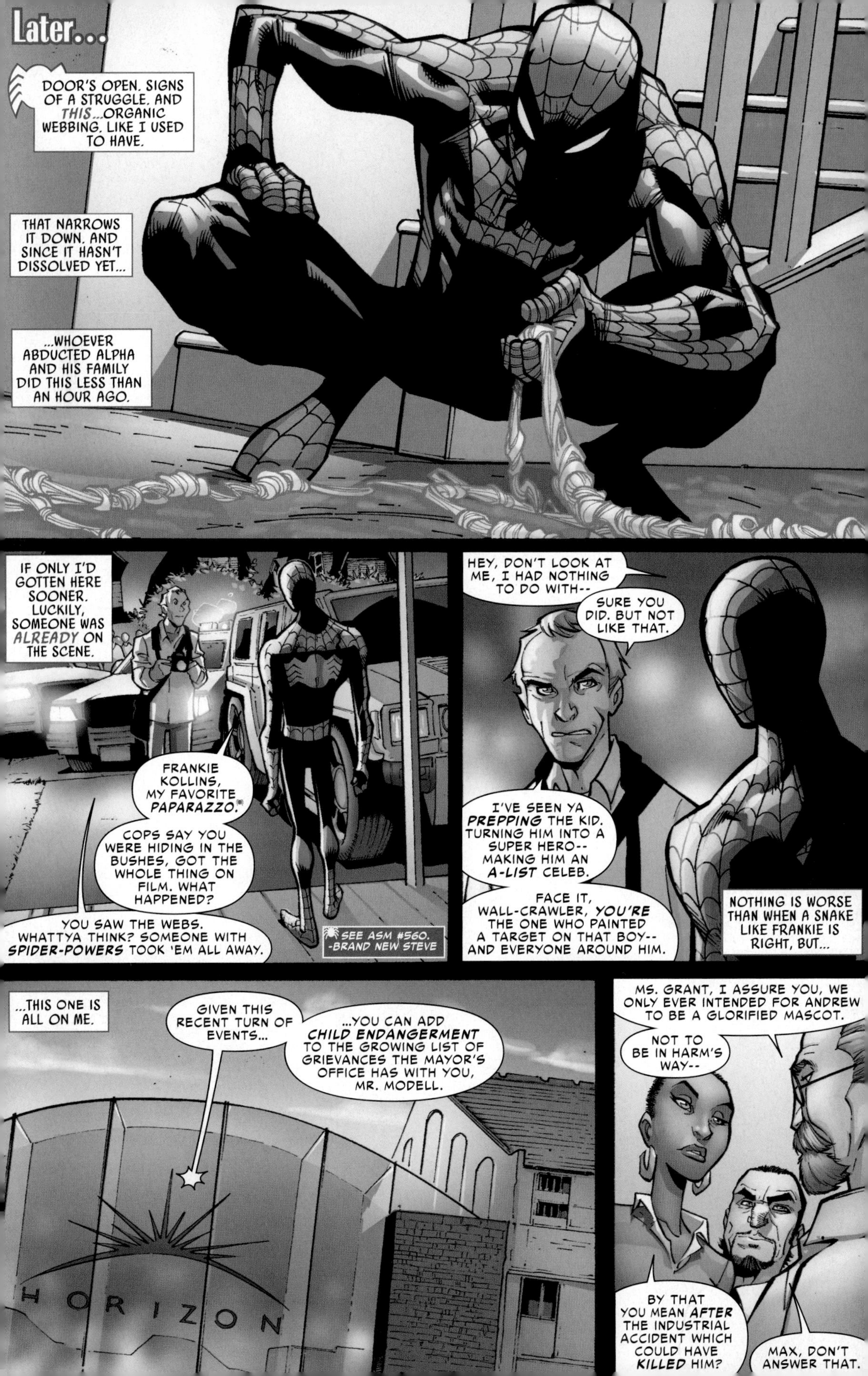

Later...
DOOR'S OPEN. SIGNS OF A STRUGGLE. AND THIS...ORGANIC WEBBING. LIKE I USED TO HAVE.
THAT NARROWS IT DOWN. AND SINCE IT HASN'T DISSOLVED YET...
...WHOEVER ABDUCTED ALPHA AND HIS FAMILY DID THIS LESS THAN AN HOUR AGO.
IF ONLY I'D GOTTEN HERE SOONER. LUCKILY, SOMEONE WAS ALREADY ON THE SCENE.
FRANKIE KOLLINS, MY FAVORITE PAPARAZZO.*
COPS SAY YOU WERE HIDING IN THE BUSHES, GOT THE WHOLE THING ON FILM. WHAT HAPPENED?
YOU SAW THE WEBS. WHATTYA THINK? SOMEONE WITH SPIDER-POWERS TOOK 'EM ALL AWAY.
*SEE ASM #560. -BRAND NEW STEVE
HEY, DON'T LOOK AT ME, I HAD NOTHING TO DO WITH--
SURE YOU DID. BUT NOT LIKE THAT.
I'VE SEEN YA PREPPING THE KID. TURNING HIM INTO A SUPER HERO-- MAKING HIM AN A-LIST CELEB.
FACE IT, WALL-CRAWLER, YOU'RE THE ONE WHO PAINTED A TARGET ON THAT BOY-- AND EVERYONE AROUND HIM.
NOTHING IS WORSE THAN WHEN A SNAKE LIKE FRANKIE IS RIGHT, BUT...
...THIS ONE IS ALL ON ME.
GIVEN THIS RECENT TURN OF EVENTS...
...YOU CAN ADD CHILD ENDANGERMENT TO THE GROWING LIST OF GRIEVANCES THE MAYOR'S OFFICE HAS WITH YOU, MR. MODELL.
HORIZON
MS. GRANT, I ASSURE YOU, WE ONLY EVER INTENDED FOR ANDREW TO BE A GLORIFIED MASCOT.
NOT TO BE IN HARM'S WAY--
BY THAT YOU MEAN AFTER THE INDUSTRIAL ACCIDENT WHICH COULD HAVE KILLED HIM?
MAX, DON'T ANSWER THAT.

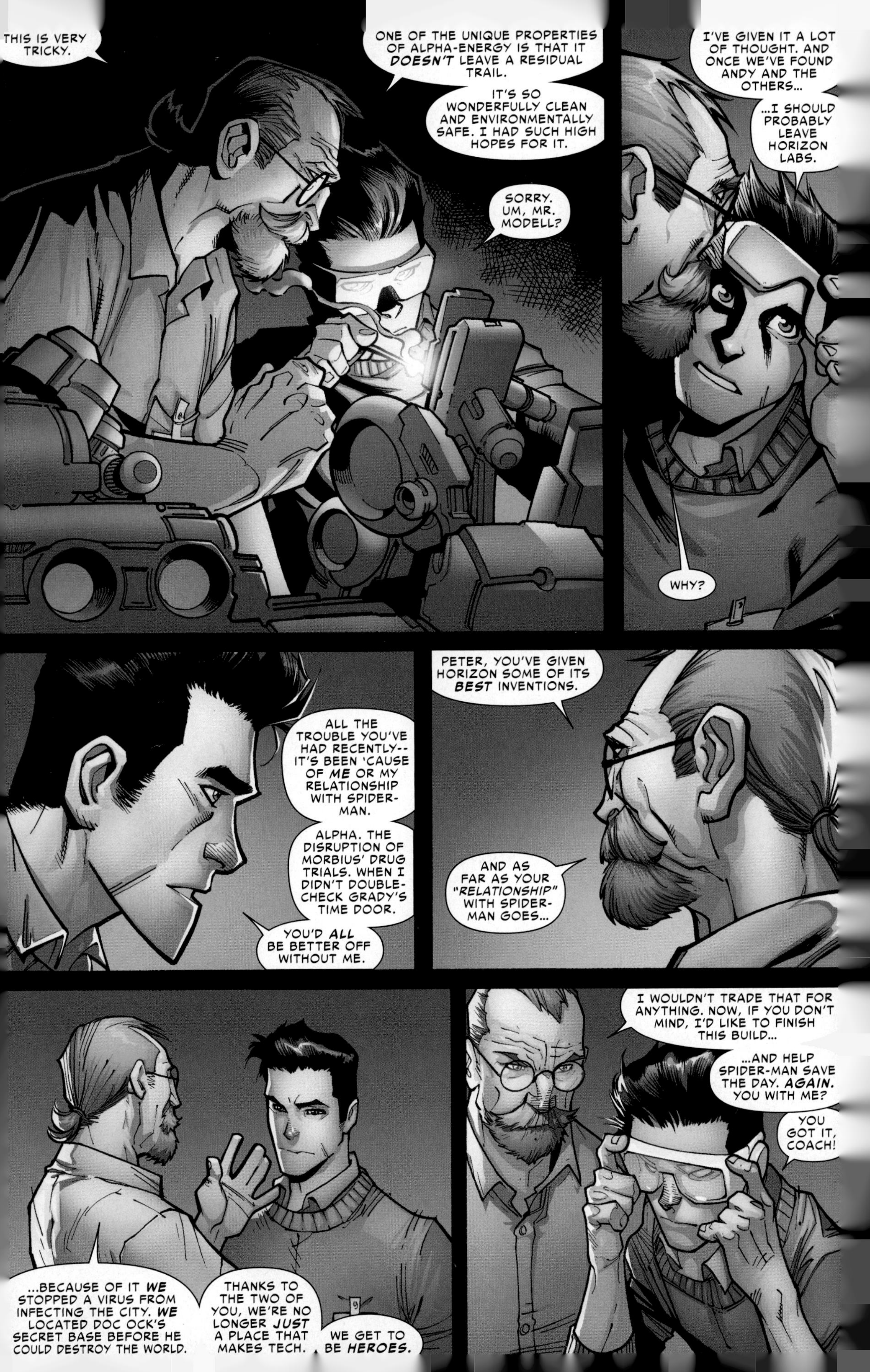
THIS IS VERY TRICKY.
ONE OF THE UNIQUE PROPERTIES OF ALPHA-ENERGY IS THAT IT DOESN'T LEAVE A RESIDUAL TRAIL.
IT'S SO WONDERFULLY CLEAN AND ENVIRONMENTALLY SAFE. I HAD SUCH HIGH HOPES FOR IT.
SORRY. UM, MR. MODELL?
I'VE GIVEN IT A LOT OF THOUGHT. AND ONCE WE'VE FOUND ANDY AND THE OTHERS...
...I SHOULD PROBABLY LEAVE HORIZON LABS.
WHY?
ALL THE TROUBLE YOU'VE HAD RECENTLY--IT'S BEEN 'CAUSE OF ME OR MY RELATIONSHIP WITH SPIDER-MAN.
ALPHA. THE DISRUPTION OF MORBIUS' DRUG TRIALS. WHEN I DIDN'T DOUBLE-CHECK GRADY'S TIME DOOR.
YOU'D ALL BE BETTER OFF WITHOUT ME.
PETER, YOU'VE GIVEN HORIZON SOME OF ITS BEST INVENTIONS.
AND AS FAR AS YOUR "RELATIONSHIP" WITH SPIDER-MAN GOES...
...BECAUSE OF IT WE STOPPED A VIRUS FROM INFECTING THE CITY. WE LOCATED DOC OCK'S SECRET BASE BEFORE HE COULD DESTROY THE WORLD.
THANKS TO THE TWO OF YOU, WE'RE NO LONGER JUST A PLACE THAT MAKES TECH.
WE GET TO BE HEROES.
I WOULDN'T TRADE THAT FOR ANYTHING. NOW, IF YOU DON'T MIND, I'D LIKE TO FINISH THIS BUILD...
...AND HELP SPIDER-MAN SAVE THE DAY. AGAIN. YOU WITH ME?
YOU GOT IT, COACH!

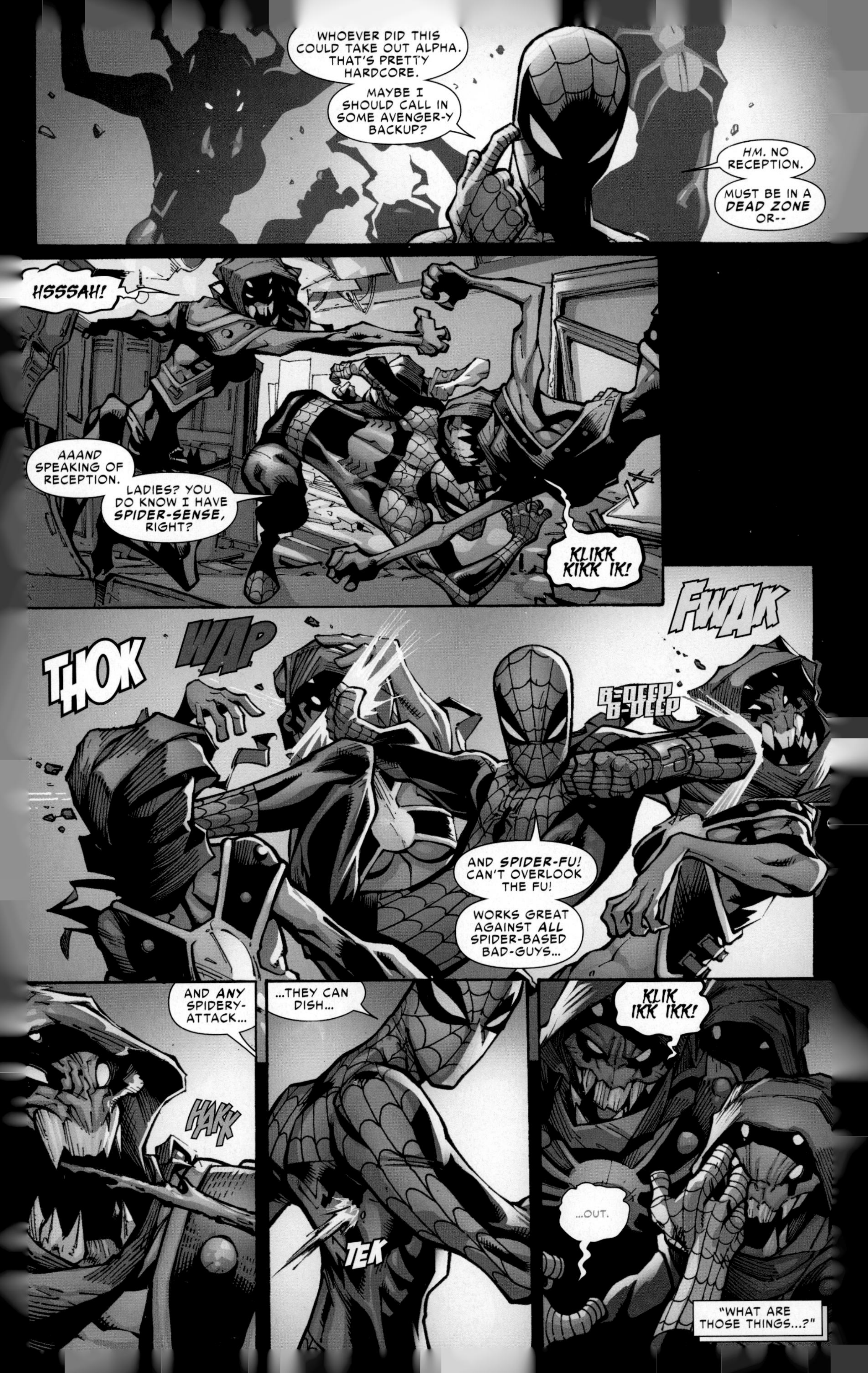
WHOEVER DID THIS COULD TAKE OUT ALPHA. THAT'S PRETTY HARDCORE.
MAYBE I SHOULD CALL IN SOME AVENGER-Y BACKUP?
HM. NO RECEPTION.
MUST BE IN A DEAD ZONE OR--
HSSSAH!
AAAND SPEAKING OF RECEPTION.
LADIES? YOU DO KNOW I HAVE SPIDER-SENSE, RIGHT?
KLIKK KIKK IK!
THOK
WAP
FWAK
B-DEEP B-DEEP
AND SPIDER-FU! CAN'T OVERLOOK THE FU!
WORKS GREAT AGAINST ALL SPIDER-BASED BAD-GUYS...
AND ANY SPIDERY-ATTACK...
HAKK
...THEY CAN DISH...
TEK
KLIK IKK IKK!
...OUT.
"WHAT ARE THOSE THINGS...?"

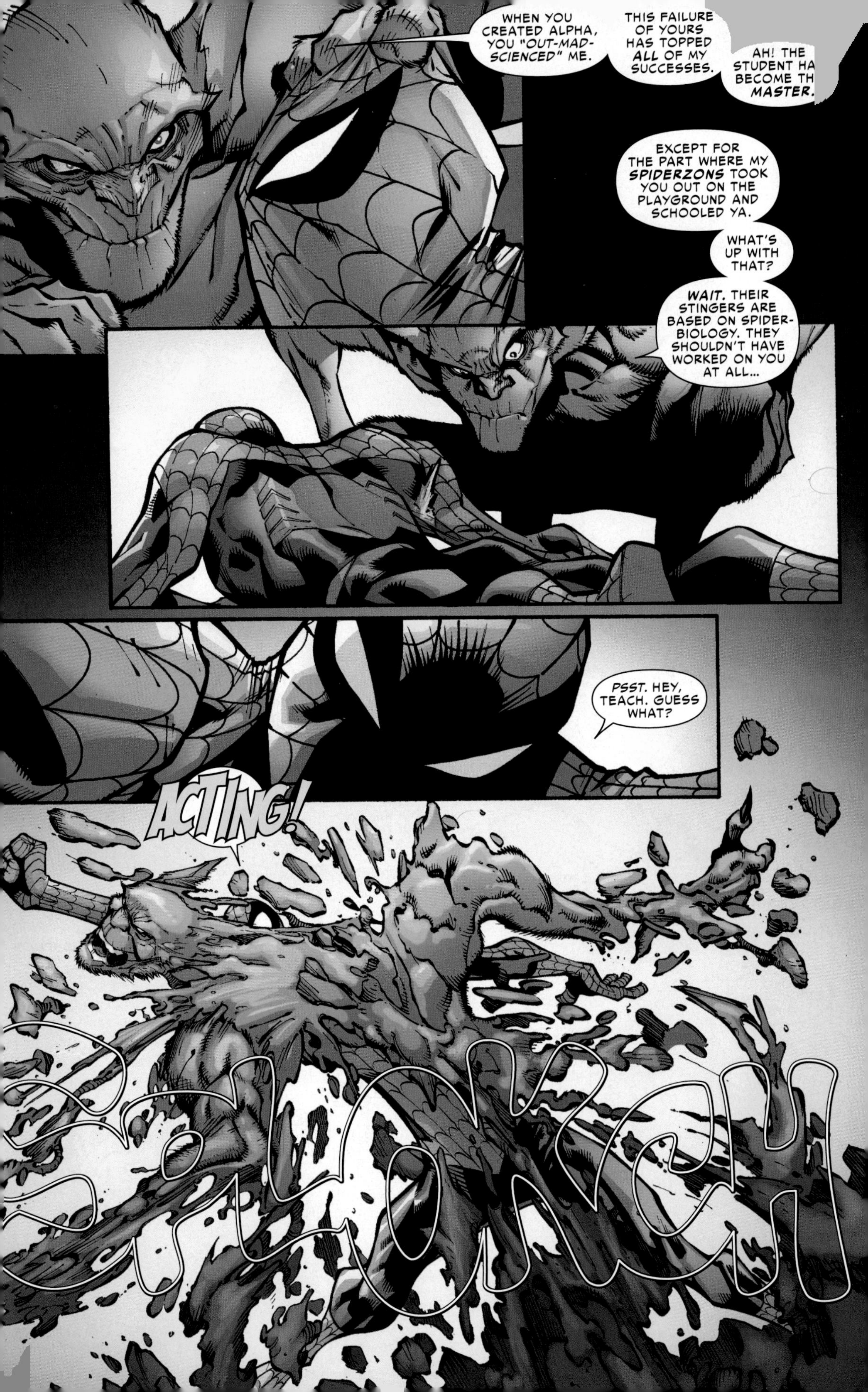
WHEN YOU CREATED ALPHA, YOU "OUT-MAD-SCIENCED" ME.
THIS FAILURE OF YOURS HAS TOPPED **ALL** OF MY SUCCESSES.
AH! THE STUDENT HA BECOME TH ***MASTER.***
EXCEPT FOR THE PART WHERE MY ***SPIDERZONS*** TOOK YOU OUT ON THE PLAYGROUND AND SCHOOLED YA.
WHAT'S UP WITH THAT?
WAIT. THEIR STINGERS ARE BASED ON SPIDER-BIOLOGY. THEY SHOULDN'T HAVE WORKED ON YOU AT ALL...
PSST. HEY, TEACH. GUESS WHAT?
ACTING!

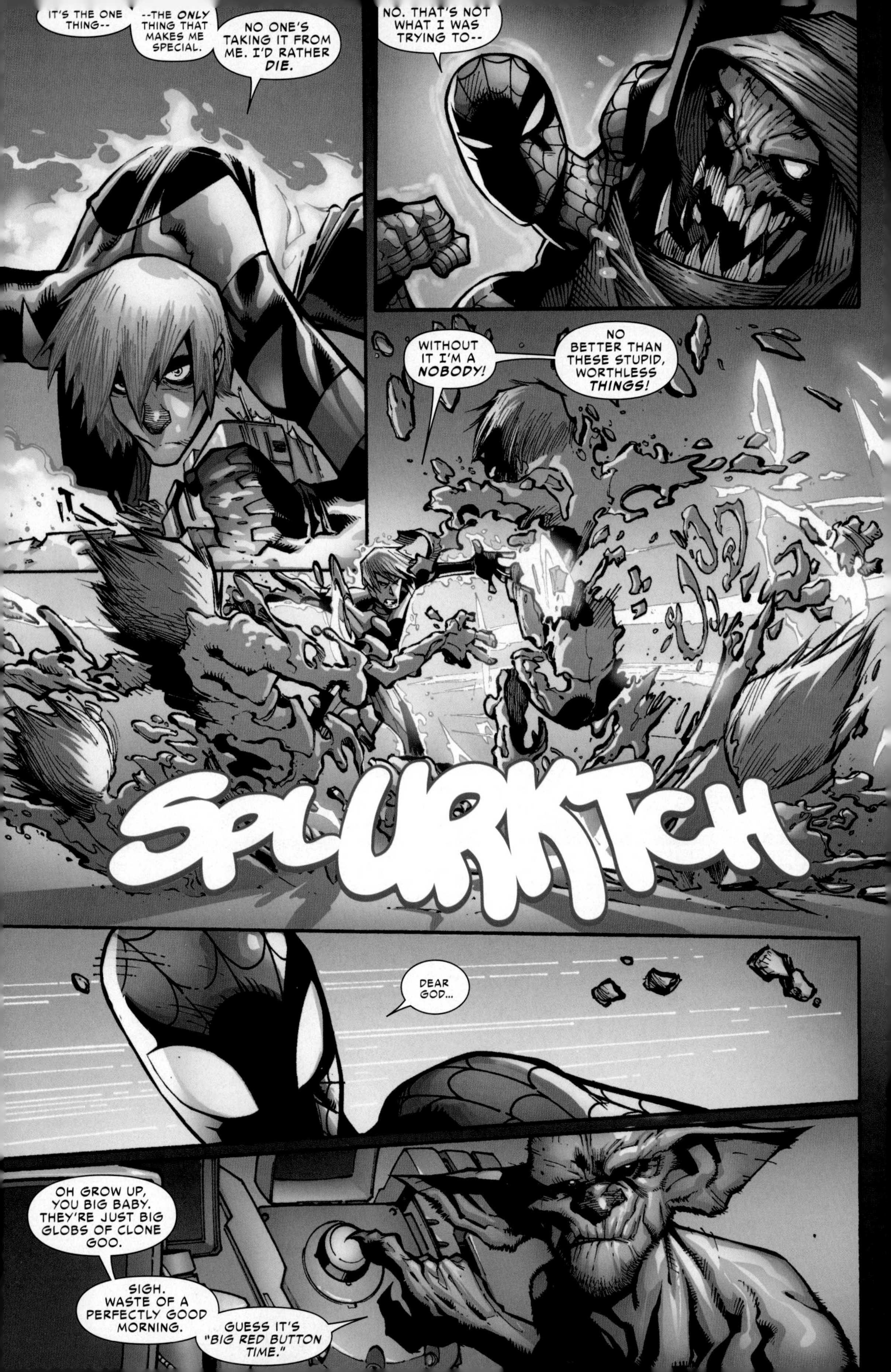
IT'S THE ONE THING--
--THE *ONLY* THING THAT MAKES ME SPECIAL.
NO ONE'S TAKING IT FROM ME. I'D RATHER *DIE.*
NO. THAT'S NOT WHAT I WAS TRYING TO--
WITHOUT IT I'M A *NOBODY!*
NO BETTER THAN THESE STUPID, WORTHLESS *THINGS!*
SPLURKTCH
DEAR GOD...
OH GROW UP, YOU BIG BABY. THEY'RE JUST BIG GLOBS OF CLONE GOO.
SIGH. WASTE OF A PERFECTLY GOOD MORNING.
GUESS IT'S *"BIG RED BUTTON TIME."*

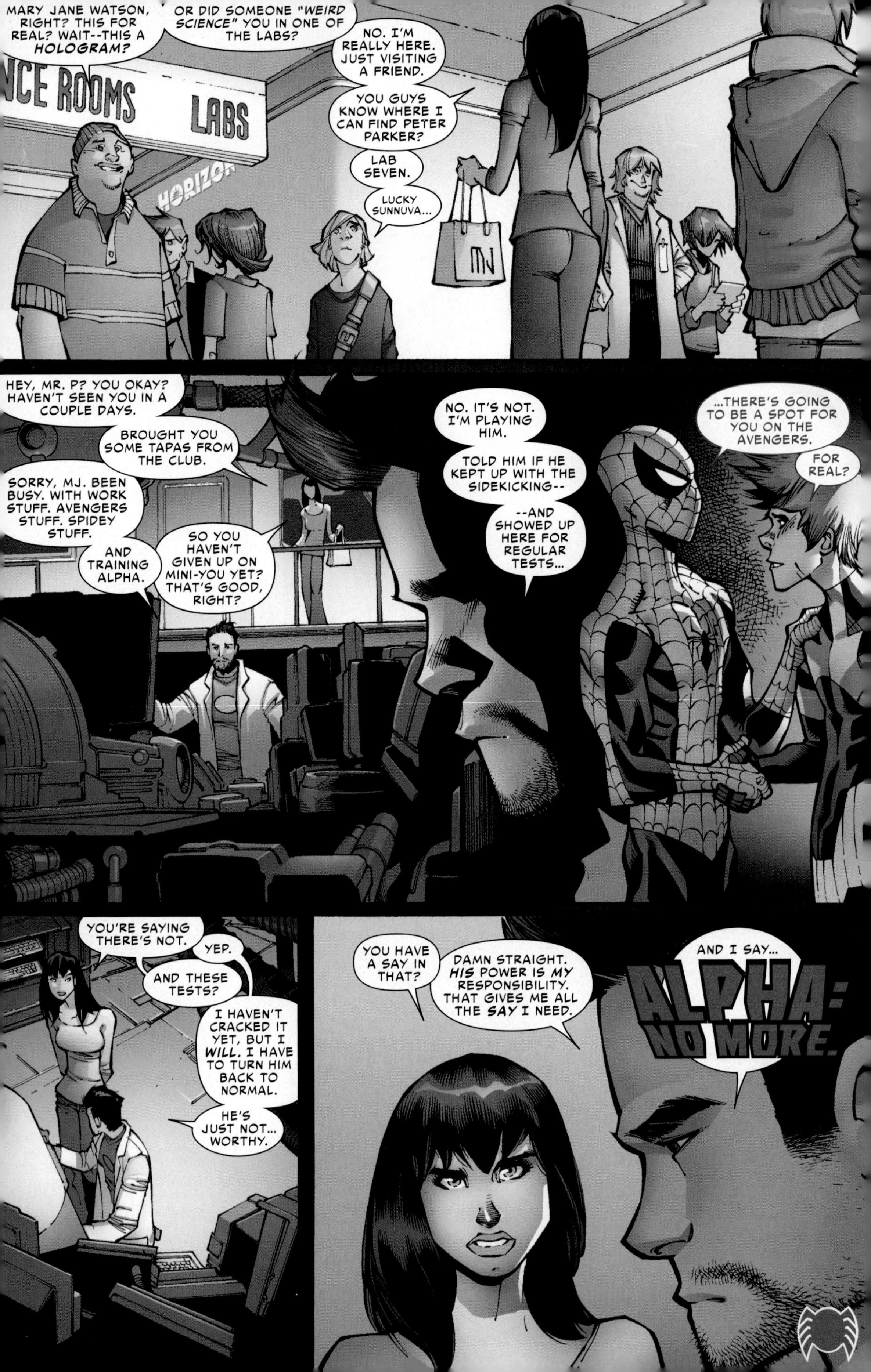
MARY JANE WATSON, RIGHT? THIS FOR REAL? WAIT--THIS A HOLOGRAM?
OR DID SOMEONE "WEIRD SCIENCE" YOU IN ONE OF THE LABS?
NCE ROOMS
LABS
HORIZON
NO. I'M REALLY HERE. JUST VISITING A FRIEND.
YOU GUYS KNOW WHERE I CAN FIND PETER PARKER?
LAB SEVEN.
LUCKY SUNNUVA...
HEY, MR. P? YOU OKAY? HAVEN'T SEEN YOU IN A COUPLE DAYS.
BROUGHT YOU SOME TAPAS FROM THE CLUB.
SORRY, MJ. BEEN BUSY. WITH WORK STUFF. AVENGERS STUFF. SPIDEY STUFF.
AND TRAINING ALPHA.
SO YOU HAVEN'T GIVEN UP ON MINI-YOU YET? THAT'S GOOD, RIGHT?
NO. IT'S NOT. I'M PLAYING HIM.
TOLD HIM IF HE KEPT UP WITH THE SIDEKICKING--
--AND SHOWED UP HERE FOR REGULAR TESTS...
...THERE'S GOING TO BE A SPOT FOR YOU ON THE AVENGERS.
FOR REAL?
YOU'RE SAYING THERE'S NOT.
YEP.
AND THESE TESTS?
I HAVEN'T CRACKED IT YET, BUT I WILL. I HAVE TO TURN HIM BACK TO NORMAL.
HE'S JUST NOT... WORTHY.
YOU HAVE A SAY IN THAT?
DAMN STRAIGHT. HIS POWER IS MY RESPONSIBILITY. THAT GIVES ME ALL THE SAY I NEED.
AND I SAY...
ALPHA: NO MORE.

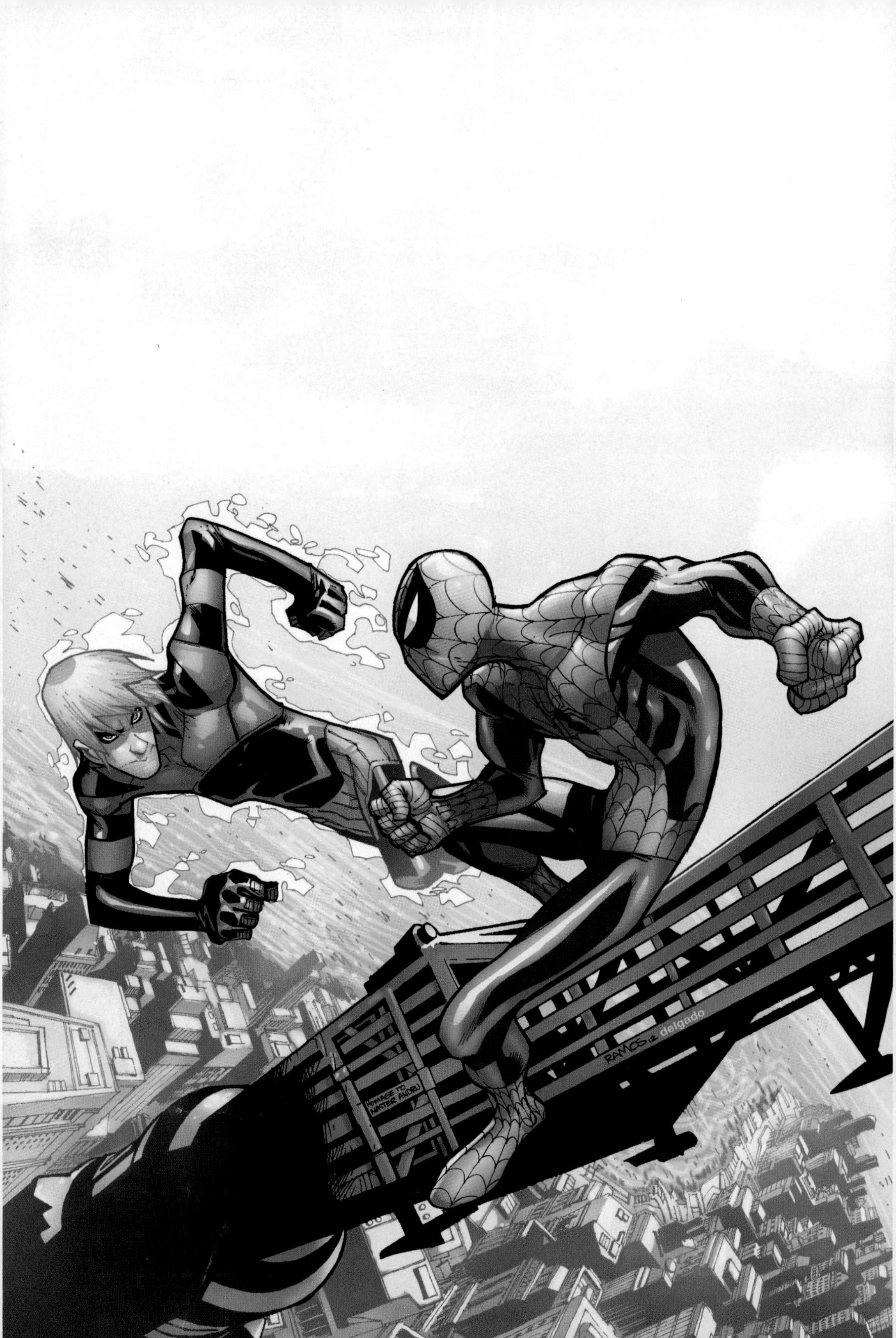

HOMMAGE TO MASTER ANDRU
RAMOS '12
delgado

SPIDER-M
& EDGAR D

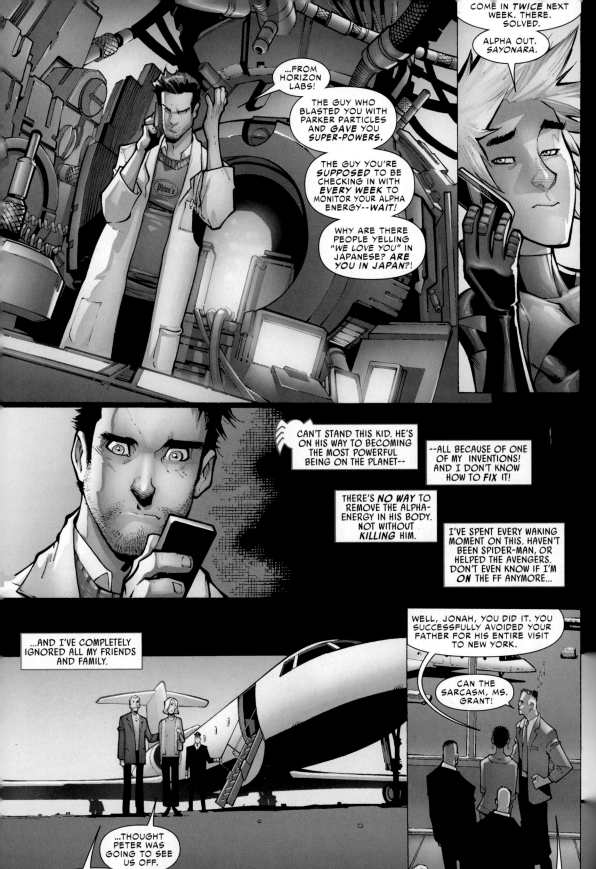

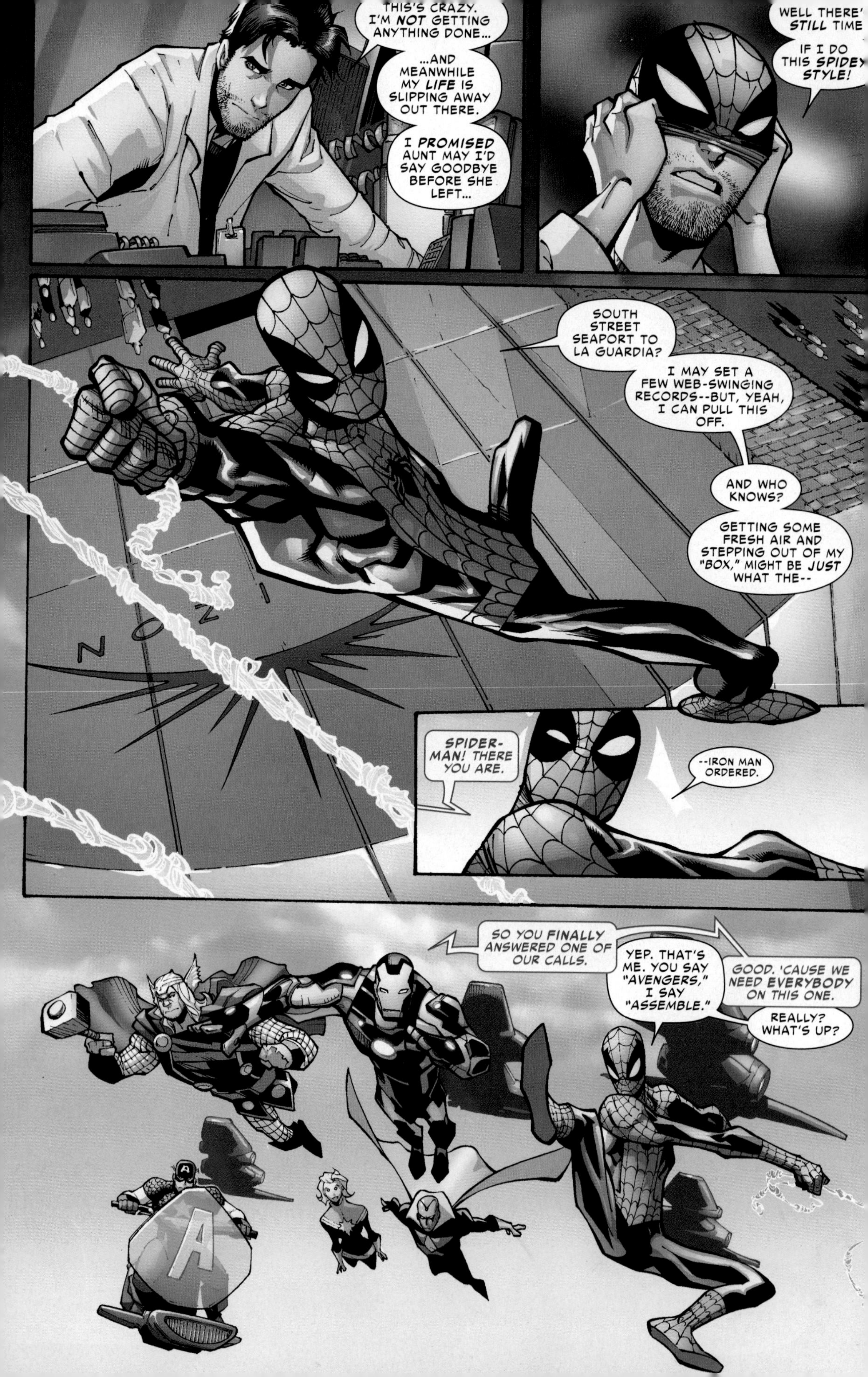
THIS'S CRAZY. I'M NOT GETTING ANYTHING DONE...
...AND MEANWHILE MY LIFE IS SLIPPING AWAY OUT THERE.
I PROMISED AUNT MAY I'D SAY GOODBYE BEFORE SHE LEFT...
WELL THERE' STILL TIME
IF I DO THIS SPIDEY STYLE!
SOUTH STREET SEAPORT TO LA GUARDIA?
I MAY SET A FEW WEB-SWINGING RECORDS--BUT, YEAH, I CAN PULL THIS OFF.
AND WHO KNOWS?
GETTING SOME FRESH AIR AND STEPPING OUT OF MY "BOX," MIGHT BE JUST WHAT THE--
SPIDER-MAN! THERE YOU ARE.
--IRON MAN ORDERED.
SO YOU FINALLY ANSWERED ONE OF OUR CALLS.
YEP. THAT'S ME. YOU SAY "AVENGERS," I SAY "ASSEMBLE."
GOOD. 'CAUSE WE NEED EVERYBODY ON THIS ONE.
REALLY? WHAT'S UP?

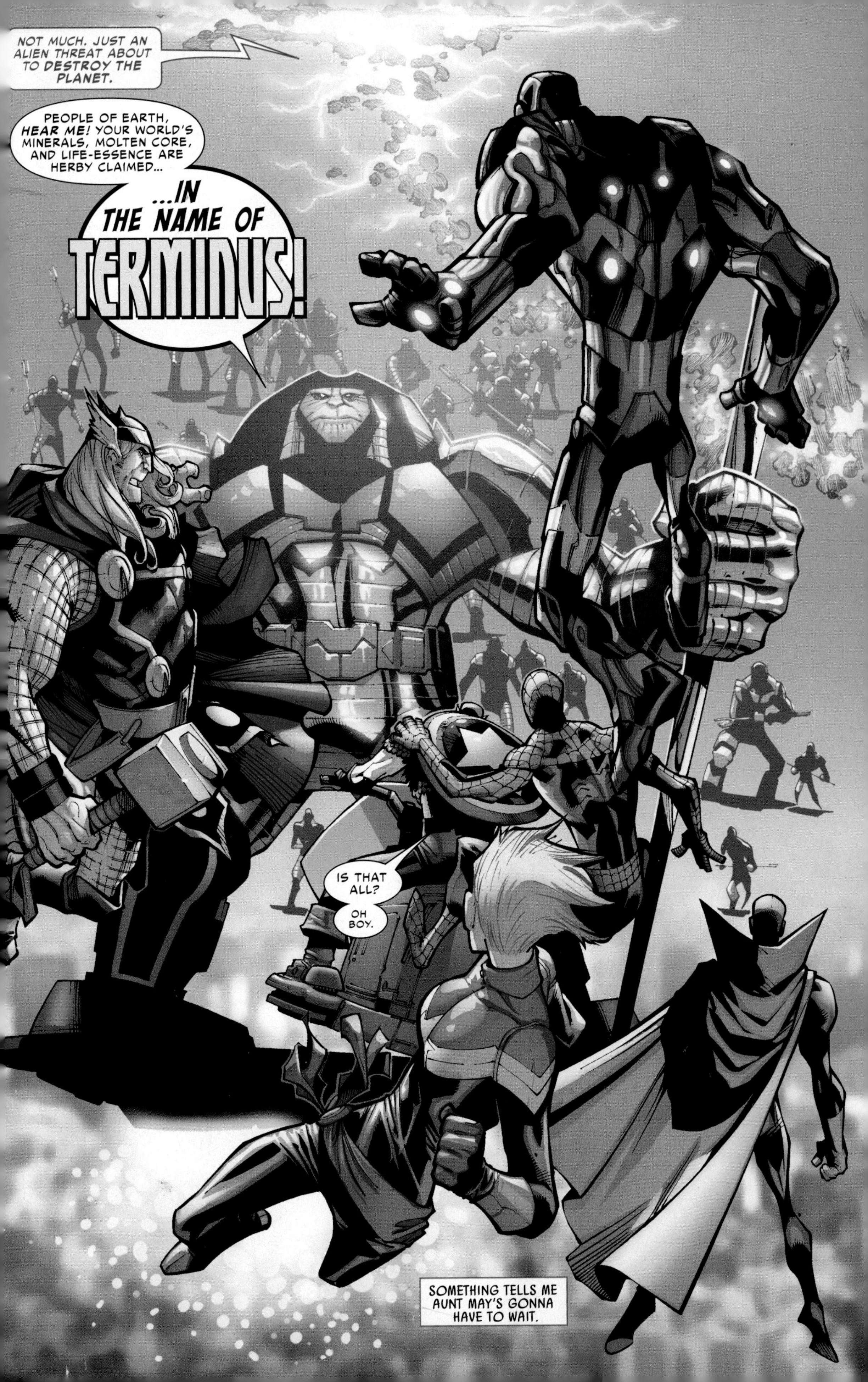
NOT MUCH. JUST AN ALIEN THREAT ABOUT TO DESTROY THE PLANET.
PEOPLE OF EARTH, HEAR ME! YOUR WORLD'S MINERALS, MOLTEN CORE, AND LIFE-ESSENCE ARE HERBY CLAIMED...
...IN THE NAME OF TERMINUS!
IS THAT ALL?
OH BOY.
SOMETHING TELLS ME AUNT MAY'S GONNA HAVE TO WAIT.

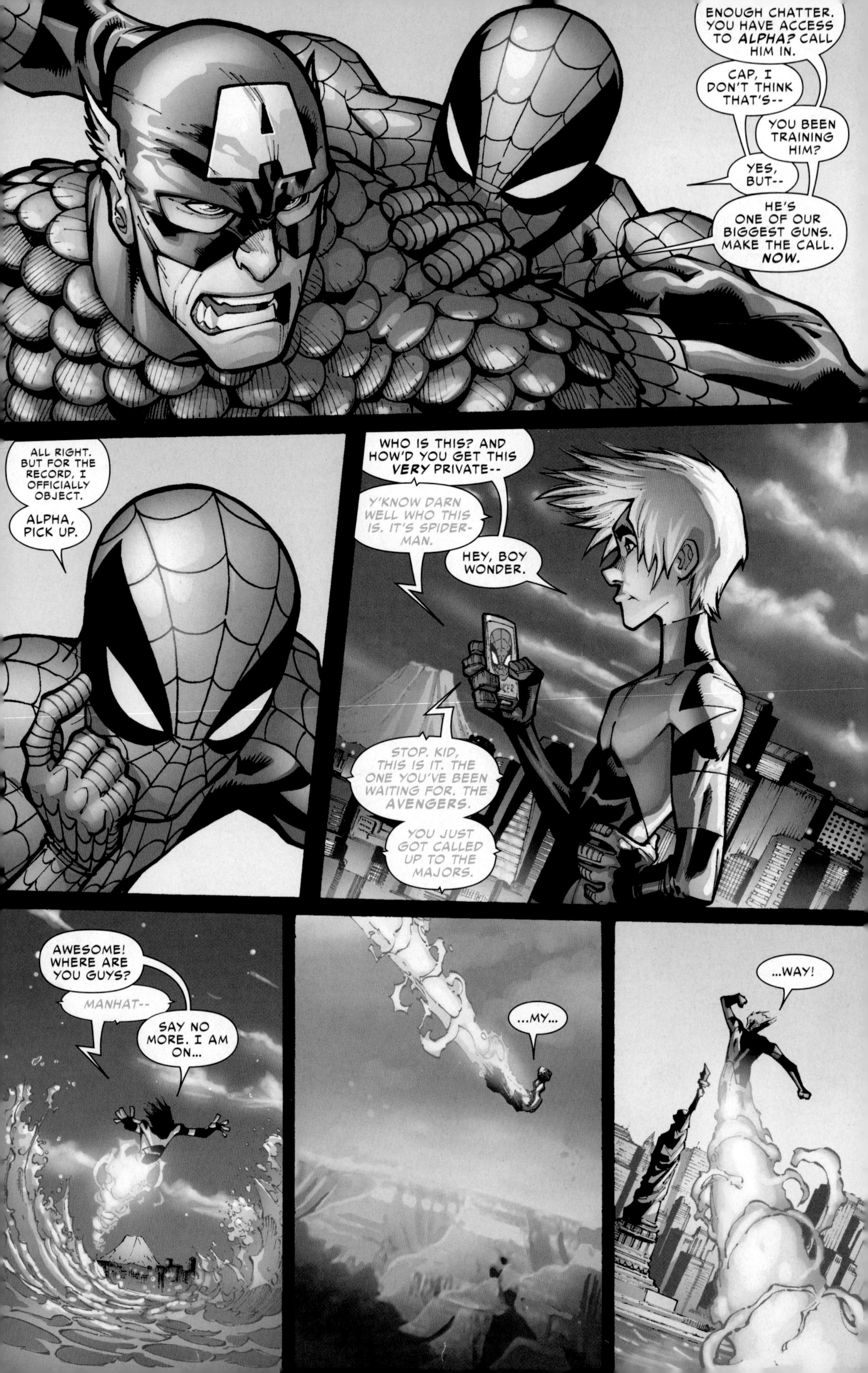
ENOUGH CHATTER. YOU HAVE ACCESS TO ALPHA? CALL HIM IN.
CAP, I DON'T THINK THAT'S--
YOU BEEN TRAINING HIM?
YES, BUT--
HE'S ONE OF OUR BIGGEST GUNS. MAKE THE CALL. NOW.
ALL RIGHT. BUT FOR THE RECORD, I OFFICIALLY OBJECT.
ALPHA, PICK UP.
WHO IS THIS? AND HOW'D YOU GET THIS VERY PRIVATE--
Y'KNOW DARN WELL WHO THIS IS. IT'S SPIDER-MAN.
HEY, BOY WONDER.
STOP. KID, THIS IS IT. THE ONE YOU'VE BEEN WAITING FOR. THE AVENGERS.
YOU JUST GOT CALLED UP TO THE MAJORS.
AWESOME! WHERE ARE YOU GUYS?
MANHAT--
SAY NO MORE. I AM ON...
...MY...
...WAY!

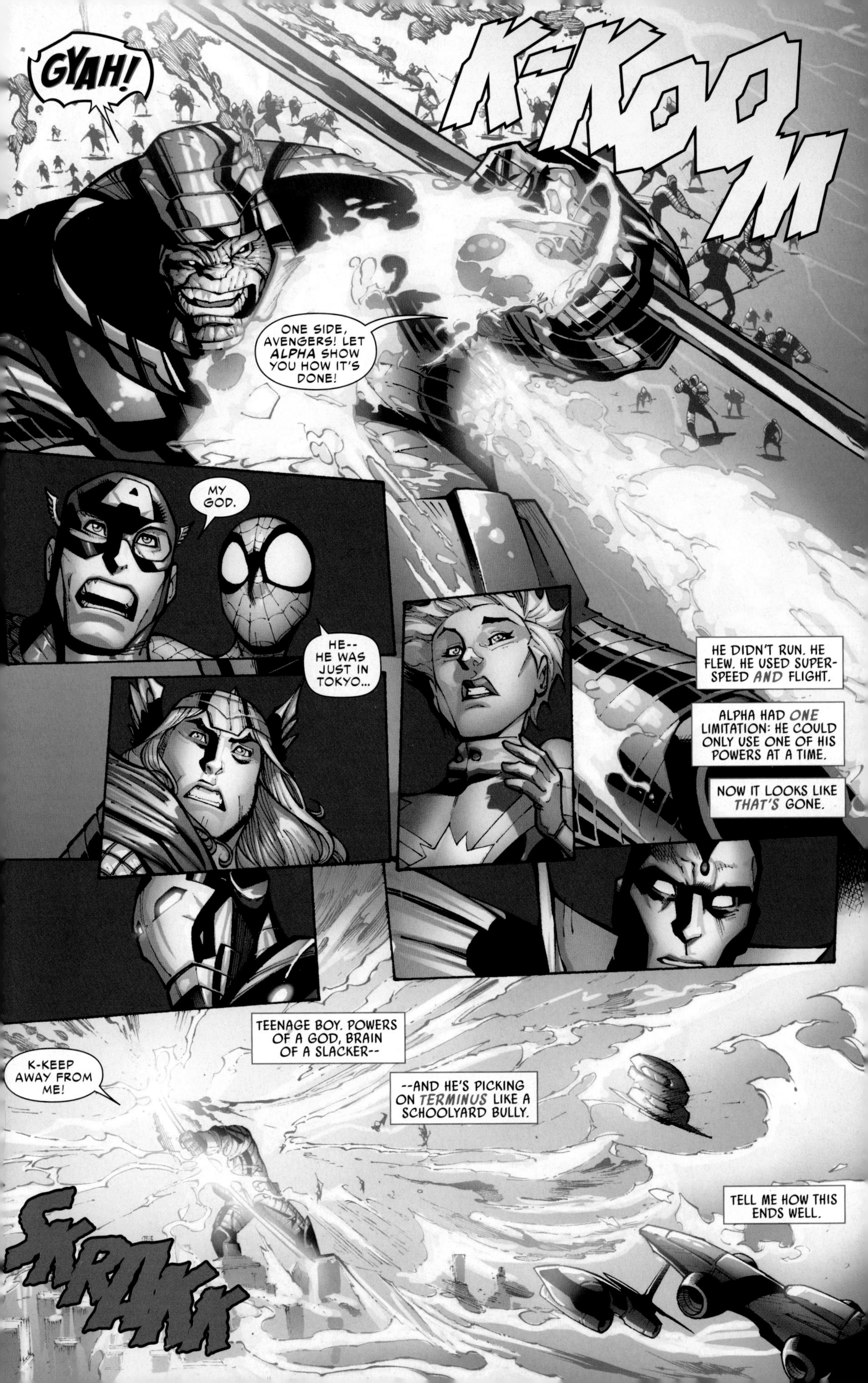
GYAH!
K-KOOM
ONE SIDE, AVENGERS! LET ALPHA SHOW YOU HOW IT'S DONE!
MY GOD.
HE-- HE WAS JUST IN TOKYO...
HE DIDN'T RUN. HE FLEW. HE USED SUPER-SPEED AND FLIGHT.
ALPHA HAD ONE LIMITATION: HE COULD ONLY USE ONE OF HIS POWERS AT A TIME.
NOW IT LOOKS LIKE THAT'S GONE.
TEENAGE BOY. POWERS OF A GOD, BRAIN OF A SLACKER--
K-KEEP AWAY FROM ME!
--AND HE'S PICKING ON TERMINUS LIKE A SCHOOLYARD BULLY.
TELL ME HOW THIS ENDS WELL.

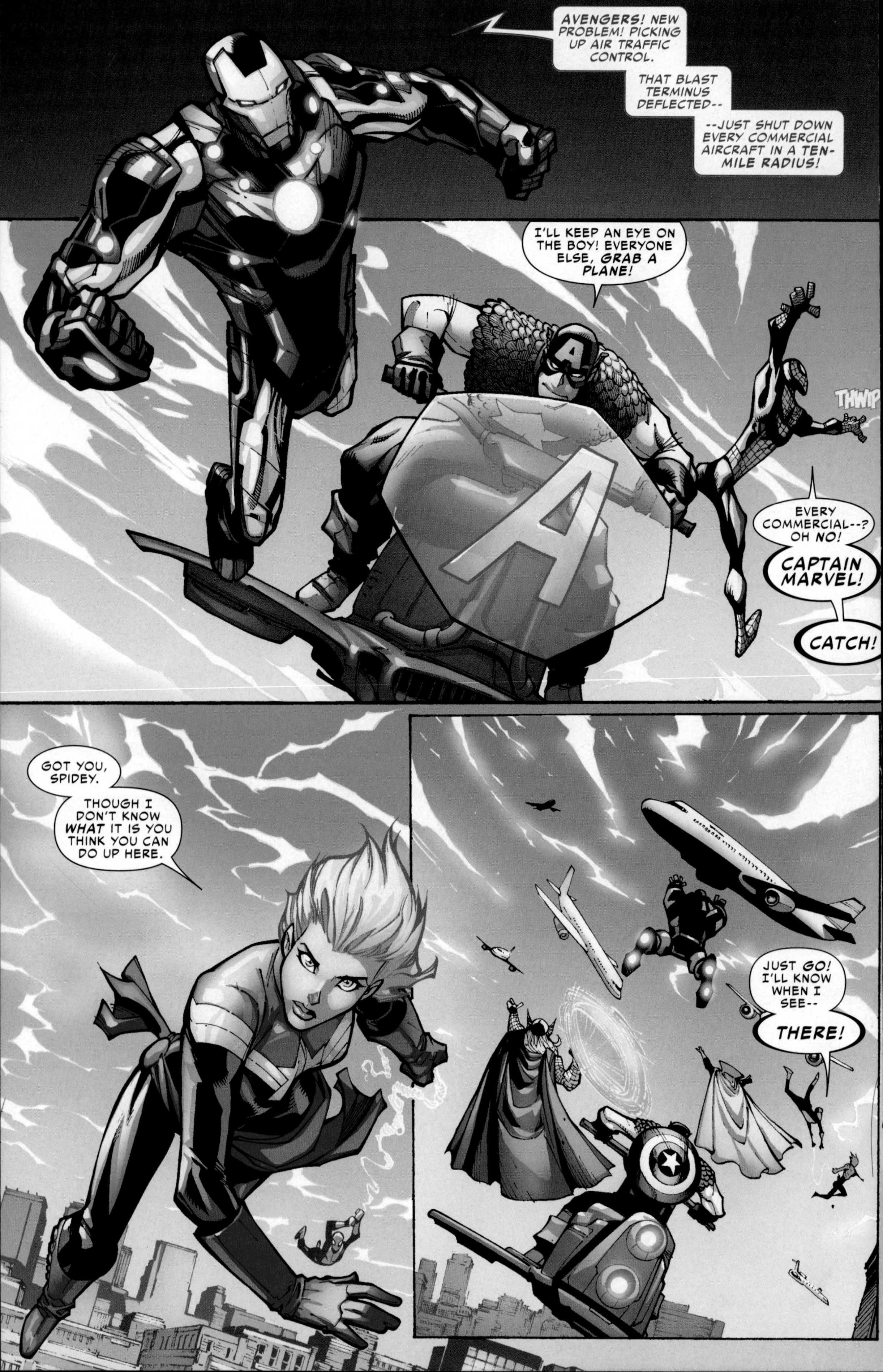
AVENGERS! NEW PROBLEM! PICKING UP AIR TRAFFIC CONTROL.
THAT BLAST TERMINUS DEFLECTED--
--JUST SHUT DOWN EVERY COMMERCIAL AIRCRAFT IN A TEN-MILE RADIUS!
I'LL KEEP AN EYE ON THE BOY! EVERYONE ELSE, GRAB A PLANE!
THWIP
EVERY COMMERCIAL--? OH NO!
CAPTAIN MARVEL!
CATCH!
GOT YOU, SPIDEY.
THOUGH I DON'T KNOW WHAT IT IS YOU THINK YOU CAN DO UP HERE.
JUST GO! I'LL KNOW WHEN I SEE--
THERE!

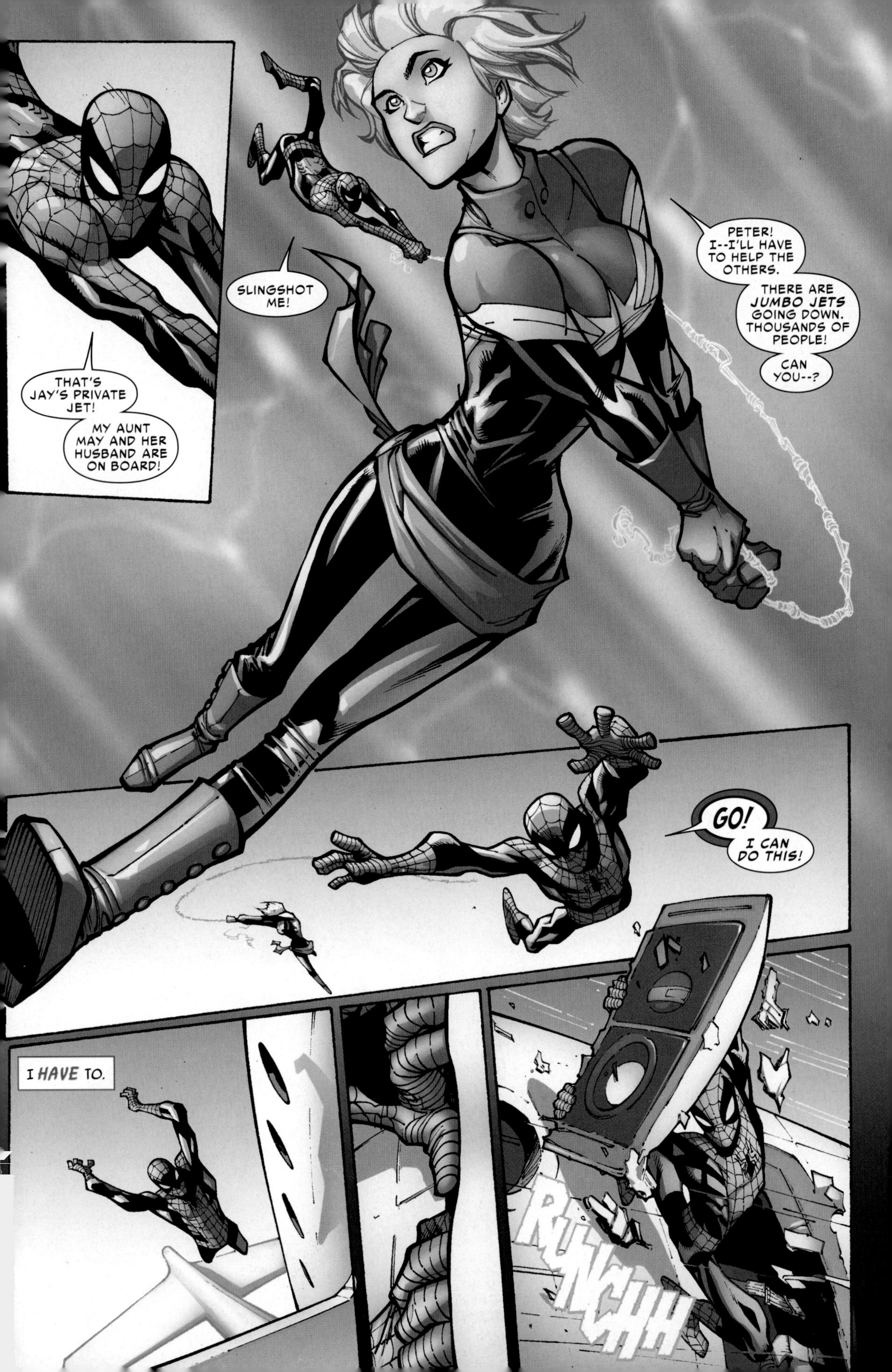
THAT'S JAY'S PRIVATE JET!
MY AUNT MAY AND HER HUSBAND ARE ON BOARD!
SLINGSHOT ME!
PETER! I--I'LL HAVE TO HELP THE OTHERS.
THERE ARE JUMBO JETS GOING DOWN. THOUSANDS OF PEOPLE!
CAN YOU--?
GO! I CAN DO THIS!
I HAVE TO.
RUNCHH

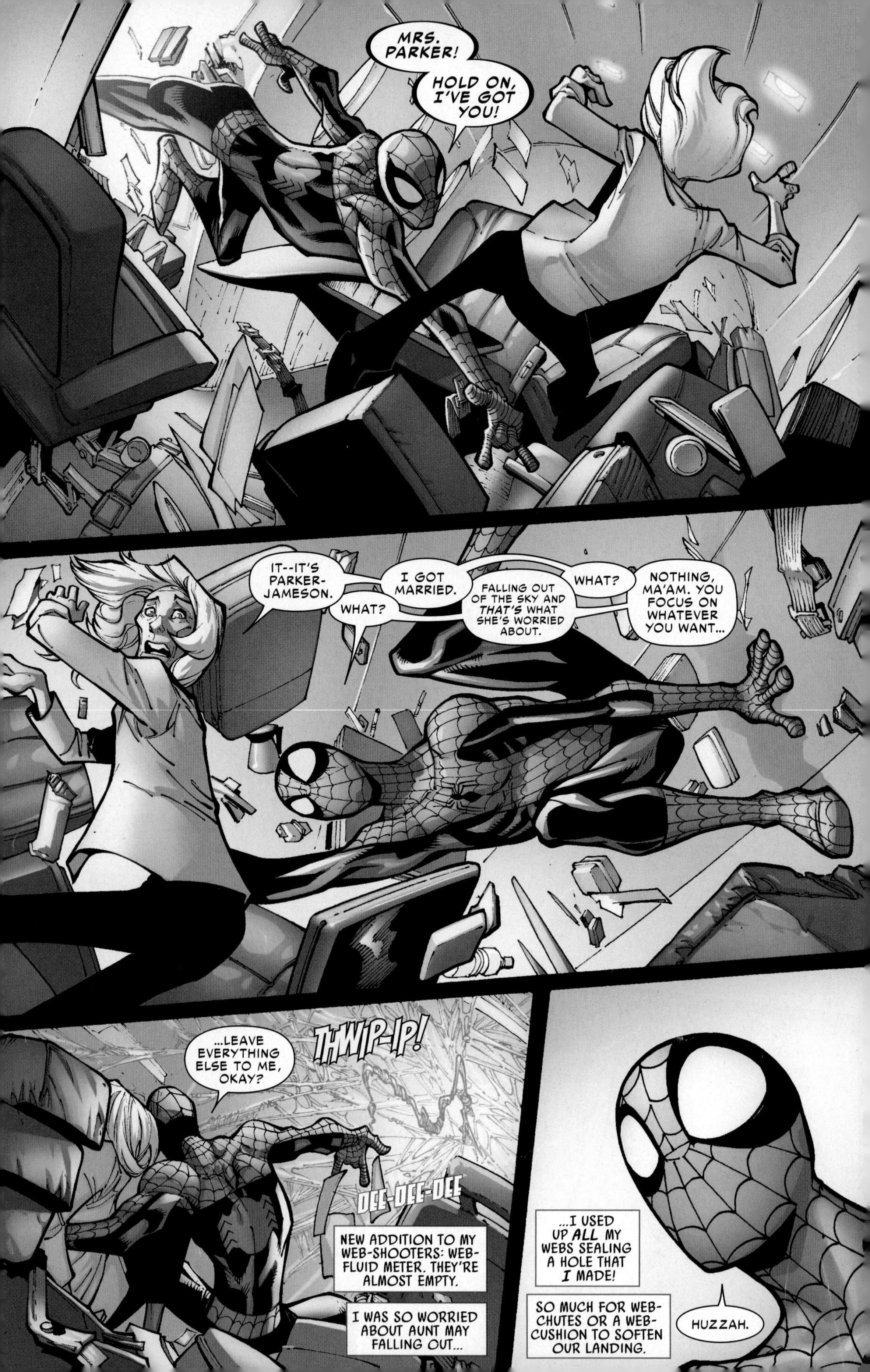
MRS. PARKER!
HOLD ON, I'VE GOT YOU!
IT--IT'S PARKER-JAMESON.
WHAT?
I GOT MARRIED.
WHAT?
FALLING OUT OF THE SKY AND THAT'S WHAT SHE'S WORRIED ABOUT.
NOTHING, MA'AM. YOU FOCUS ON WHATEVER YOU WANT...
...LEAVE EVERYTHING ELSE TO ME, OKAY?
THWIP-IP!
DEE-DEE-DEE
NEW ADDITION TO MY WEB-SHOOTERS: WEB-FLUID METER. THEY'RE ALMOST EMPTY.
I WAS SO WORRIED ABOUT AUNT MAY FALLING OUT...
...I USED UP ALL MY WEBS SEALING A HOLE THAT I MADE!
SO MUCH FOR WEB-CHUTES OR A WEB-CUSHION TO SOFTEN OUR LANDING.
HUZZAH.

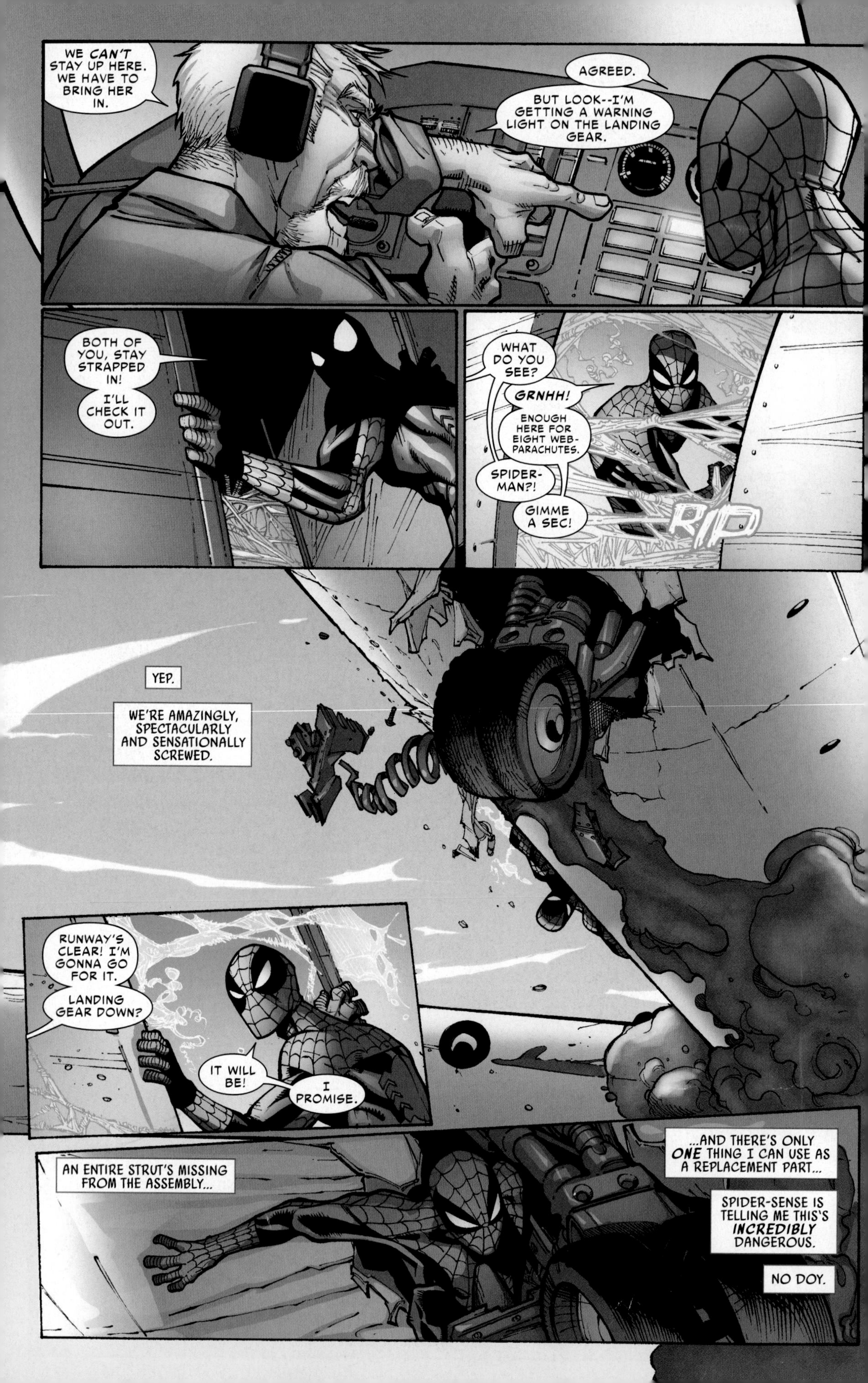
WE CAN'T STAY UP HERE. WE HAVE TO BRING HER IN.
AGREED.
BUT LOOK--I'M GETTING A WARNING LIGHT ON THE LANDING GEAR.
BOTH OF YOU, STAY STRAPPED IN!
I'LL CHECK IT OUT.
WHAT DO YOU SEE?
GRNHH!
ENOUGH HERE FOR EIGHT WEB-PARACHUTES.
SPIDER-MAN?!
GIMME A SEC!
RIP
YEP.
WE'RE AMAZINGLY, SPECTACULARLY AND SENSATIONALLY SCREWED.
RUNWAY'S CLEAR! I'M GONNA GO FOR IT.
LANDING GEAR DOWN?
IT WILL BE!
I PROMISE.
AN ENTIRE STRUT'S MISSING FROM THE ASSEMBLY...
...AND THERE'S ONLY ONE THING I CAN USE AS A REPLACEMENT PART...
SPIDER-SENSE IS TELLING ME THIS'S INCREDIBLY DANGEROUS.
NO DOY.

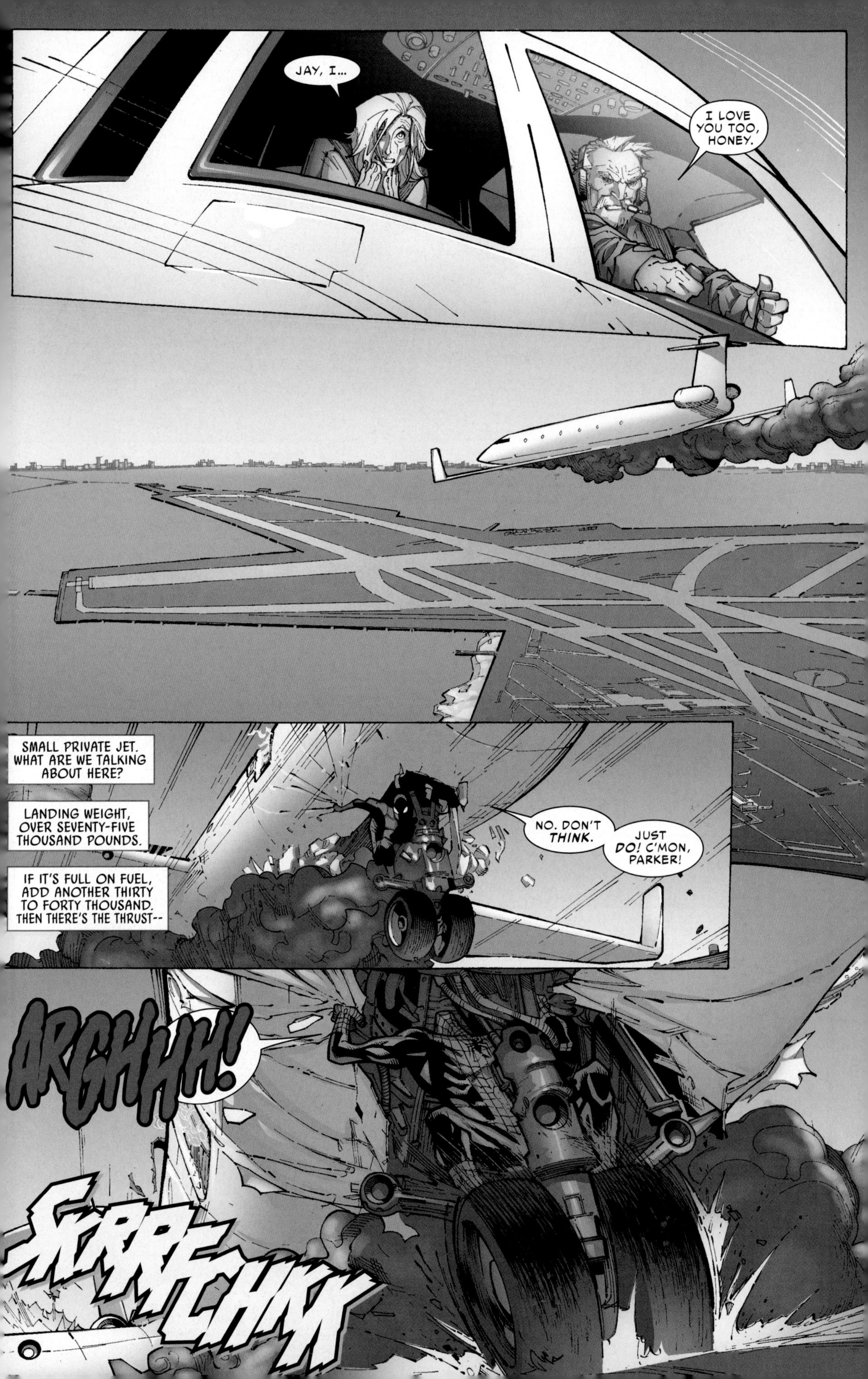
JAY, I...
I LOVE YOU TOO, HONEY.
SMALL PRIVATE JET. WHAT ARE WE TALKING ABOUT HERE?
LANDING WEIGHT, OVER SEVENTY-FIVE THOUSAND POUNDS.
IF IT'S FULL ON FUEL, ADD ANOTHER THIRTY TO FORTY THOUSAND. THEN THERE'S THE THRUST--
NO. DON'T THINK.
JUST DO! C'MON, PARKER!
ARGHHH!
SKRRECHKK

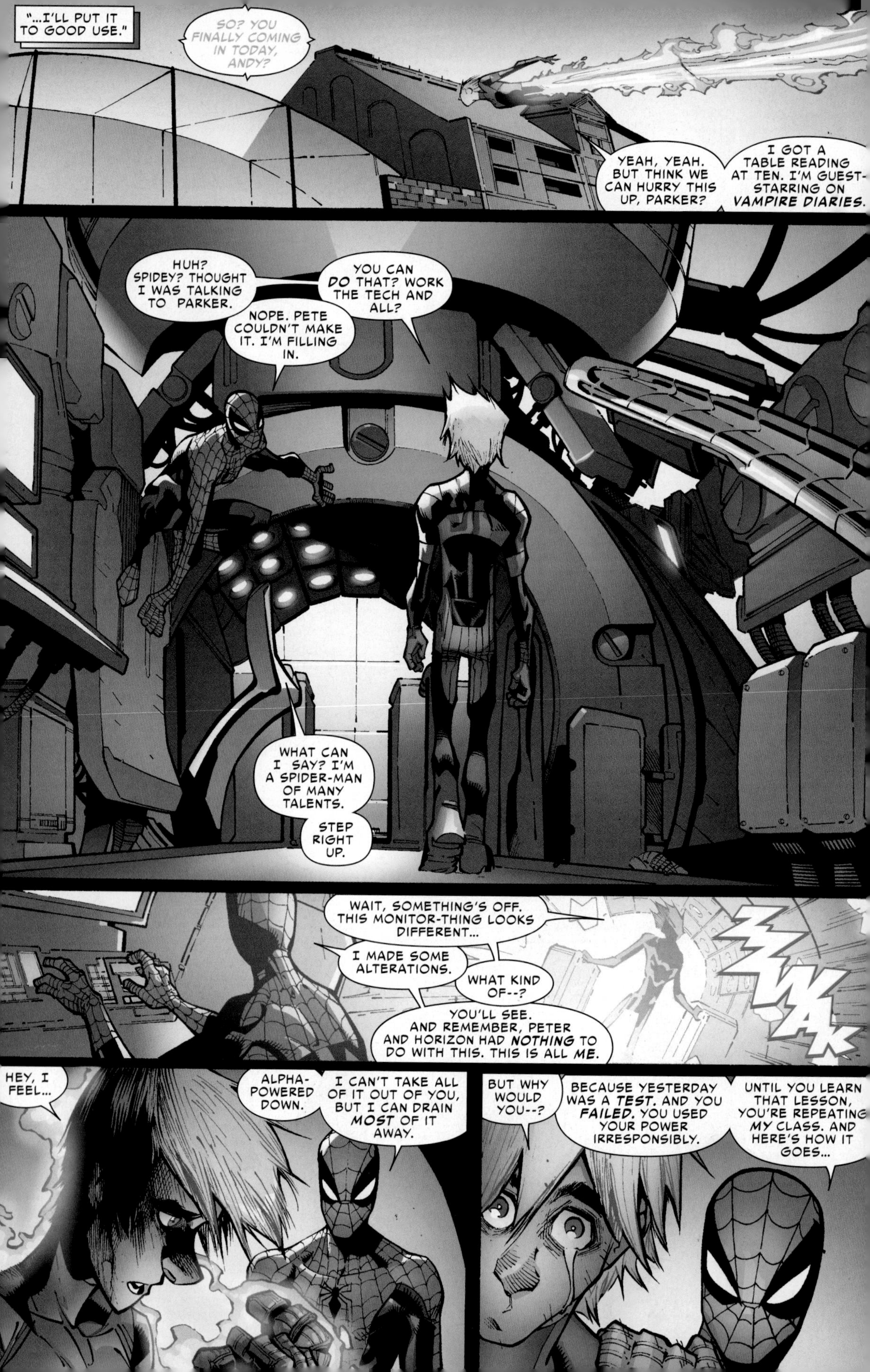
"...I'LL PUT IT TO GOOD USE."
SO? YOU FINALLY COMING IN TODAY, ANDY?
YEAH, YEAH. BUT THINK WE CAN HURRY THIS UP, PARKER?
I GOT A TABLE READING AT TEN. I'M GUEST-STARRING ON VAMPIRE DIARIES.
HUH? SPIDEY? THOUGHT I WAS TALKING TO PARKER.
NOPE. PETE COULDN'T MAKE IT. I'M FILLING IN.
YOU CAN DO THAT? WORK THE TECH AND ALL?
WHAT CAN I SAY? I'M A SPIDER-MAN OF MANY TALENTS.
STEP RIGHT UP.
WAIT, SOMETHING'S OFF. THIS MONITOR-THING LOOKS DIFFERENT...
I MADE SOME ALTERATIONS.
WHAT KIND OF--?
YOU'LL SEE. AND REMEMBER, PETER AND HORIZON HAD NOTHING TO DO WITH THIS. THIS IS ALL ME.
ZWAK
HEY, I FEEL...
ALPHA-POWERED DOWN.
I CAN'T TAKE ALL OF IT OUT OF YOU, BUT I CAN DRAIN MOST OF IT AWAY.
BUT WHY WOULD YOU--?
BECAUSE YESTERDAY WAS A TEST. AND YOU FAILED. YOU USED YOUR POWER IRRESPONSIBLY.
UNTIL YOU LEARN THAT LESSON, YOU'RE REPEATING MY CLASS. AND HERE'S HOW IT GOES...

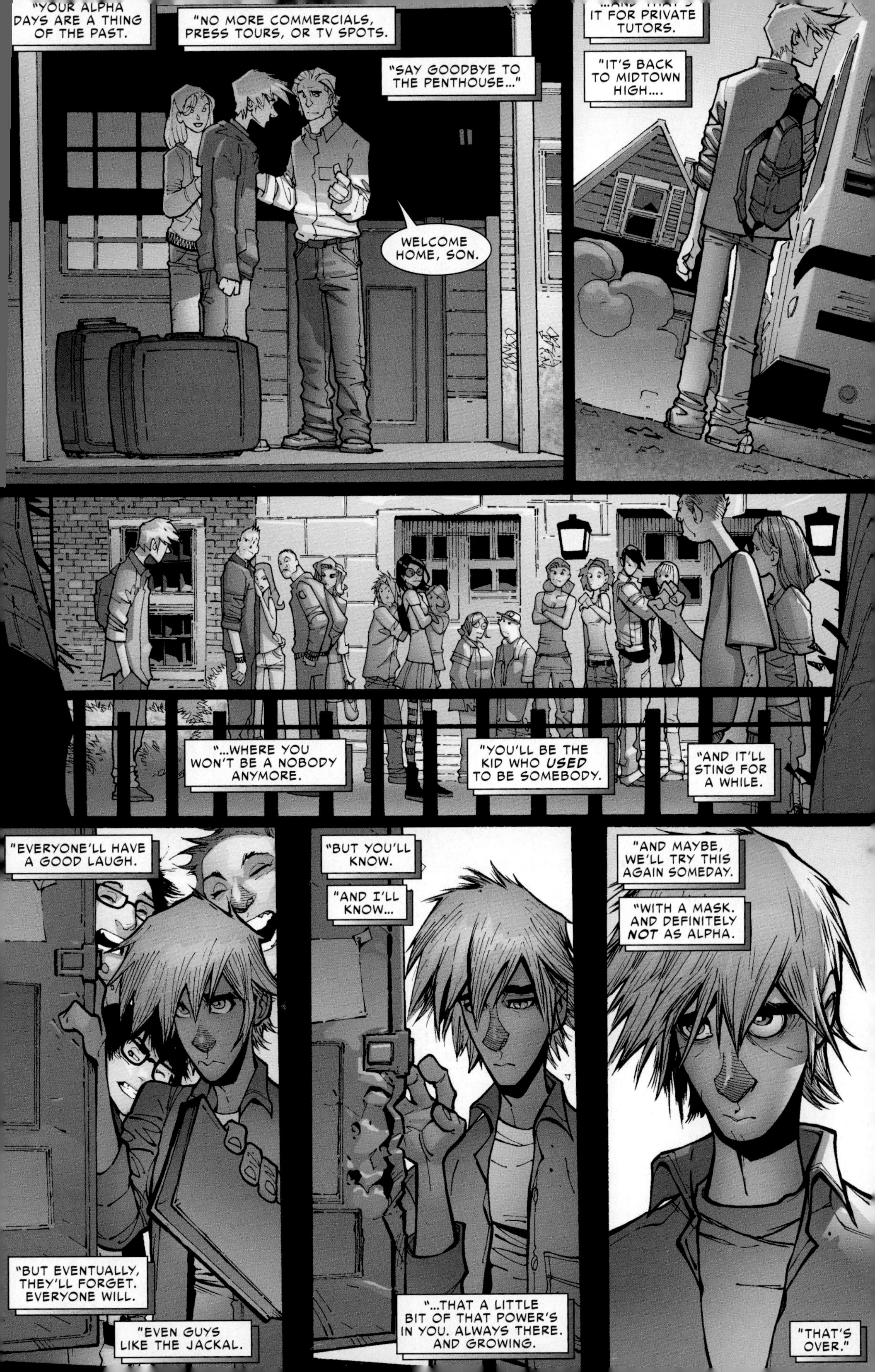
"YOUR ALPHA DAYS ARE A THING OF THE PAST.
"NO MORE COMMERCIALS, PRESS TOURS, OR TV SPOTS.
"SAY GOODBYE TO THE PENTHOUSE..."
WELCOME HOME, SON.
...AND THAT'S IT FOR PRIVATE TUTORS.
"IT'S BACK TO MIDTOWN HIGH....
"...WHERE YOU WON'T BE A NOBODY ANYMORE.
"YOU'LL BE THE KID WHO *USED* TO BE SOMEBODY.
"AND IT'LL STING FOR A WHILE.
"EVERYONE'LL HAVE A GOOD LAUGH.
"BUT EVENTUALLY, THEY'LL FORGET. EVERYONE WILL.
"EVEN GUYS LIKE THE JACKAL.
"BUT YOU'LL KNOW.
"AND I'LL KNOW...
"...THAT A LITTLE BIT OF THAT POWER'S IN YOU. ALWAYS THERE. AND GROWING.
"AND MAYBE, WE'LL TRY THIS AGAIN SOMEDAY.
"WITH A MASK. AND DEFINITELY *NOT* AS ALPHA.
"THAT'S OVER."

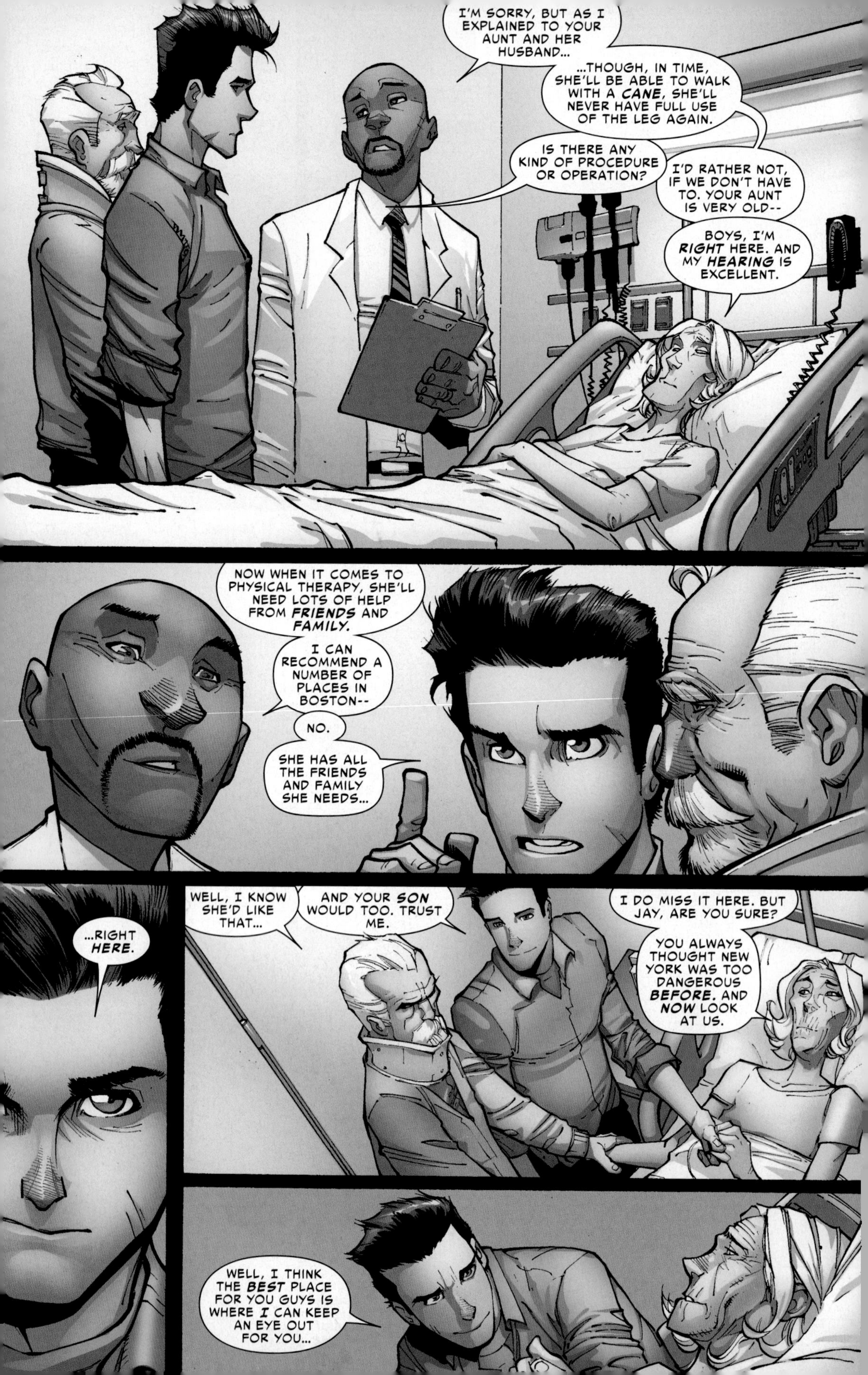
I'M SORRY, BUT AS I EXPLAINED TO YOUR AUNT AND HER HUSBAND...
...THOUGH, IN TIME, SHE'LL BE ABLE TO WALK WITH A CANE, SHE'LL NEVER HAVE FULL USE OF THE LEG AGAIN.
IS THERE ANY KIND OF PROCEDURE OR OPERATION?
I'D RATHER NOT, IF WE DON'T HAVE TO. YOUR AUNT IS VERY OLD--
BOYS, I'M RIGHT HERE. AND MY HEARING IS EXCELLENT.
NOW WHEN IT COMES TO PHYSICAL THERAPY, SHE'LL NEED LOTS OF HELP FROM FRIENDS AND FAMILY.
I CAN RECOMMEND A NUMBER OF PLACES IN BOSTON--
NO.
SHE HAS ALL THE FRIENDS AND FAMILY SHE NEEDS...
...RIGHT HERE.
WELL, I KNOW SHE'D LIKE THAT...
AND YOUR SON WOULD TOO. TRUST ME.
I DO MISS IT HERE. BUT JAY, ARE YOU SURE?
YOU ALWAYS THOUGHT NEW YORK WAS TOO DANGEROUS BEFORE. AND NOW LOOK AT US.
WELL, I THINK THE BEST PLACE FOR YOU GUYS IS WHERE I CAN KEEP AN EYE OUT FOR YOU...

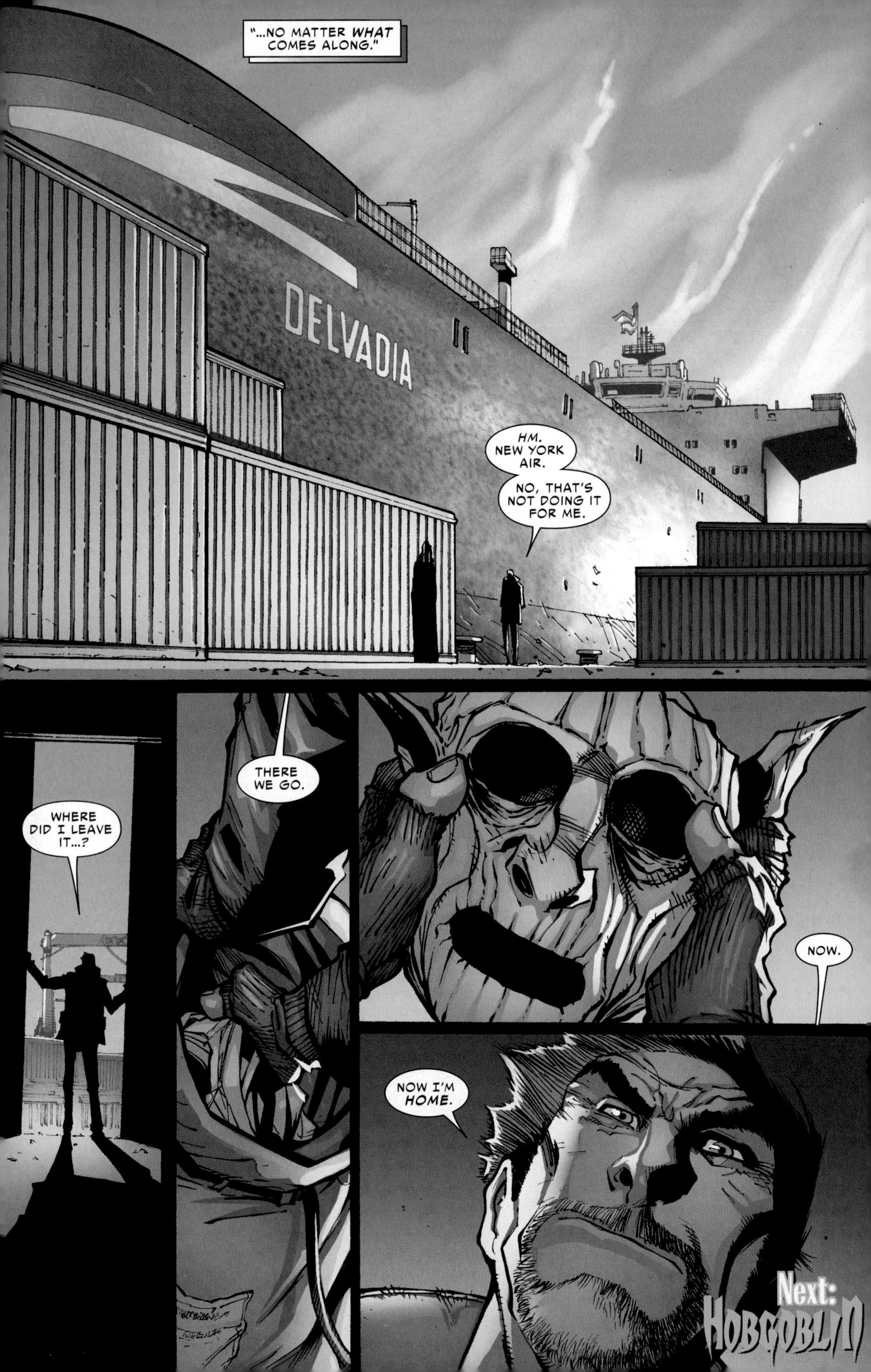
"...NO MATTER WHAT COMES ALONG."
DELVADIA
HM. NEW YORK AIR.
NO, THAT'S NOT DOING IT FOR ME.
WHERE DID I LEAVE IT...?
THERE WE GO.
NOW.
NOW I'M HOME.
Next: HOBGOBLIN

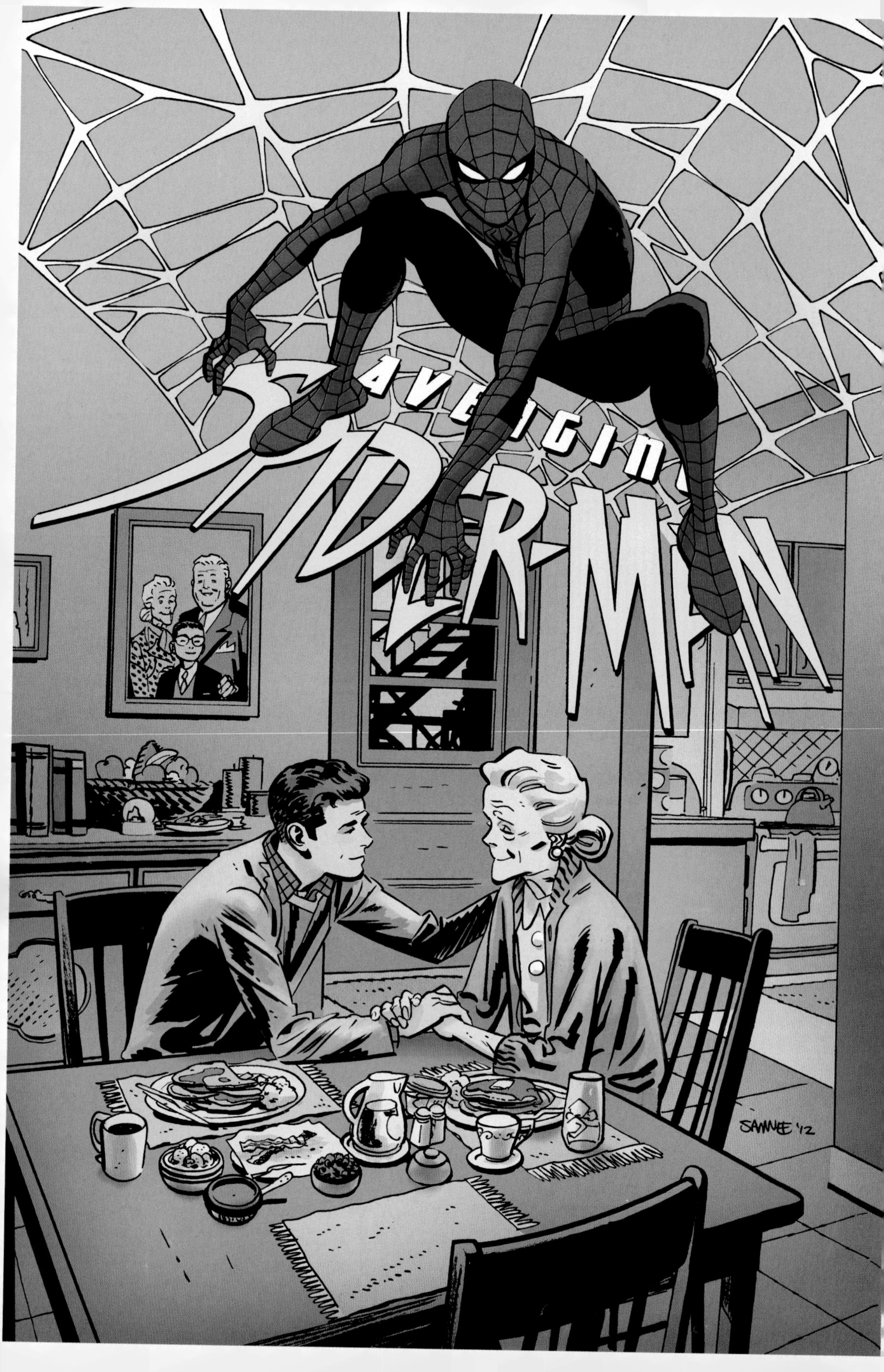
SAMNEE '12

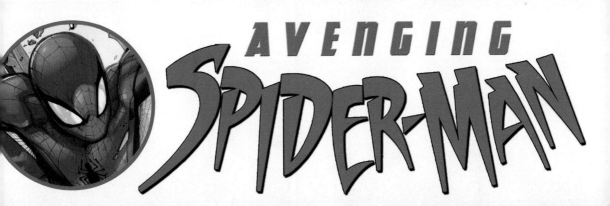

AVENGING SPIDER-MAN

PREVIOUSLY...

AS YOU MAY HAVE GATHERED, PETER PARKER WAS FAR FROM BEING THE BIGGEST MAN ON CAMPUS! BUT, HIS UNCLE BEN THOUGHT HE WAS A PRETTY SPECIAL LAD...
YOU'RE NOT FOOLIN' ME, PETEY! I KNOW YOU'RE AWAKE -- AND IT'S TIME FOR SCHOOL!
GOSH, UNCLE BEN--YOU'RE WORSE THAN A ROOM FULL OF ALARM CLOCKS!
AS FOR PETE'S AUNT MAY, SHE THOUGHT THE SUN ROSE AND SET UPON HER NEPHEW!
I COOKED YOUR FAVORITE BREAKFAST, PETEY--WHEATCAKES!
DON'T FATTEN HIM UP TOO MUCH, DEAR! I CAN HARDLY OUT-WRESTLE HIM NOW!

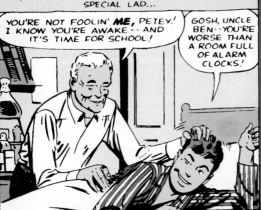

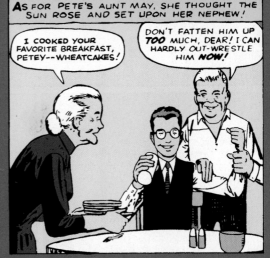

WRITER: **ZEB WELLS** ARTIST: **STEVE DILLON**

COLORS: **FRANK MARTIN JR.** LETTERER: **VC's JOE CARAMAGNA**

COVER: **CHRIS SAMNEE & JAVIER RODRIGUEZ**

ASSISTANT EDITOR: **ELLIE PYLE** ASSOCIATE EDITOR: **SANA AMANAT** SENIOR EDITOR: **STEPHEN WACKER**

EXECUTIVE EDITOR: **TOM BREVOORT** EDITOR IN CHIEF: **AXEL ALONSO**

CHIEF CREATIVE OFFICER: **JOE QUESADA** PUBLISHER: **DAN BUCKLEY** EXECUTIVE PRODUCER: **ALAN FINE**

FIFTY YEARS AGO **STAN LEE** AND **STEVE DITKO** GAVE THE WORLD SPIDER-MAN. WE THANK THEM AND DEDICATE THIS ISSUE TO THEIR LEGACY.

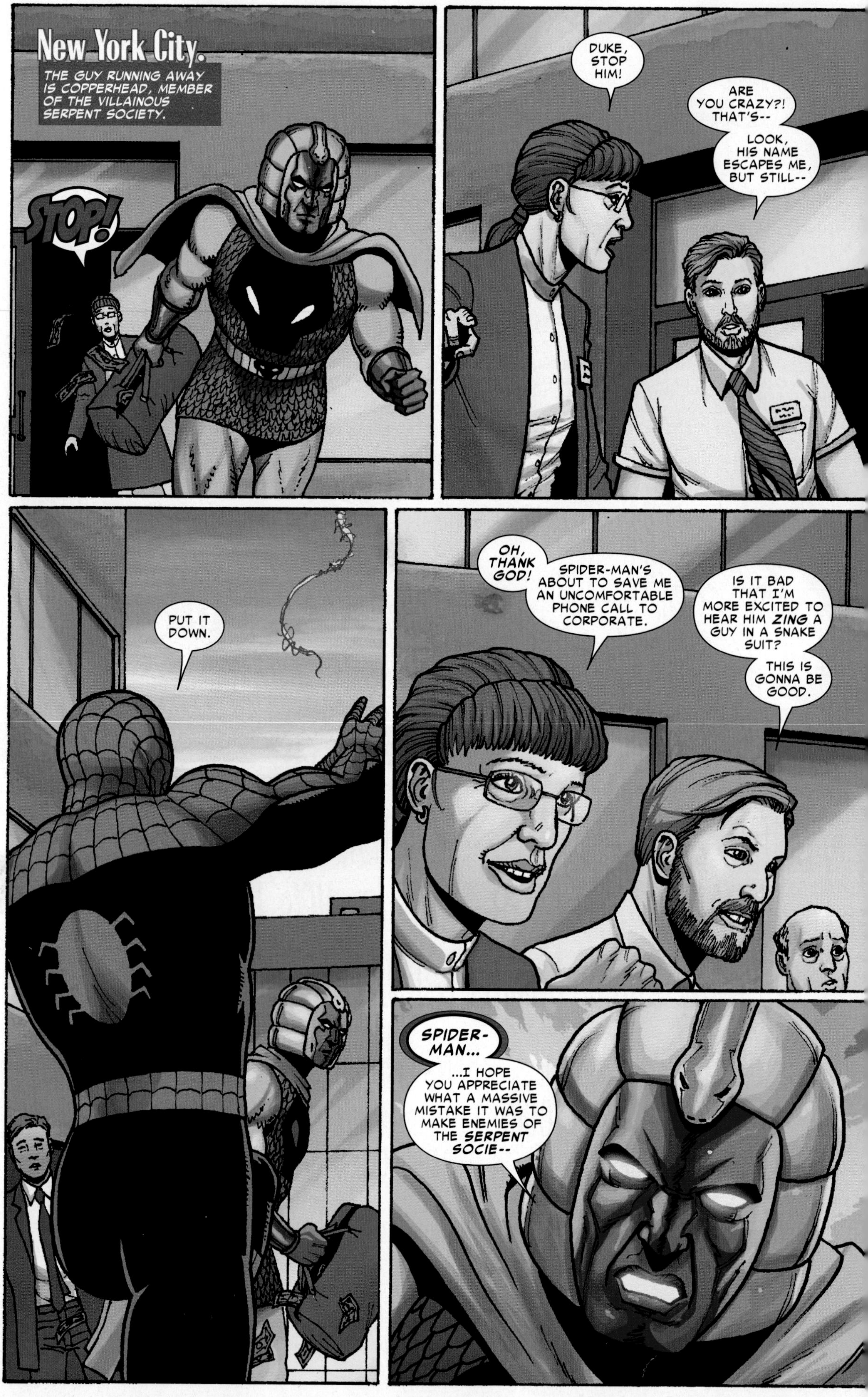
New York City.
THE GUY RUNNING AWAY IS COPPERHEAD, MEMBER OF THE VILLAINOUS SERPENT SOCIETY.
STOP!
DUKE, STOP HIM!
ARE YOU CRAZY?! THAT'S--
LOOK, HIS NAME ESCAPES ME, BUT STILL--
PUT IT DOWN.
OH, THANK GOD!
SPIDER-MAN'S ABOUT TO SAVE ME AN UNCOMFORTABLE PHONE CALL TO CORPORATE.
IS IT BAD THAT I'M MORE EXCITED TO HEAR HIM ZING A GUY IN A SNAKE SUIT?
THIS IS GONNA BE GOOD.
SPIDER-MAN...
...I HOPE YOU APPRECIATE WHAT A MASSIVE MISTAKE IT WAS TO MAKE ENEMIES OF THE SERPENT SOCIE--

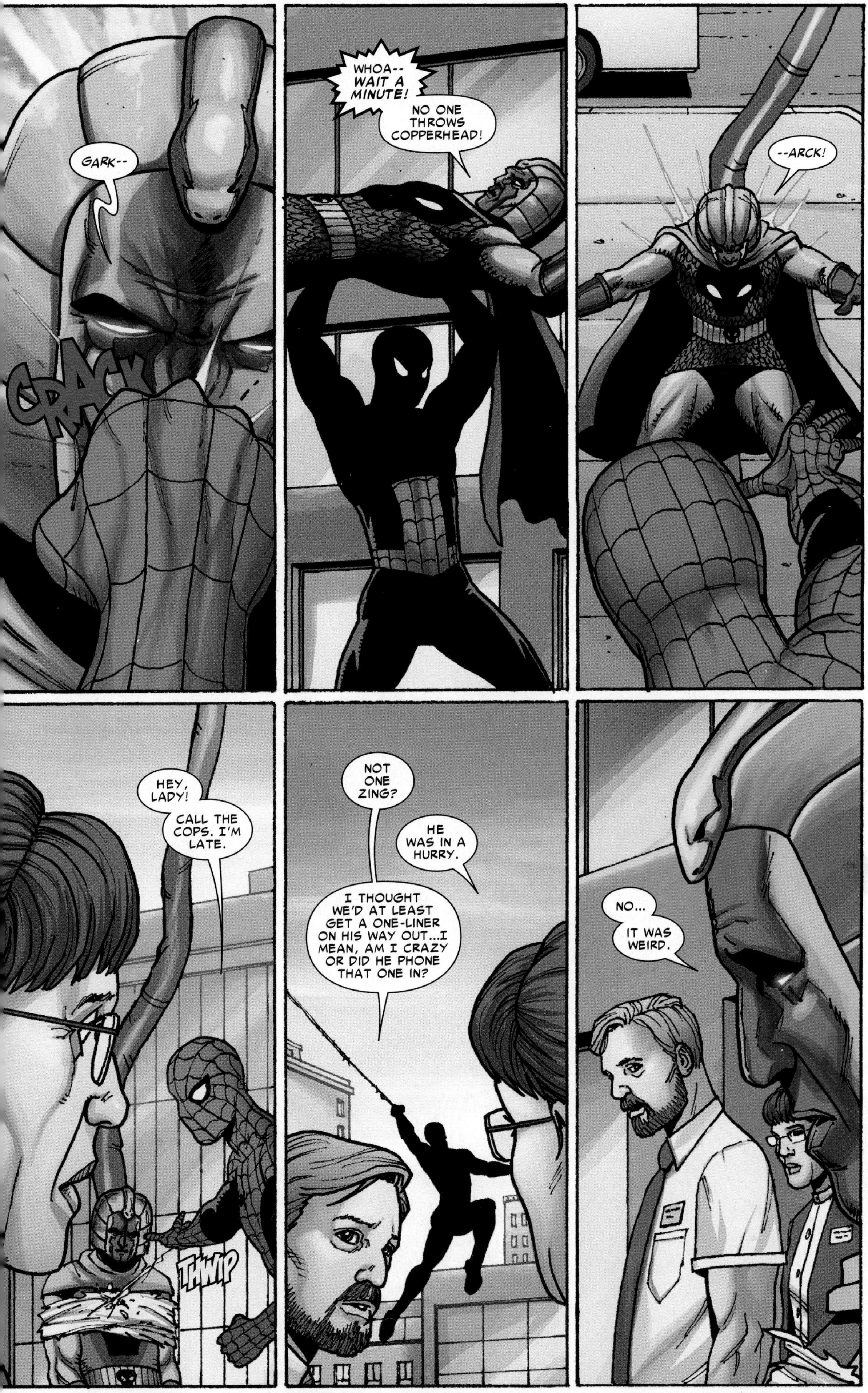
GARK--
CRACK
WHOA-- WAIT A MINUTE!
NO ONE THROWS COPPERHEAD!
--ARCK!
HEY, LADY!
CALL THE COPS. I'M LATE.
THWIP
NOT ONE ZING?
HE WAS IN A HURRY.
I THOUGHT WE'D AT LEAST GET A ONE-LINER ON HIS WAY OUT...I MEAN, AM I CRAZY OR DID HE PHONE THAT ONE IN?
NO...
IT WAS WEIRD.

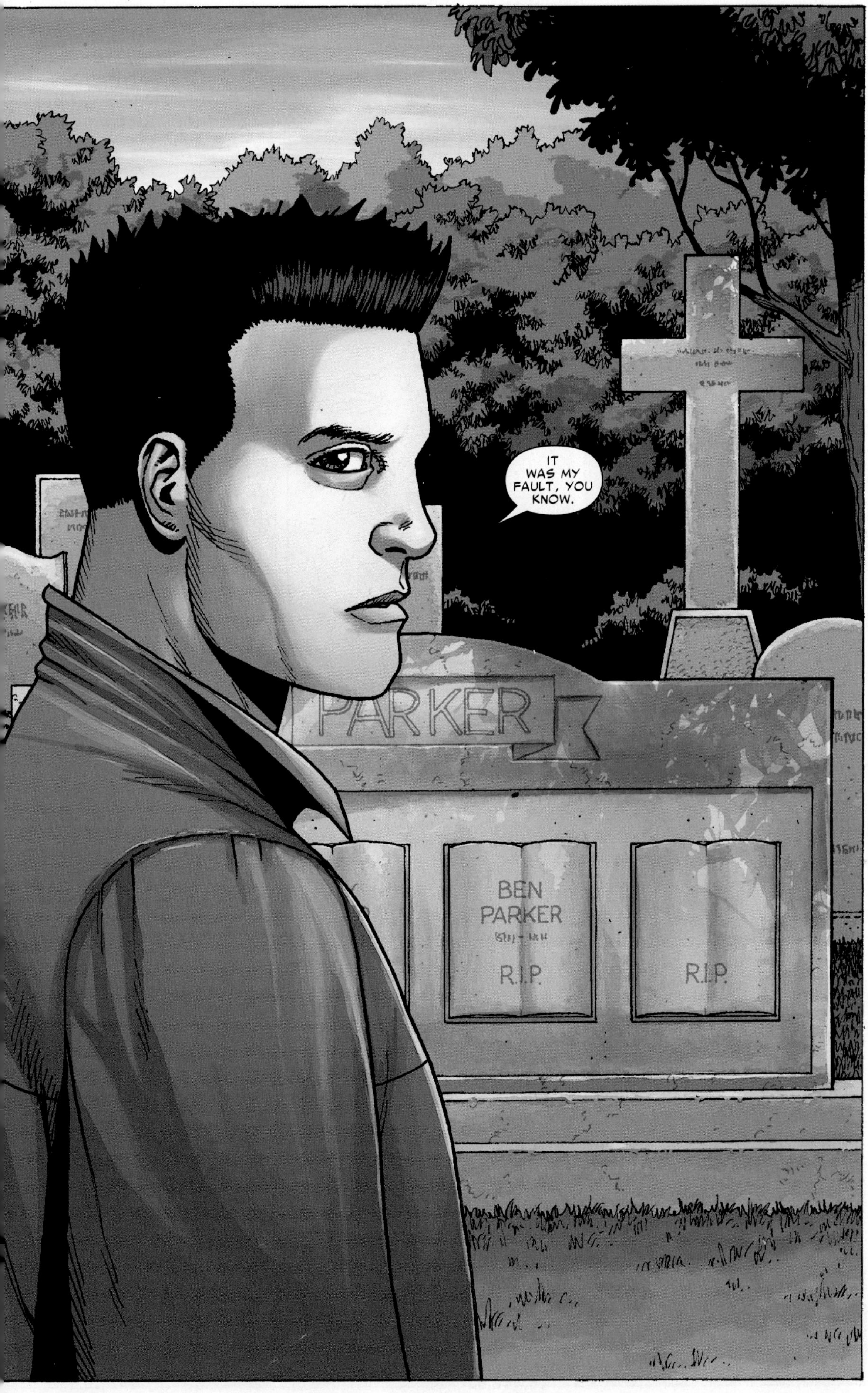
IT WAS MY FAULT, YOU KNOW.
PARKER
BEN PARKER
R.I.P.
R.I.P.

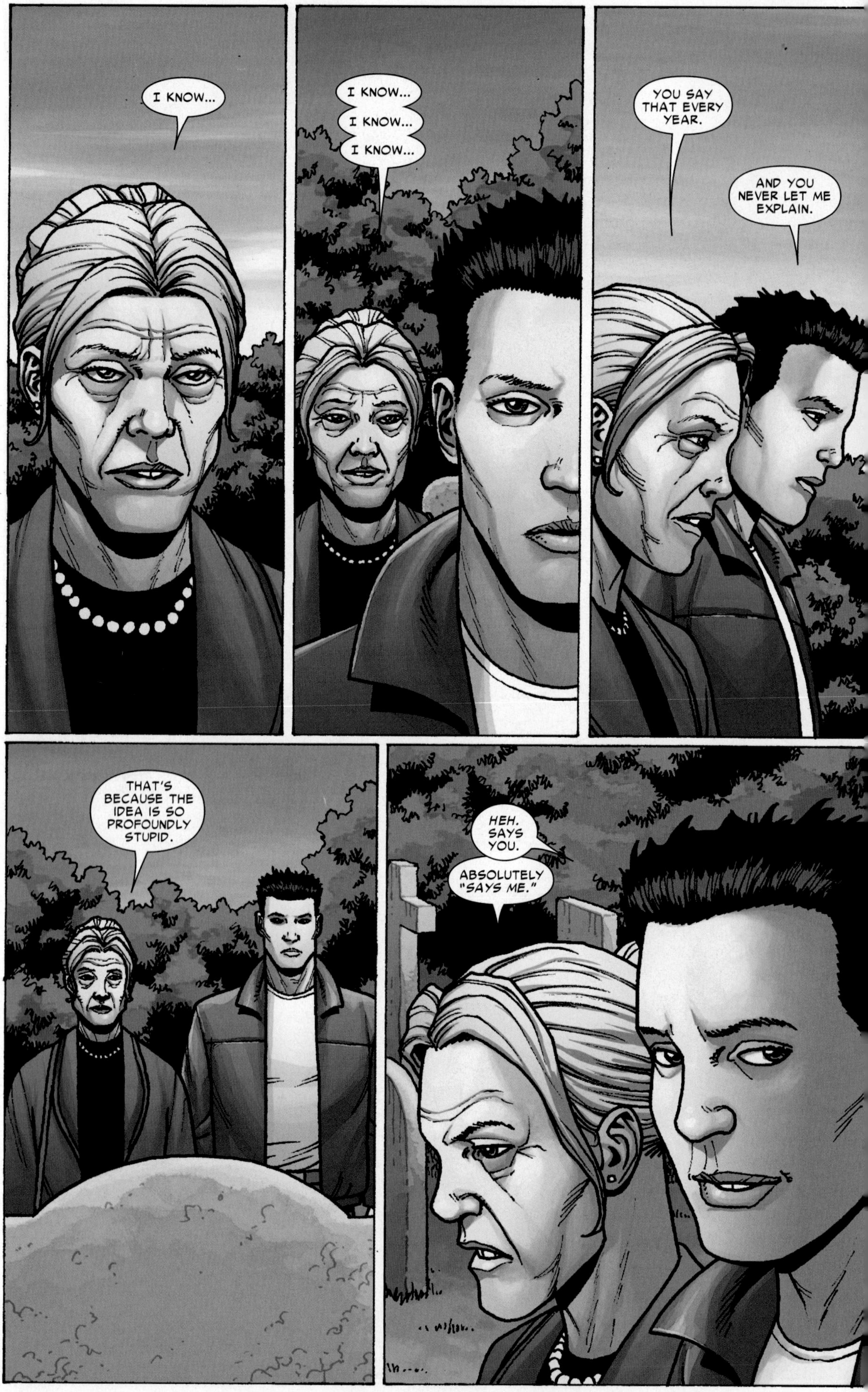
I KNOW...
I KNOW...
I KNOW...
I KNOW...
YOU SAY THAT EVERY YEAR.
AND YOU NEVER LET ME EXPLAIN.
THAT'S BECAUSE THE IDEA IS SO PROFOUNDLY STUPID.
HEH. SAYS YOU.
ABSOLUTELY "SAYS ME."

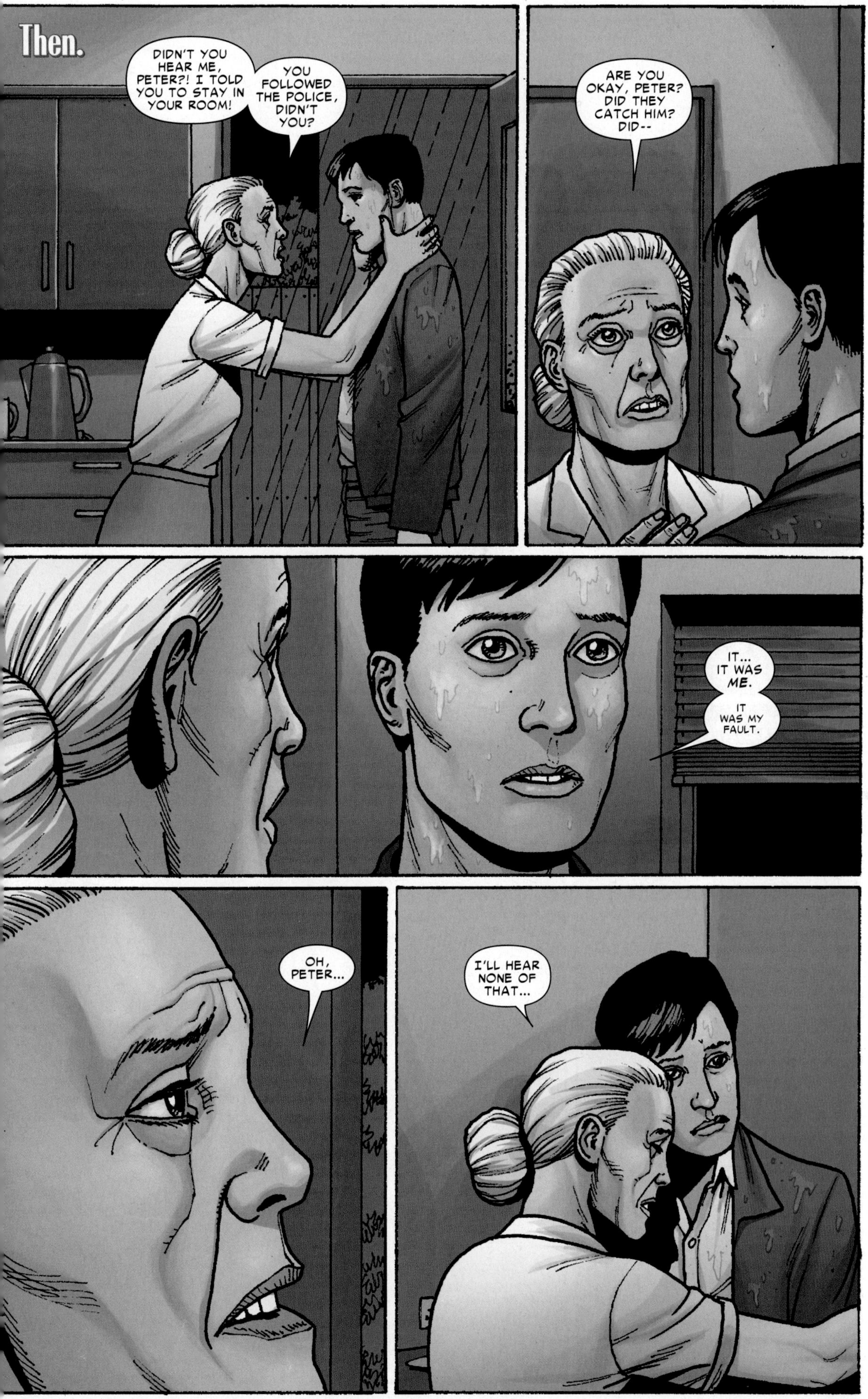
Then.
DIDN'T YOU HEAR ME, PETER?! I TOLD YOU TO STAY IN YOUR ROOM!
YOU FOLLOWED THE POLICE, DIDN'T YOU?
ARE YOU OKAY, PETER? DID THEY CATCH HIM? DID--
IT... IT WAS ME.
IT WAS MY FAULT.
OH, PETER...
I'LL HEAR NONE OF THAT...

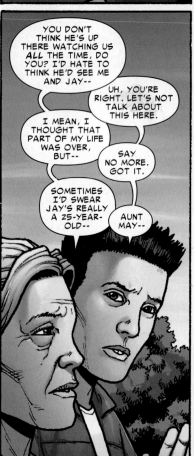

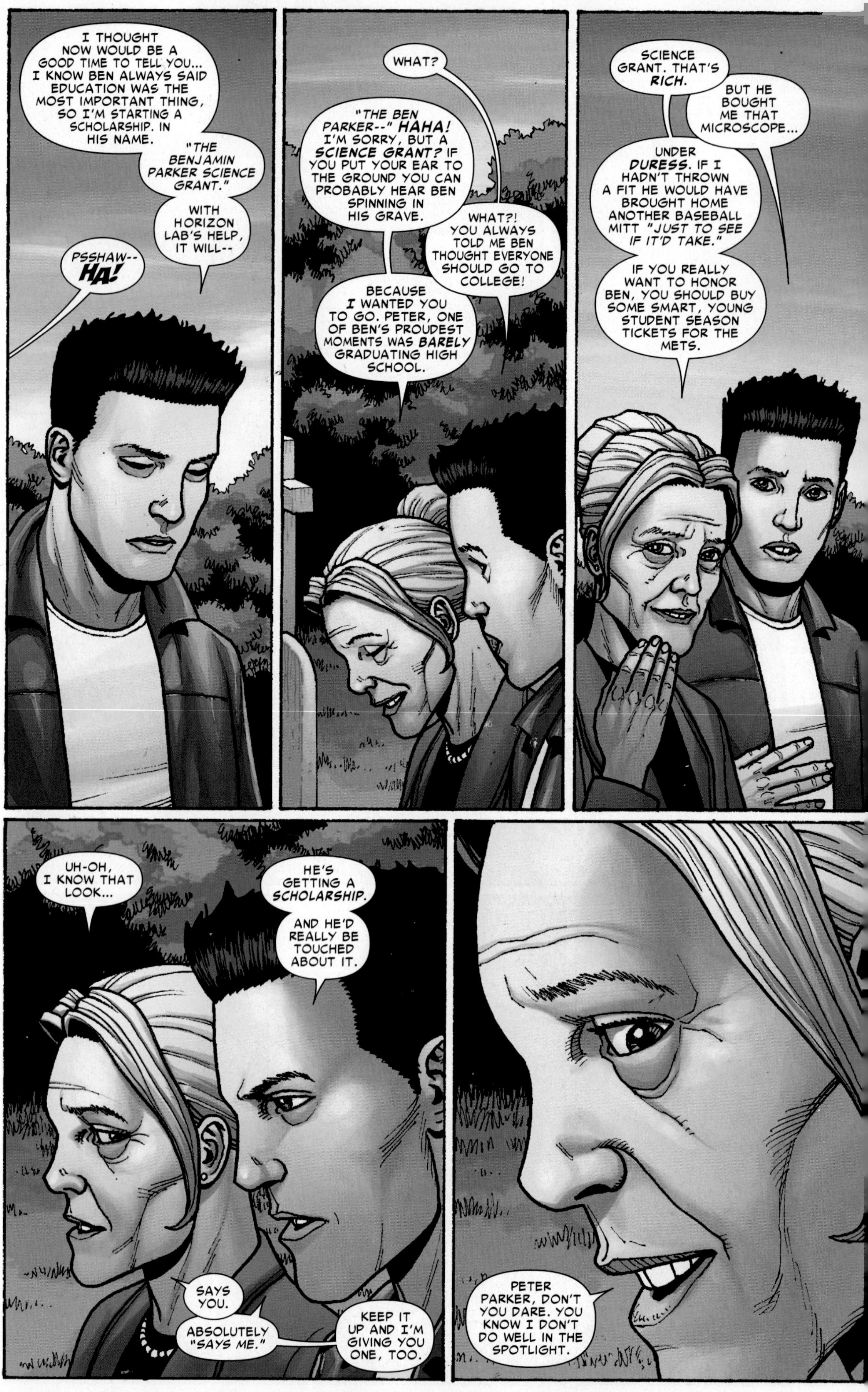
I THOUGHT NOW WOULD BE A GOOD TIME TO TELL YOU... I KNOW BEN ALWAYS SAID EDUCATION WAS THE MOST IMPORTANT THING, SO I'M STARTING A SCHOLARSHIP. IN HIS NAME.
"THE BENJAMIN PARKER SCIENCE GRANT."
PSSHAW-- HA!
WITH HORIZON LAB'S HELP, IT WILL--
WHAT?
"THE BEN PARKER--" HAHA! I'M SORRY, BUT A SCIENCE GRANT? IF YOU PUT YOUR EAR TO THE GROUND YOU CAN PROBABLY HEAR BEN SPINNING IN HIS GRAVE.
WHAT?! YOU ALWAYS TOLD ME BEN THOUGHT EVERYONE SHOULD GO TO COLLEGE!
BECAUSE I WANTED YOU TO GO. PETER, ONE OF BEN'S PROUDEST MOMENTS WAS BARELY GRADUATING HIGH SCHOOL.
SCIENCE GRANT. THAT'S RICH.
BUT HE BOUGHT ME THAT MICROSCOPE...
UNDER DURESS. IF I HADN'T THROWN A FIT HE WOULD HAVE BROUGHT HOME ANOTHER BASEBALL MITT "JUST TO SEE IF IT'D TAKE."
IF YOU REALLY WANT TO HONOR BEN, YOU SHOULD BUY SOME SMART, YOUNG STUDENT SEASON TICKETS FOR THE METS.
UH-OH, I KNOW THAT LOOK...
HE'S GETTING A SCHOLARSHIP.
AND HE'D REALLY BE TOUCHED ABOUT IT.
SAYS YOU.
ABSOLUTELY "SAYS ME."
KEEP IT UP AND I'M GIVING YOU ONE, TOO.
PETER PARKER, DON'T YOU DARE. YOU KNOW I DON'T DO WELL IN THE SPOTLIGHT.

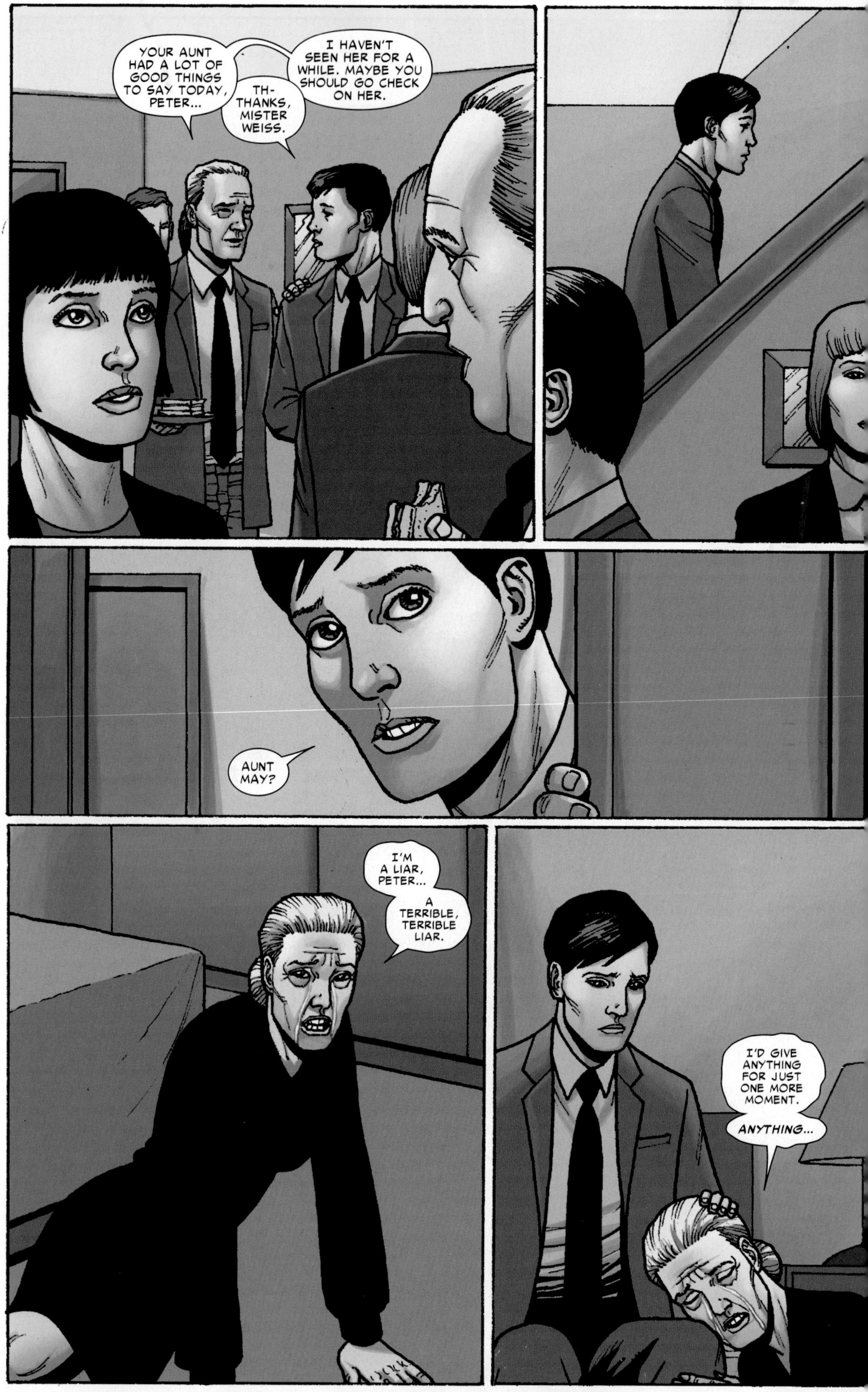
YOUR AUNT HAD A LOT OF GOOD THINGS TO SAY TODAY, PETER...
TH-THANKS, MISTER WEISS.
I HAVEN'T SEEN HER FOR A WHILE. MAYBE YOU SHOULD GO CHECK ON HER.
AUNT MAY?
I'M A LIAR, PETER...
A TERRIBLE, TERRIBLE LIAR.
I'D GIVE ANYTHING FOR JUST ONE MORE MOMENT.
ANYTHING...

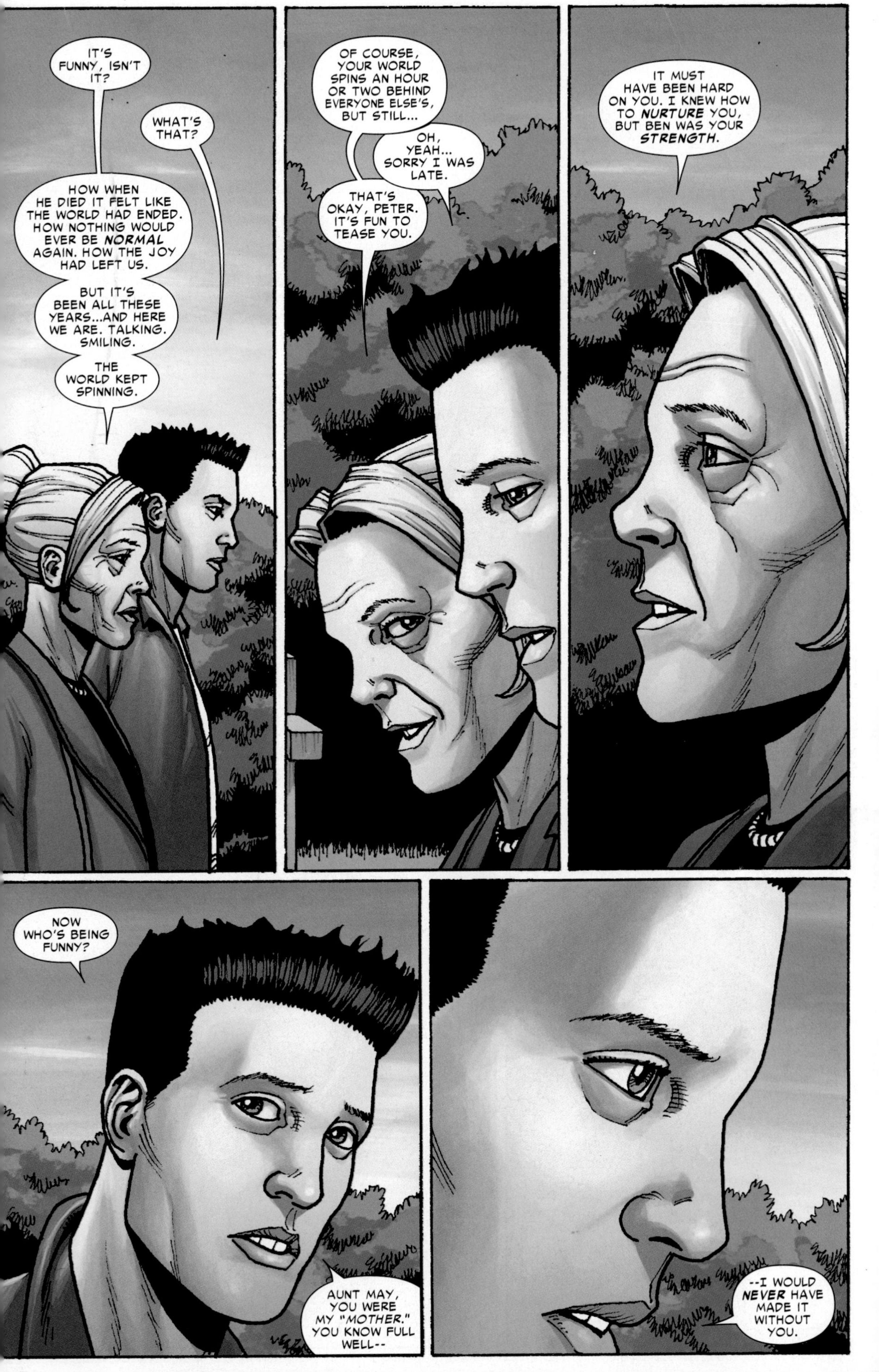
IT'S FUNNY, ISN'T IT?
WHAT'S THAT?
HOW WHEN HE DIED IT FELT LIKE THE WORLD HAD ENDED. HOW NOTHING WOULD EVER BE NORMAL AGAIN. HOW THE JOY HAD LEFT US.
BUT IT'S BEEN ALL THESE YEARS...AND HERE WE ARE. TALKING. SMILING.
THE WORLD KEPT SPINNING.
OF COURSE, YOUR WORLD SPINS AN HOUR OR TWO BEHIND EVERYONE ELSE'S, BUT STILL...
OH, YEAH... SORRY I WAS LATE.
THAT'S OKAY, PETER. IT'S FUN TO TEASE YOU.
IT MUST HAVE BEEN HARD ON YOU. I KNEW HOW TO NURTURE YOU, BUT BEN WAS YOUR STRENGTH.
NOW WHO'S BEING FUNNY?
AUNT MAY, YOU WERE MY "MOTHER." YOU KNOW FULL WELL--
--I WOULD NEVER HAVE MADE IT WITHOUT YOU.

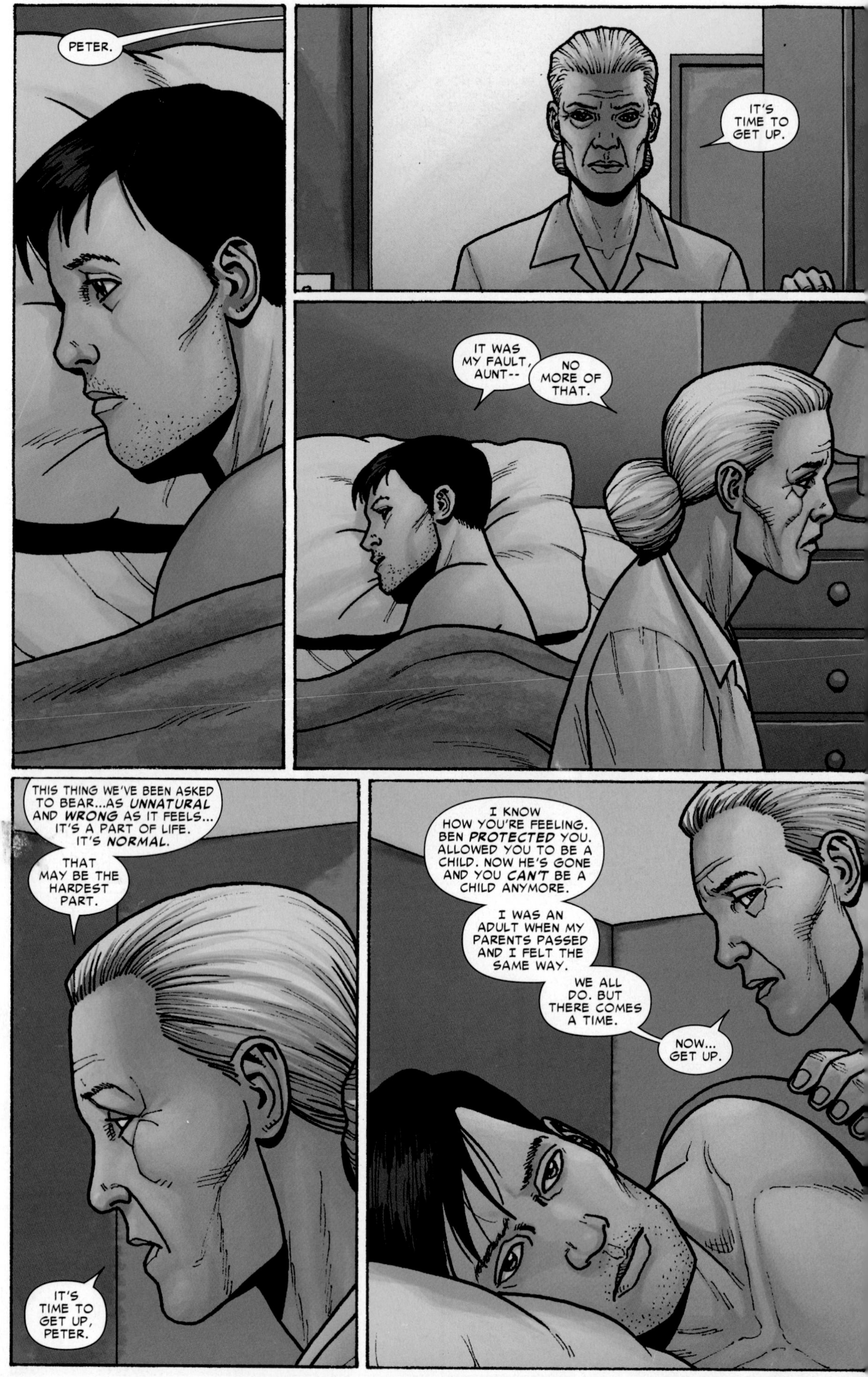
PETER.
IT'S TIME TO GET UP.
IT WAS MY FAULT, AUNT--
NO MORE OF THAT.
THIS THING WE'VE BEEN ASKED TO BEAR...AS *UNNATURAL* AND *WRONG* AS IT FEELS... IT'S A PART OF LIFE. IT'S *NORMAL*.
THAT MAY BE THE HARDEST PART.
IT'S TIME TO GET UP, PETER.
I KNOW HOW YOU'RE FEELING. BEN *PROTECTED* YOU. ALLOWED YOU TO BE A CHILD. NOW HE'S GONE AND YOU *CAN'T* BE A CHILD ANYMORE.
I WAS AN ADULT WHEN MY PARENTS PASSED AND I FELT THE SAME WAY.
WE ALL DO. BUT THERE COMES A TIME.
NOW... GET UP.

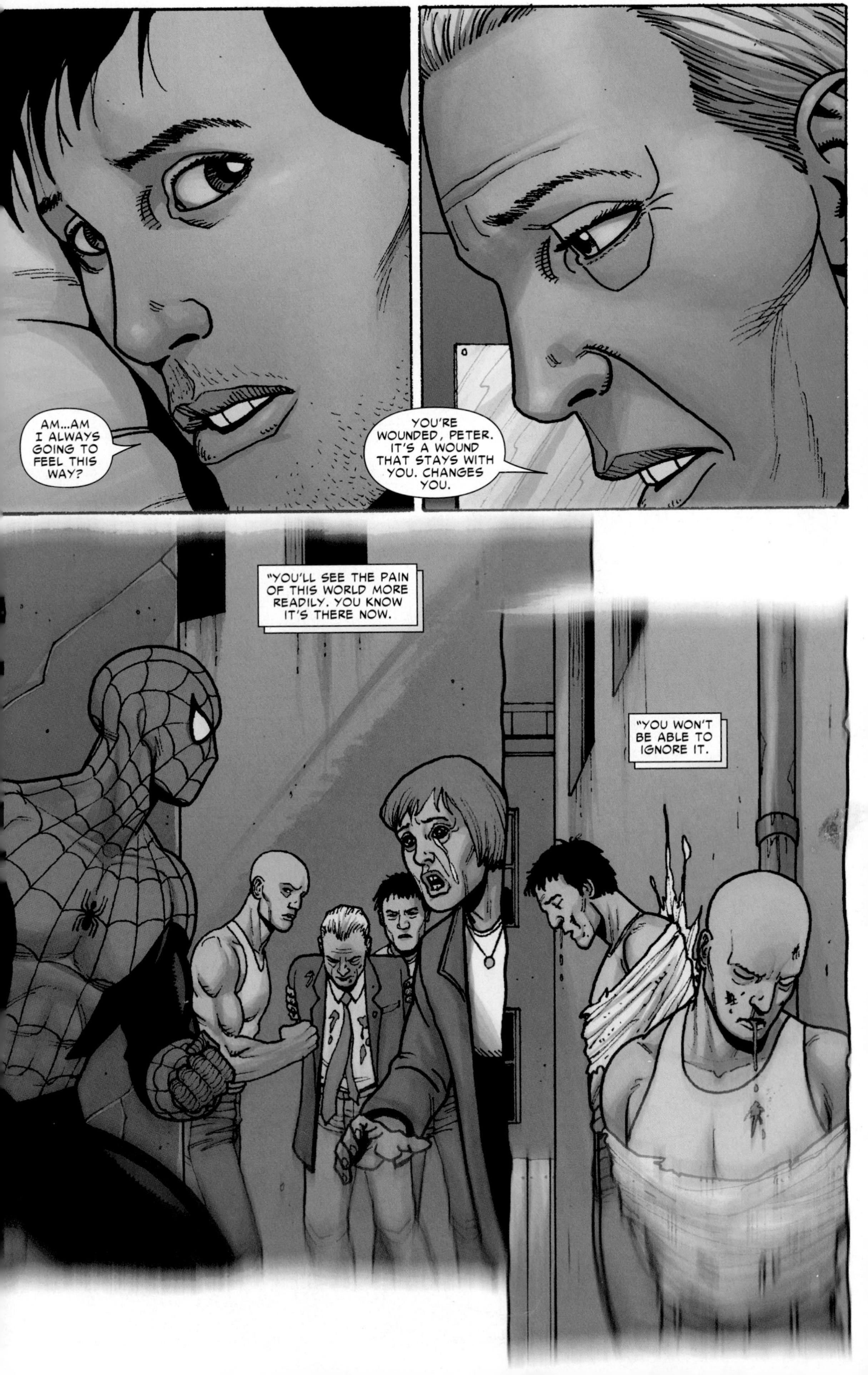
AM...AM I ALWAYS GOING TO FEEL THIS WAY?
YOU'RE WOUNDED, PETER. IT'S A WOUND THAT STAYS WITH YOU. CHANGES YOU.
"YOU'LL SEE THE PAIN OF THIS WORLD MORE READILY. YOU KNOW IT'S THERE NOW.
"YOU WON'T BE ABLE TO IGNORE IT.

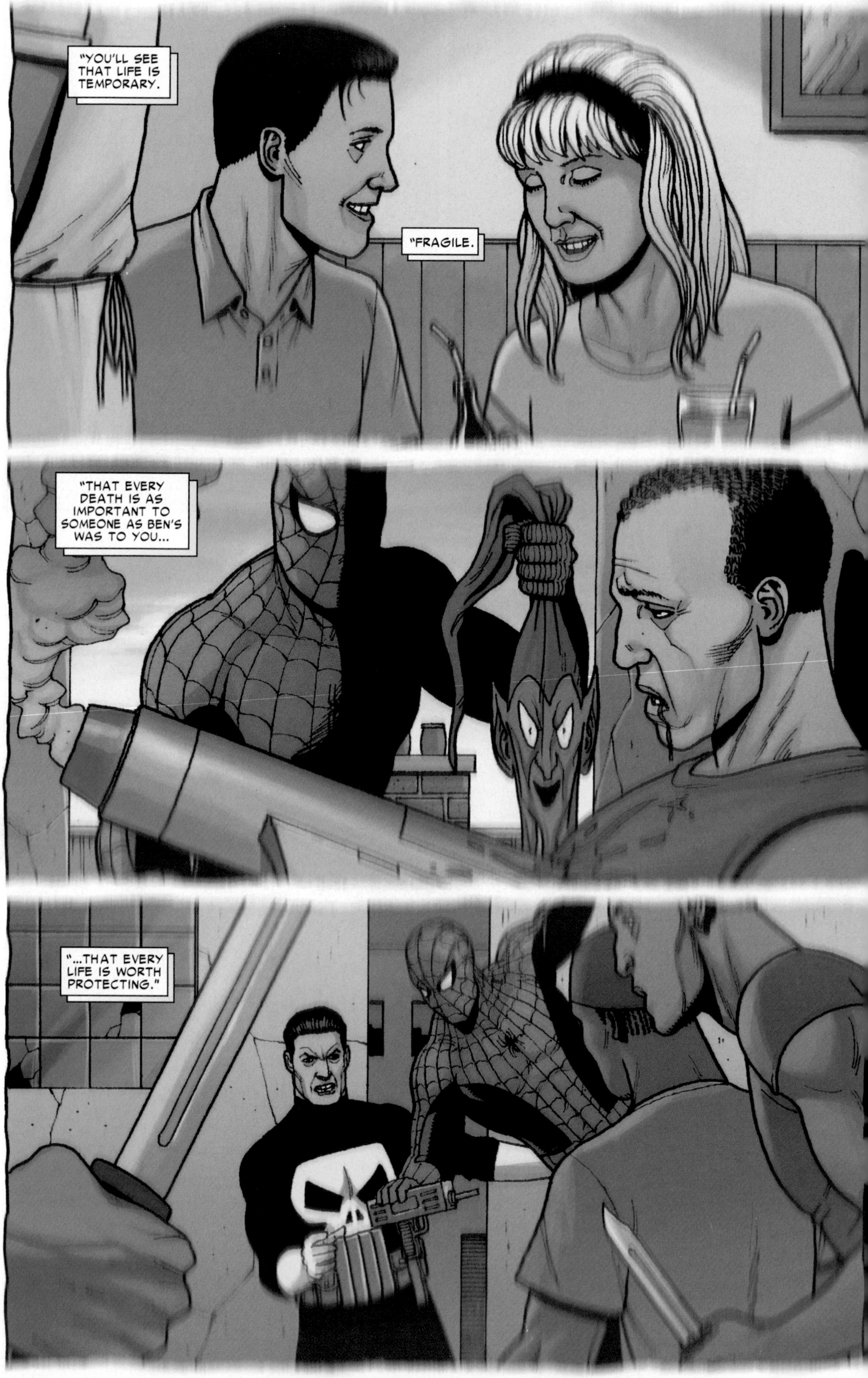
"YOU'LL SEE THAT LIFE IS TEMPORARY.
"FRAGILE.
"THAT EVERY DEATH IS AS IMPORTANT TO SOMEONE AS BEN'S WAS TO YOU...
"...THAT EVERY LIFE IS WORTH PROTECTING."

"UNTIL NOW YOU HAVEN'T HAD TO BE."

I SAID ALL THAT?

I THINK SO. THAT'S HOW I REMEMBER IT, AT LEAST.

WELL, THEN. MAYBE I DO DESERVE A SCHOLARSHIP.

OR AT LEAST LUNCH. ARE YOU HUNGRY, PETER? WE COULD--

WAIT.

I...I WANT YOU TO KNOW THAT I DO...YOU KNOW...

I DO HELP PEOPLE.

I KNOW I'VE SEEN...

NO, I MEAN...I KNOW I COME OFF AS A BIT OF A SCREW-UP, BUT I WANT YOU TO KNOW...

I MEAN, ALL THAT STUFF YOU SAID I'D DO...I...

...I THINK BEN WOULD...

PETER.

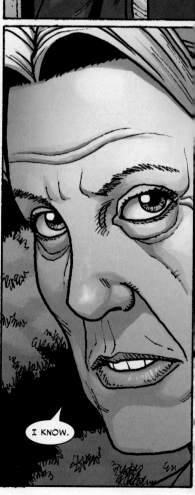

I KNOW.

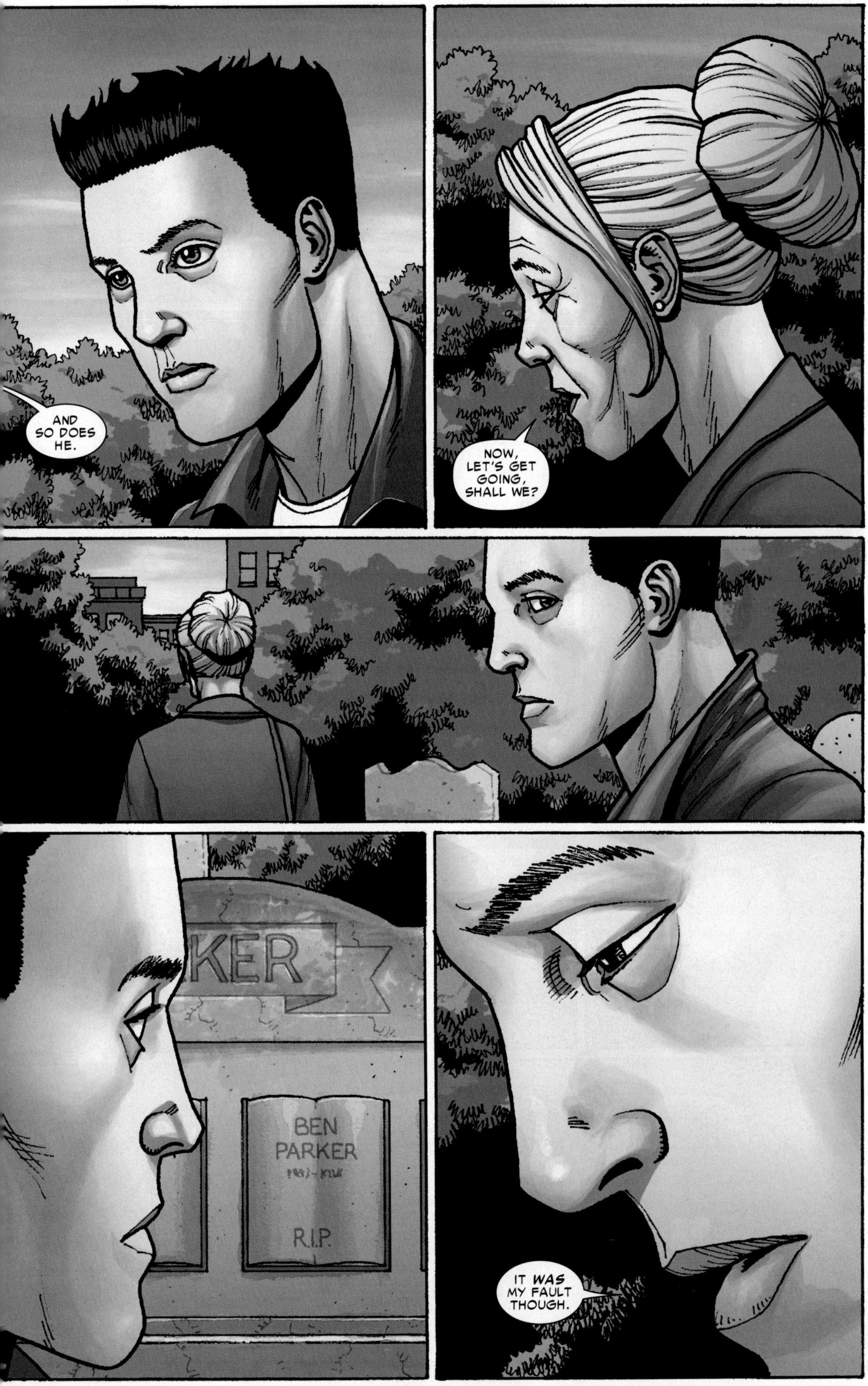
AND SO DOES HE.
NOW, LET'S GET GOING, SHALL WE?
KER
BEN PARKER
R.I.P.
IT WAS MY FAULT THOUGH.

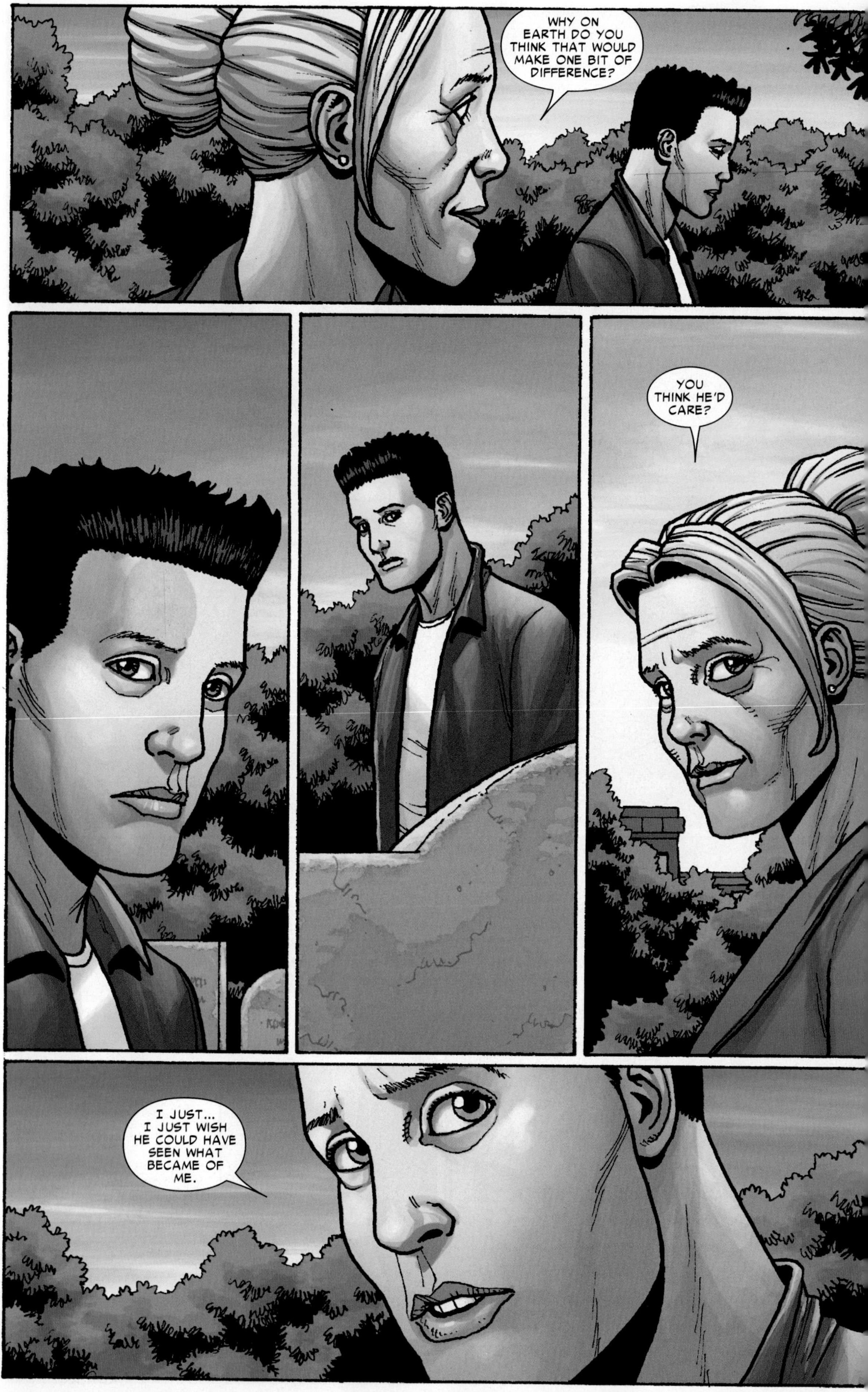
WHY ON EARTH DO YOU THINK THAT WOULD MAKE ONE BIT OF DIFFERENCE?
YOU THINK HE'D CARE?
I JUST... I JUST WISH HE COULD HAVE SEEN WHAT BECAME OF ME.

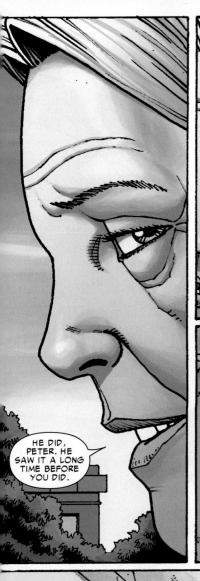

NOW, LET'S LET HIM GET SOME REST.

HE DID, PETER. HE SAW IT A LONG TIME BEFORE YOU DID.

BEN PARKER

1945-1962

R.I.P.   R.I.P.

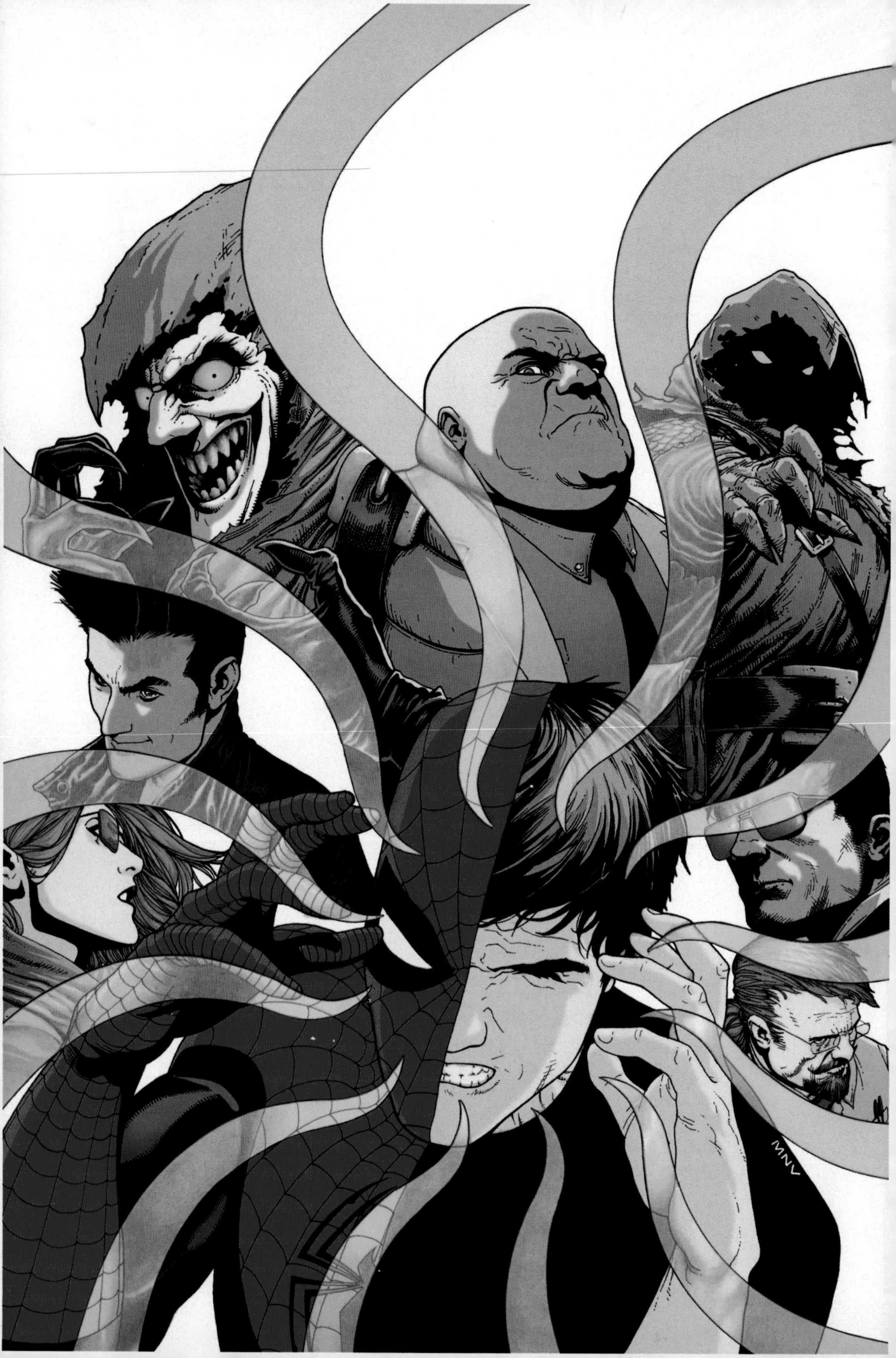

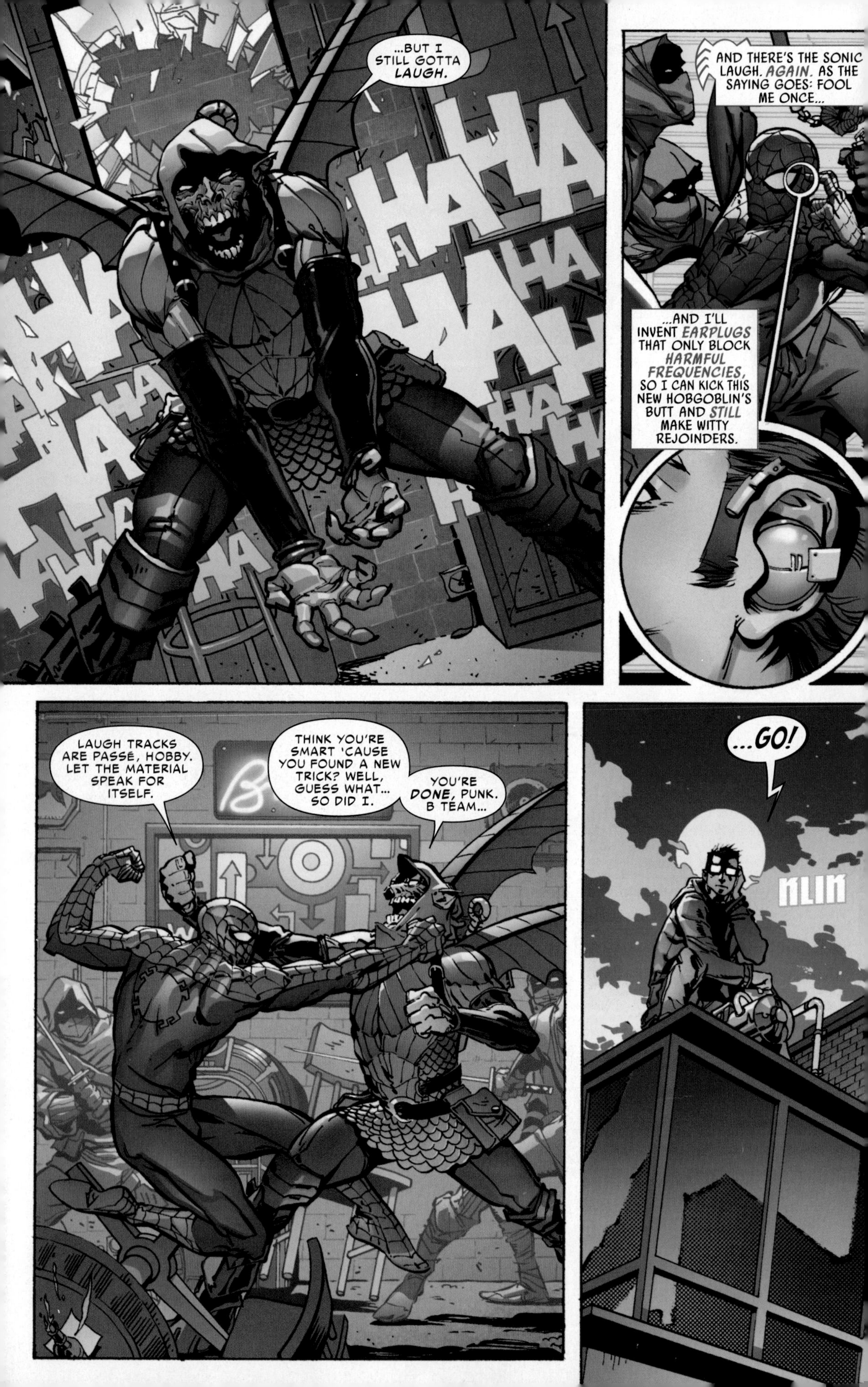

...BUT I STILL GOTTA LAUGH.
HAHAHAHA
AND THERE'S THE SONIC LAUGH. AGAIN. AS THE SAYING GOES: FOOL ME ONCE...
...AND I'LL INVENT EARPLUGS THAT ONLY BLOCK HARMFUL FREQUENCIES, SO I CAN KICK THIS NEW HOBGOBLIN'S BUTT AND STILL MAKE WITTY REJOINDERS.
LAUGH TRACKS ARE PASSÉ, HOBBY. LET THE MATERIAL SPEAK FOR ITSELF.
THINK YOU'RE SMART 'CAUSE YOU FOUND A NEW TRICK? WELL, GUESS WHAT... SO DID I.
YOU'RE DONE, PUNK. B TEAM...
...GO!
KLIK

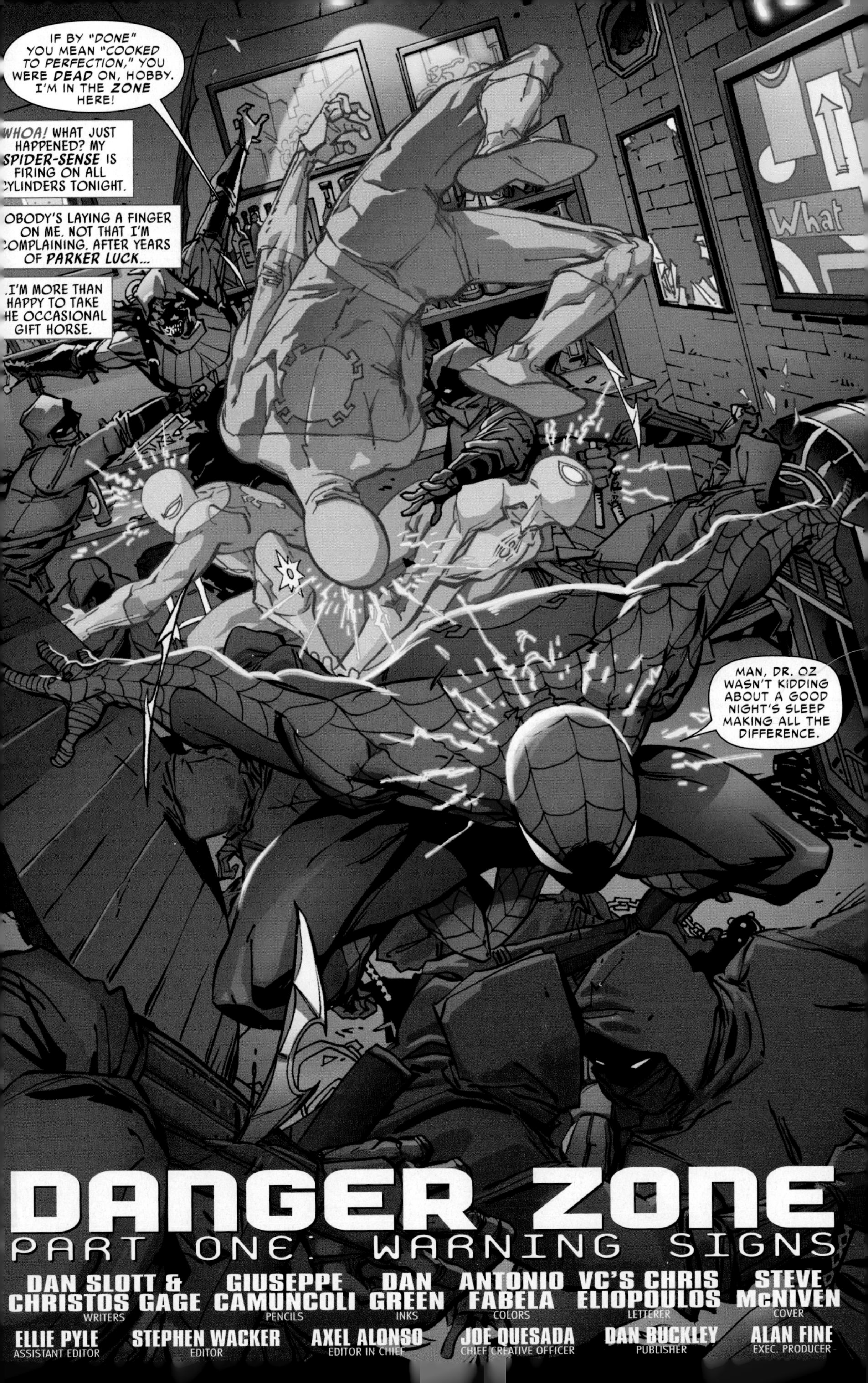
IF BY "DONE" YOU MEAN "COOKED TO PERFECTION," YOU WERE DEAD ON, HOBBY. I'M IN THE ZONE HERE!
WHOA! WHAT JUST HAPPENED? MY SPIDER-SENSE IS FIRING ON ALL CYLINDERS TONIGHT.
OBODY'S LAYING A FINGER ON ME. NOT THAT I'M COMPLAINING. AFTER YEARS OF PARKER LUCK...
.I'M MORE THAN HAPPY TO TAKE HE OCCASIONAL GIFT HORSE.
What
MAN, DR. OZ WASN'T KIDDING ABOUT A GOOD NIGHT'S SLEEP MAKING ALL THE DIFFERENCE.
DANGER ZONE
PART ONE: WARNING SIGNS
DAN SLOTT & CHRISTOS GAGE WRITERS
GIUSEPPE CAMUNCOLI PENCILS
DAN GREEN INKS
ANTONIO FABELA COLORS
VC'S CHRIS ELIOPOULOS LETTERER
STEVE McNIVEN COVER
ELLIE PYLE ASSISTANT EDITOR
STEPHEN WACKER EDITOR
AXEL ALONSO EDITOR IN CHIEF
JOE QUESADA CHIEF CREATIVE OFFICER
DAN BUCKLEY PUBLISHER
ALAN FINE EXEC. PRODUCER

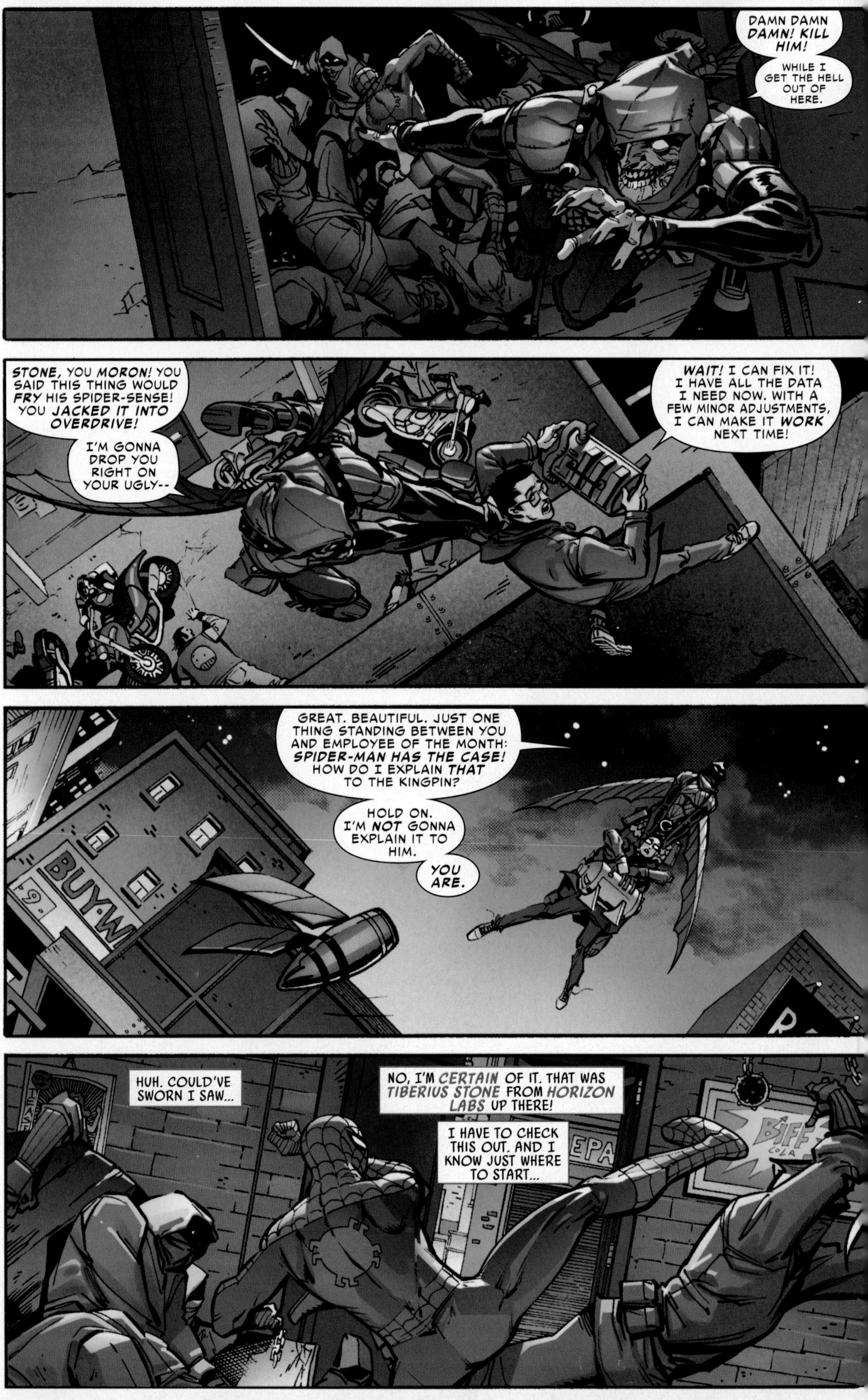
DAMN DAMN DAMN! KILL HIM!
WHILE I GET THE HELL OUT OF HERE.
STONE, YOU MORON! YOU SAID THIS THING WOULD FRY HIS SPIDER-SENSE! YOU JACKED IT INTO OVERDRIVE!
I'M GONNA DROP YOU RIGHT ON YOUR UGLY--
WAIT! I CAN FIX IT! I HAVE ALL THE DATA I NEED NOW. WITH A FEW MINOR ADJUSTMENTS, I CAN MAKE IT WORK NEXT TIME!
GREAT. BEAUTIFUL. JUST ONE THING STANDING BETWEEN YOU AND EMPLOYEE OF THE MONTH: SPIDER-MAN HAS THE CASE! HOW DO I EXPLAIN THAT TO THE KINGPIN?
HOLD ON. I'M NOT GONNA EXPLAIN IT TO HIM.
YOU ARE.
BUY-M
HUH. COULD'VE SWORN I SAW...
NO, I'M CERTAIN OF IT. THAT WAS TIBERIUS STONE FROM HORIZON LABS UP THERE!
I HAVE TO CHECK THIS OUT. AND I KNOW JUST WHERE TO START...
BIFF COLA

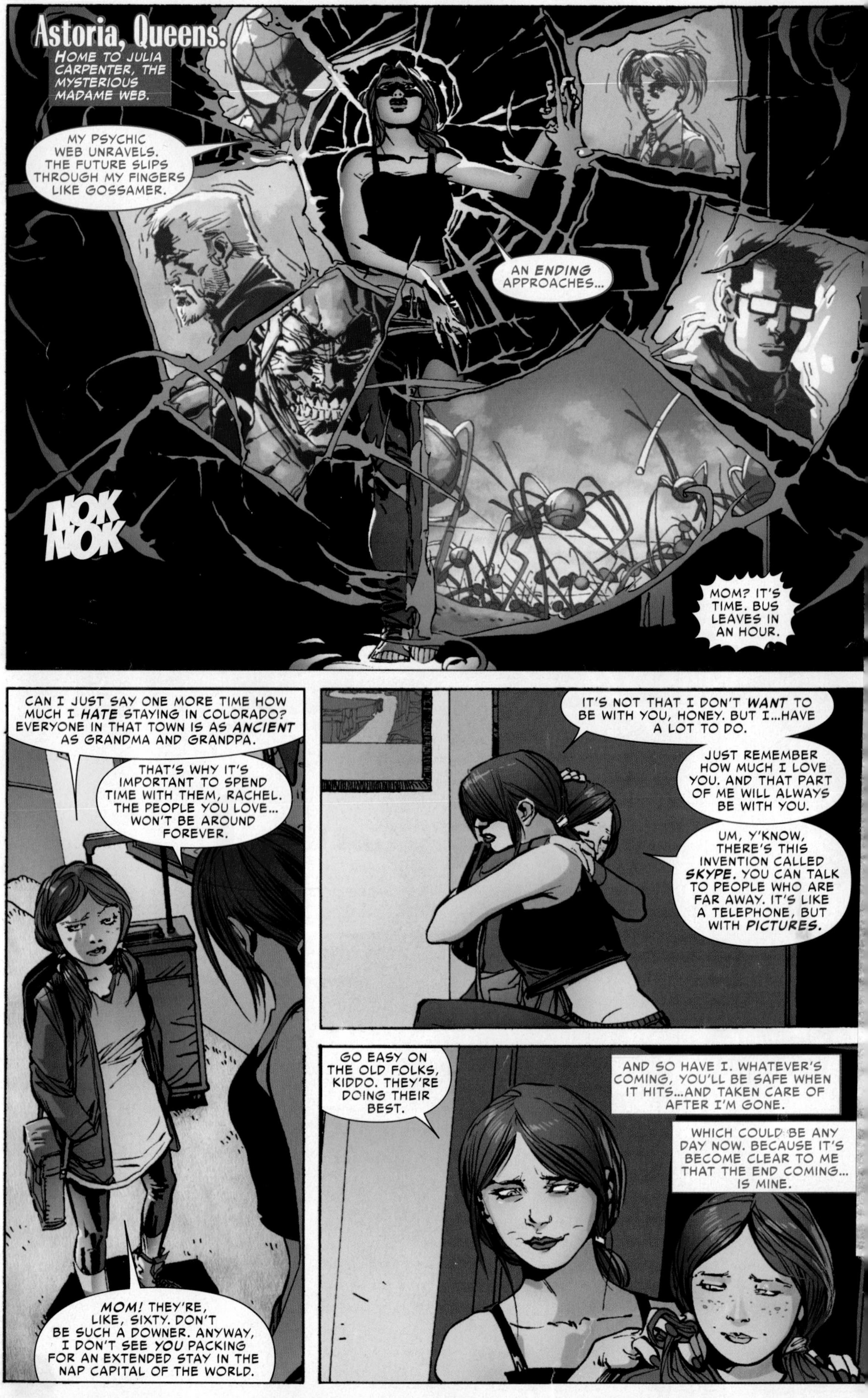
Astoria, Queens.
HOME TO JULIA CARPENTER, THE MYSTERIOUS MADAME WEB.
MY PSYCHIC WEB UNRAVELS. THE FUTURE SLIPS THROUGH MY FINGERS LIKE GOSSAMER.
AN ENDING APPROACHES...
NOK NOK
MOM? IT'S TIME. BUS LEAVES IN AN HOUR.
CAN I JUST SAY ONE MORE TIME HOW MUCH I HATE STAYING IN COLORADO? EVERYONE IN THAT TOWN IS AS ANCIENT AS GRANDMA AND GRANDPA.
THAT'S WHY IT'S IMPORTANT TO SPEND TIME WITH THEM, RACHEL. THE PEOPLE YOU LOVE... WON'T BE AROUND FOREVER.
MOM! THEY'RE, LIKE, SIXTY. DON'T BE SUCH A DOWNER. ANYWAY, I DON'T SEE YOU PACKING FOR AN EXTENDED STAY IN THE NAP CAPITAL OF THE WORLD.
IT'S NOT THAT I DON'T WANT TO BE WITH YOU, HONEY. BUT I...HAVE A LOT TO DO.
JUST REMEMBER HOW MUCH I LOVE YOU. AND THAT PART OF ME WILL ALWAYS BE WITH YOU.
UM, Y'KNOW, THERE'S THIS INVENTION CALLED SKYPE. YOU CAN TALK TO PEOPLE WHO ARE FAR AWAY. IT'S LIKE A TELEPHONE, BUT WITH PICTURES.
GO EASY ON THE OLD FOLKS, KIDDO. THEY'RE DOING THEIR BEST.
AND SO HAVE I. WHATEVER'S COMING, YOU'LL BE SAFE WHEN IT HITS...AND TAKEN CARE OF AFTER I'M GONE.
WHICH COULD BE ANY DAY NOW. BECAUSE IT'S BECOME CLEAR TO ME THAT THE END COMING... IS MINE.

I'M DYING TO KNOW WHAT'S SO IMPORTANT THE GOBLIN CULT, HOBGOBLIN AND THE KINGPIN ARE ALL HOT TO GET THEIR HANDS ON THIS BRIEFCASE...

...BUT IT IS OBVIOUSLY *BOOBY-TRAPPED*, AND BEFORE I CAN PUT IN THE TIME TO CRACK IT, I'VE GOT TO FIND OUT IF TIBERIUS IS HERE, OR--

SLOW DOWN, PETE. JUST 'CAUSE YOU DON'T LIKE THE GUY DOESN'T MEAN HE'S WORKING WITH HOBGOBLIN. YOU'RE A SCIENTIST. SUPPORT YOUR HYPOTHESIS WITH *FACTS*.

THERE. IT'LL BE SAFE IN MY *SPIDEY-VAULT* WHILE I SHAKE THE RUST OFF MY JOURNALISM SKILLS. I STILL REMEMBER LESSON ONE: FOR ANSWERS, YOU GO TO THE *TOP*.

HEY, MAX, HAVE YOU SEEN-- OH, SORRY.

NOT AT ALL, COME IN. PETER, DO YOU KNOW *SALLY FLOYD?* SHE'S DOING A PROFILE ON US FOR THE *DAILY BUGLE*.

I HOPE YOU'LL GIVE HER A MINUTE. WITH ALL THE PRESSURE *MAYOR JAMESON'S* BEEN PUTTING ON US LATELY, WE COULD STAND SOME GOOD PRESS.

SURE, I REMEMBER SALLY...FROM THE *OLD* BUGLE. SEEING YOU MAKES ME ALL KINDS OF NOSTALGIC.

YOU'VE COME A LONG WAY SINCE THEN. FREELANCE SHUTTERBUG TO BIG-TIME RESEARCHER...AND THE GUY WHO DESIGNS TECH FOR *SPIDER-MAN*.

WHAT? YOU'RE, UH, YOU'RE NOT PUTTING THAT IN THE *ARTICLE*, ARE YOU?

SORRY, PETER. LOOKS LIKE SOME OF OUR STAFF SPOKE OUT OF TURN. MS. FLOYD, I'M GOING TO HAVE TO ASK YOU TO REMOVE--

NO CAN DO, MR. MODELL. LOOK, PETE, I'M NOT TRYING TO MAKE YOUR LIFE DIFFICULT, BUT THIS IS *GOLD*...AND *ON THE RECORD*. YOU WANT THE STORY KILLED, YOU'RE GONNA HAVE TO REMEMBER THE OLD REPORTER'S RULE...

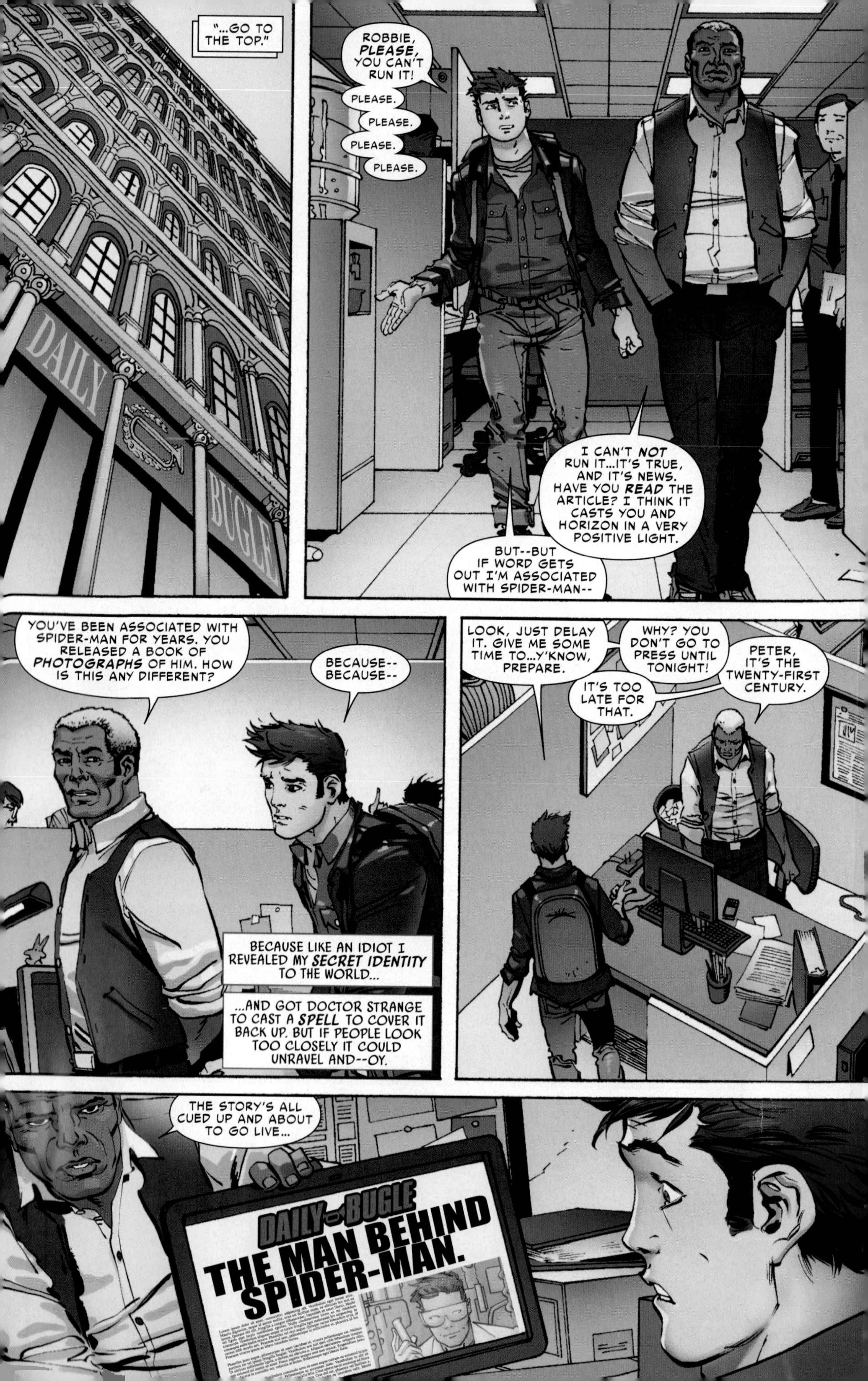
"...GO TO THE TOP."
DAILY BUGLE
ROBBIE, PLEASE, YOU CAN'T RUN IT!
PLEASE.
PLEASE.
PLEASE.
PLEASE.
I CAN'T NOT RUN IT...IT'S TRUE, AND IT'S NEWS. HAVE YOU READ THE ARTICLE? I THINK IT CASTS YOU AND HORIZON IN A VERY POSITIVE LIGHT.
BUT--BUT IF WORD GETS OUT I'M ASSOCIATED WITH SPIDER-MAN--
YOU'VE BEEN ASSOCIATED WITH SPIDER-MAN FOR YEARS. YOU RELEASED A BOOK OF PHOTOGRAPHS OF HIM. HOW IS THIS ANY DIFFERENT?
BECAUSE-- BECAUSE--
BECAUSE LIKE AN IDIOT I REVEALED MY SECRET IDENTITY TO THE WORLD...
...AND GOT DOCTOR STRANGE TO CAST A SPELL TO COVER IT BACK UP. BUT IF PEOPLE LOOK TOO CLOSELY IT COULD UNRAVEL AND--OY.
LOOK, JUST DELAY IT. GIVE ME SOME TIME TO...Y'KNOW, PREPARE.
IT'S TOO LATE FOR THAT.
WHY? YOU DON'T GO TO PRESS UNTIL TONIGHT!
PETER, IT'S THE TWENTY-FIRST CENTURY.
THE STORY'S ALL CUED UP AND ABOUT TO GO LIVE...
DAILY BUGLE
THE MAN BEHIND SPIDER-MAN.

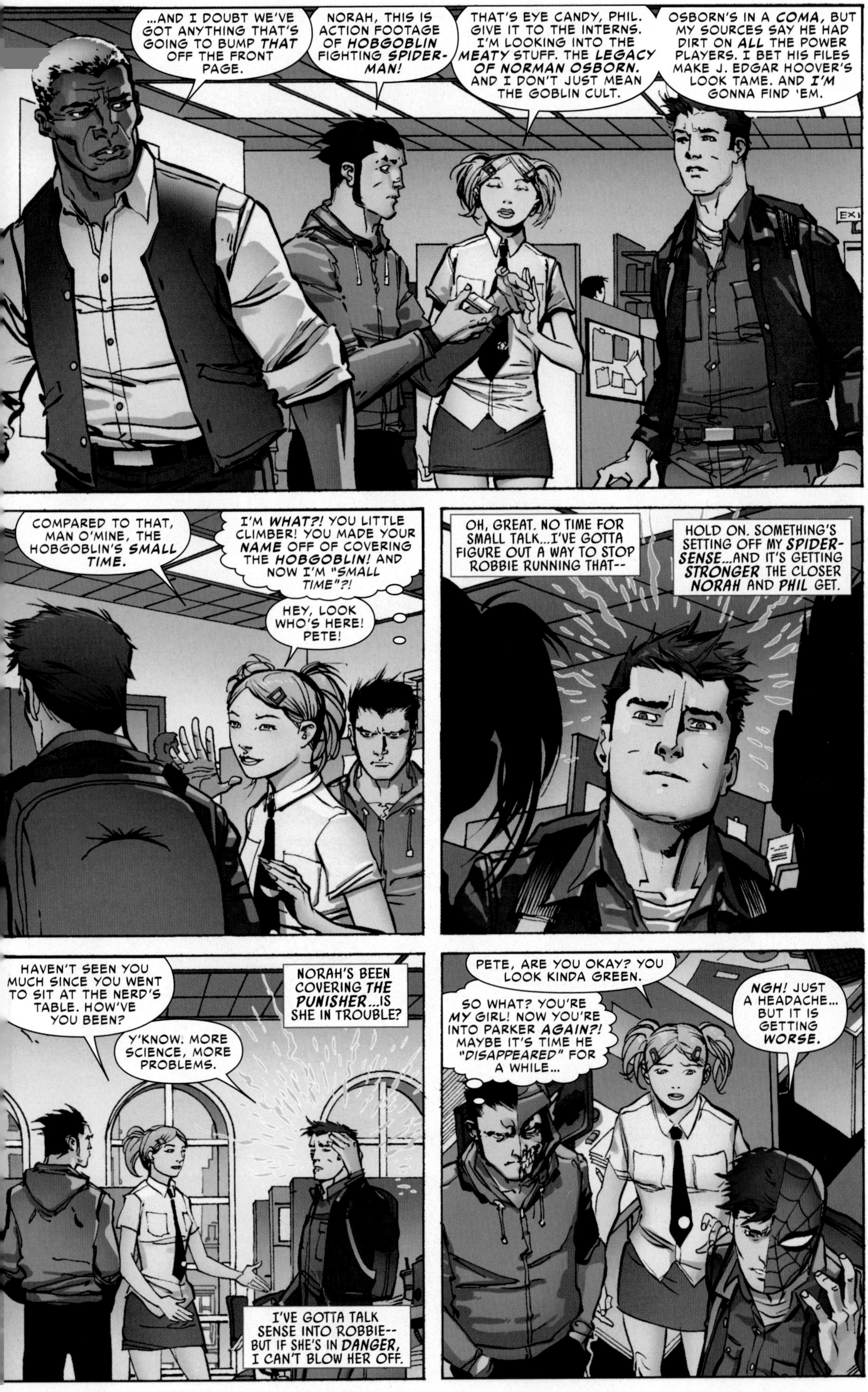

...AND I DOUBT WE'VE GOT ANYTHING THAT'S GOING TO BUMP THAT OFF THE FRONT PAGE.
NORAH, THIS IS ACTION FOOTAGE OF HOBGOBLIN FIGHTING SPIDER-MAN!
THAT'S EYE CANDY, PHIL. GIVE IT TO THE INTERNS. I'M LOOKING INTO THE MEATY STUFF. THE LEGACY OF NORMAN OSBORN. AND I DON'T JUST MEAN THE GOBLIN CULT.
OSBORN'S IN A COMA, BUT MY SOURCES SAY HE HAD DIRT ON ALL THE POWER PLAYERS. I BET HIS FILES MAKE J. EDGAR HOOVER'S LOOK TAME. AND I'M GONNA FIND 'EM.
COMPARED TO THAT, MAN O'MINE, THE HOBGOBLIN'S SMALL TIME.
I'M WHAT?! YOU LITTLE CLIMBER! YOU MADE YOUR NAME OFF OF COVERING THE HOBGOBLIN! AND NOW I'M "SMALL TIME"?!
HEY, LOOK WHO'S HERE! PETE!
OH, GREAT. NO TIME FOR SMALL TALK...I'VE GOTTA FIGURE OUT A WAY TO STOP ROBBIE RUNNING THAT--
HOLD ON. SOMETHING'S SETTING OFF MY SPIDER-SENSE...AND IT'S GETTING STRONGER THE CLOSER NORAH AND PHIL GET.
HAVEN'T SEEN YOU MUCH SINCE YOU WENT TO SIT AT THE NERD'S TABLE. HOW'VE YOU BEEN?
Y'KNOW. MORE SCIENCE, MORE PROBLEMS.
NORAH'S BEEN COVERING THE PUNISHER...IS SHE IN TROUBLE?
I'VE GOTTA TALK SENSE INTO ROBBIE-- BUT IF SHE'S IN DANGER, I CAN'T BLOW HER OFF.
PETE, ARE YOU OKAY? YOU LOOK KINDA GREEN.
SO WHAT? YOU'RE MY GIRL! NOW YOU'RE INTO PARKER AGAIN?! MAYBE IT'S TIME HE "DISAPPEARED" FOR A WHILE...
NGH! JUST A HEADACHE... BUT IT IS GETTING WORSE.

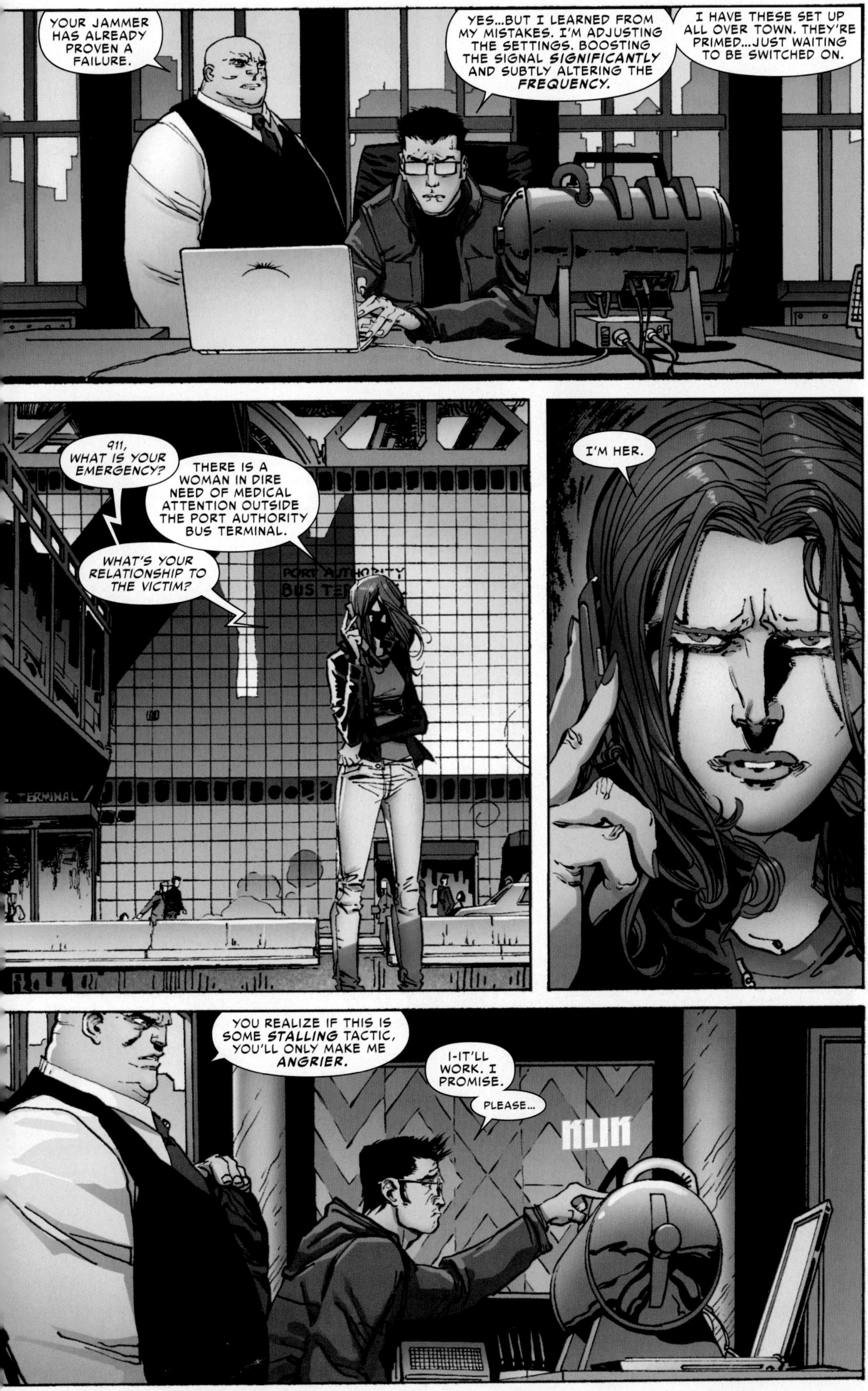

YOUR JAMMER HAS ALREADY PROVEN A FAILURE.
YES...BUT I LEARNED FROM MY MISTAKES. I'M ADJUSTING THE SETTINGS. BOOSTING THE SIGNAL SIGNIFICANTLY AND SUBTLY ALTERING THE FREQUENCY.
I HAVE THESE SET UP ALL OVER TOWN. THEY'RE PRIMED...JUST WAITING TO BE SWITCHED ON.
911, WHAT IS YOUR EMERGENCY?
THERE IS A WOMAN IN DIRE NEED OF MEDICAL ATTENTION OUTSIDE THE PORT AUTHORITY BUS TERMINAL.
WHAT'S YOUR RELATIONSHIP TO THE VICTIM?
PORT AUTHORITY BUS TER
TERMINAL
I'M HER.
YOU REALIZE IF THIS IS SOME STALLING TACTIC, YOU'LL ONLY MAKE ME ANGRIER.
I-IT'LL WORK. I PROMISE.
PLEASE...
KLIK

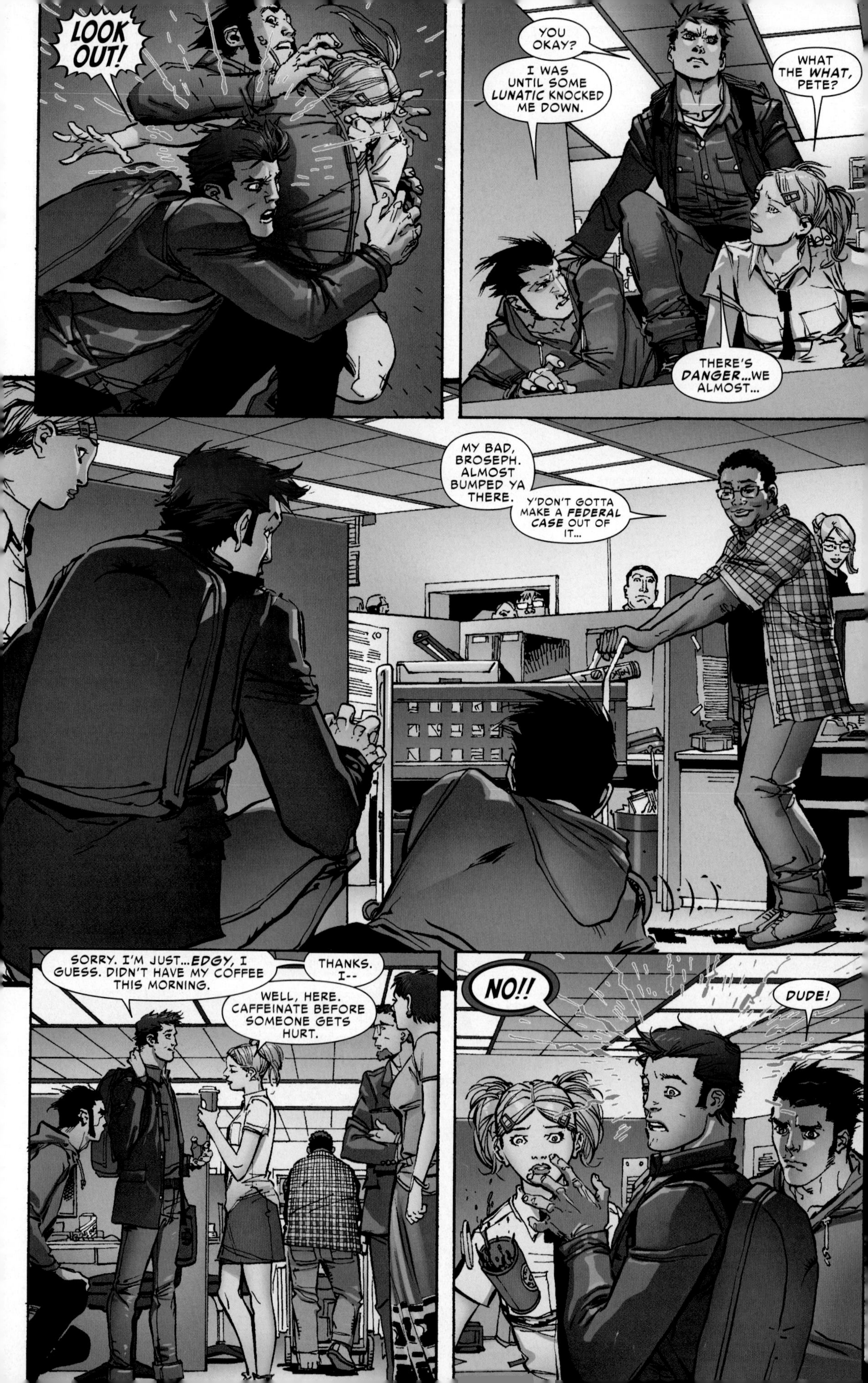
LOOK OUT!
YOU OKAY?
I WAS UNTIL SOME LUNATIC KNOCKED ME DOWN.
WHAT THE WHAT, PETE?
THERE'S DANGER...WE ALMOST...
MY BAD, BROSEPH. ALMOST BUMPED YA THERE.
Y'DON'T GOTTA MAKE A FEDERAL CASE OUT OF IT...
SORRY. I'M JUST...EDGY, I GUESS. DIDN'T HAVE MY COFFEE THIS MORNING.
THANKS. I--
WELL, HERE. CAFFEINATE BEFORE SOMEONE GETS HURT.
NO!!
DUDE!

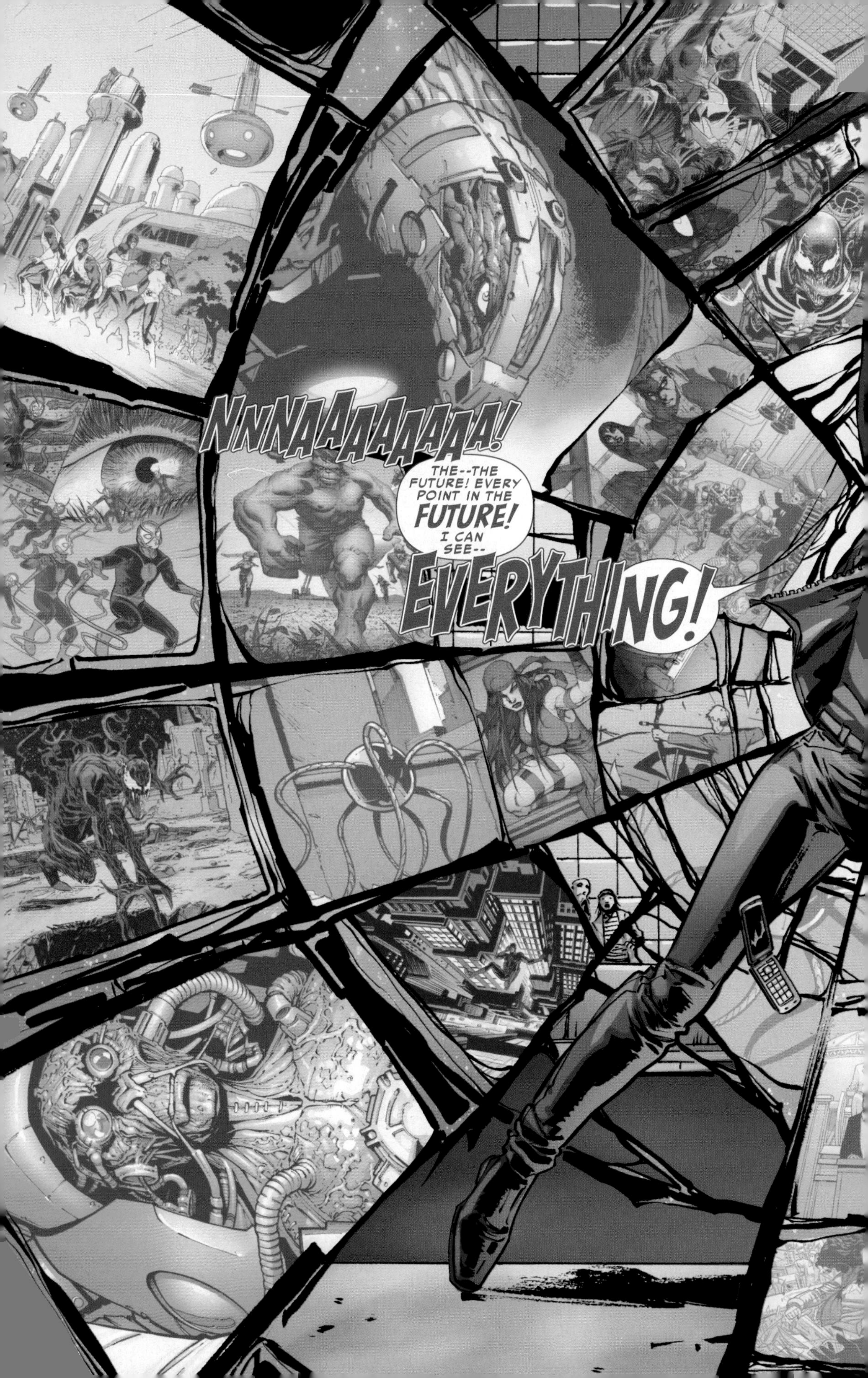
NNNAAAAAAAA!
THE--THE FUTURE! EVERY POINT IN THE FUTURE! I CAN SEE--
EVERYTHING!

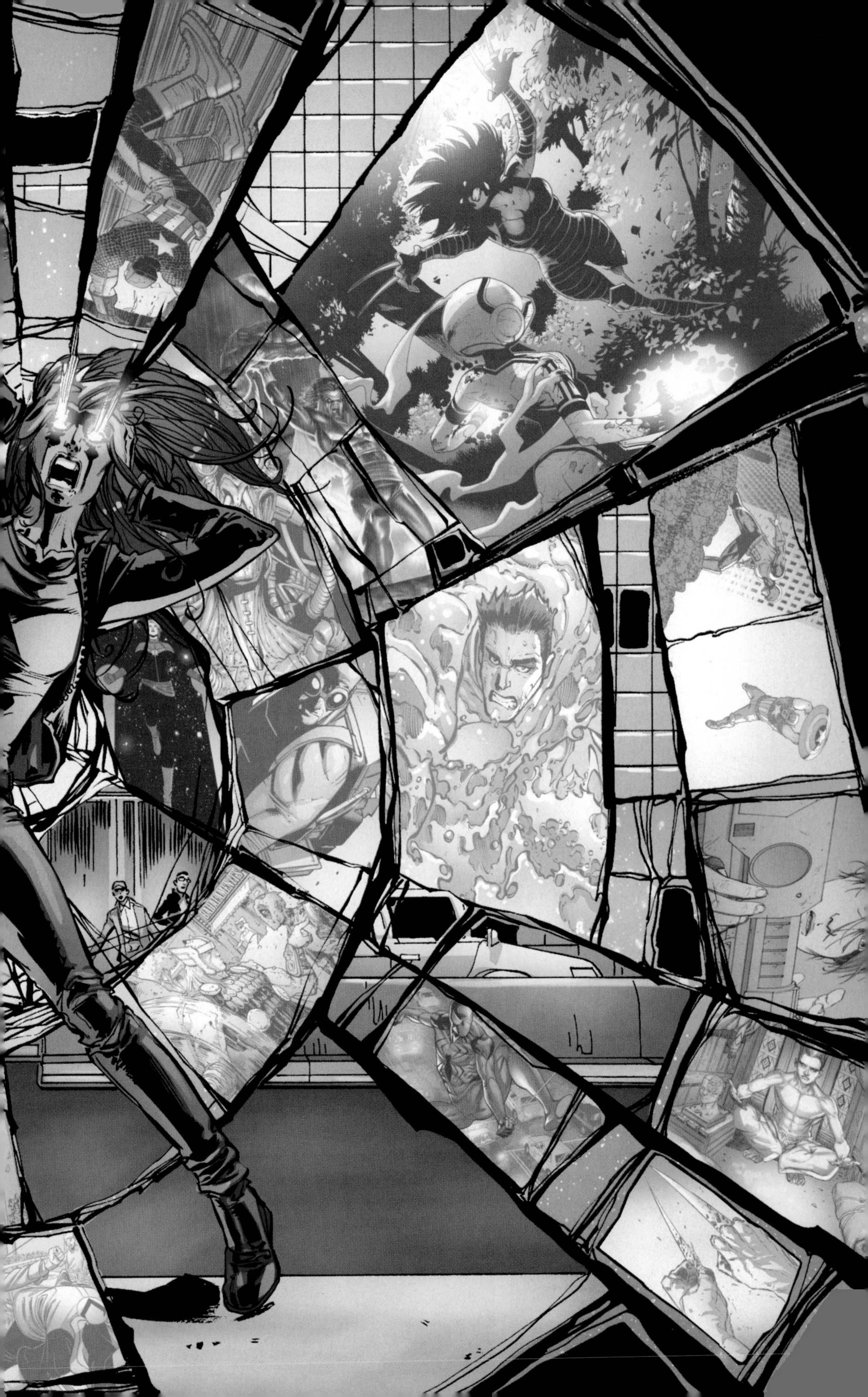

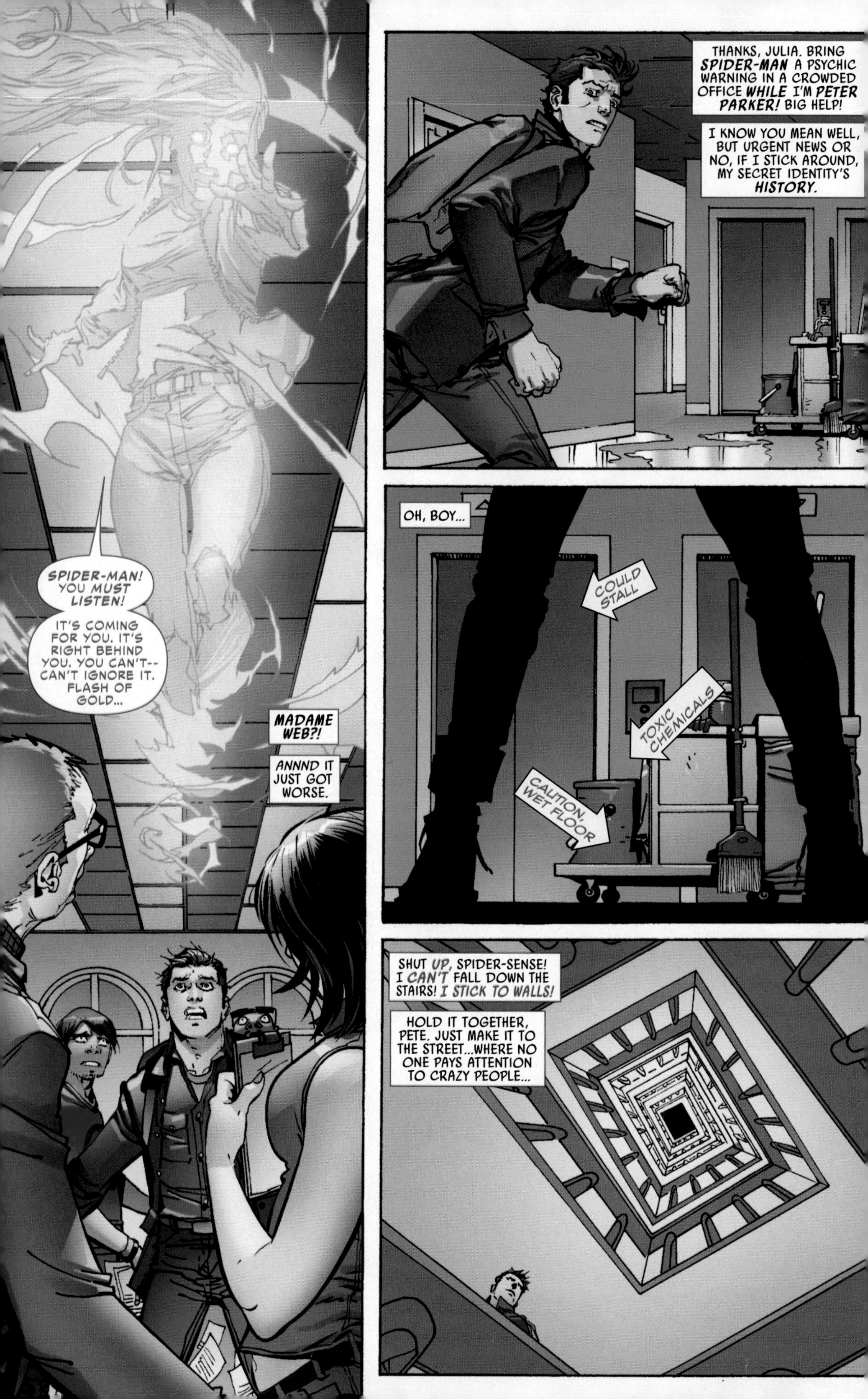
SPIDER-MAN! YOU MUST LISTEN!
IT'S COMING FOR YOU. IT'S RIGHT BEHIND YOU. YOU CAN'T-- CAN'T IGNORE IT. FLASH OF GOLD...
MADAME WEB?!
ANNND IT JUST GOT WORSE.
THANKS, JULIA. BRING SPIDER-MAN A PSYCHIC WARNING IN A CROWDED OFFICE WHILE I'M PETER PARKER! BIG HELP!
I KNOW YOU MEAN WELL, BUT URGENT NEWS OR NO, IF I STICK AROUND, MY SECRET IDENTITY'S HISTORY.
OH, BOY...
COULD STALL
TOXIC CHEMICALS
CAUTION, WET FLOOR
SHUT UP, SPIDER-SENSE! I CAN'T FALL DOWN THE STAIRS! I STICK TO WALLS!
HOLD IT TOGETHER, PETE. JUST MAKE IT TO THE STREET...WHERE NO ONE PAYS ATTENTION TO CRAZY PEOPLE...

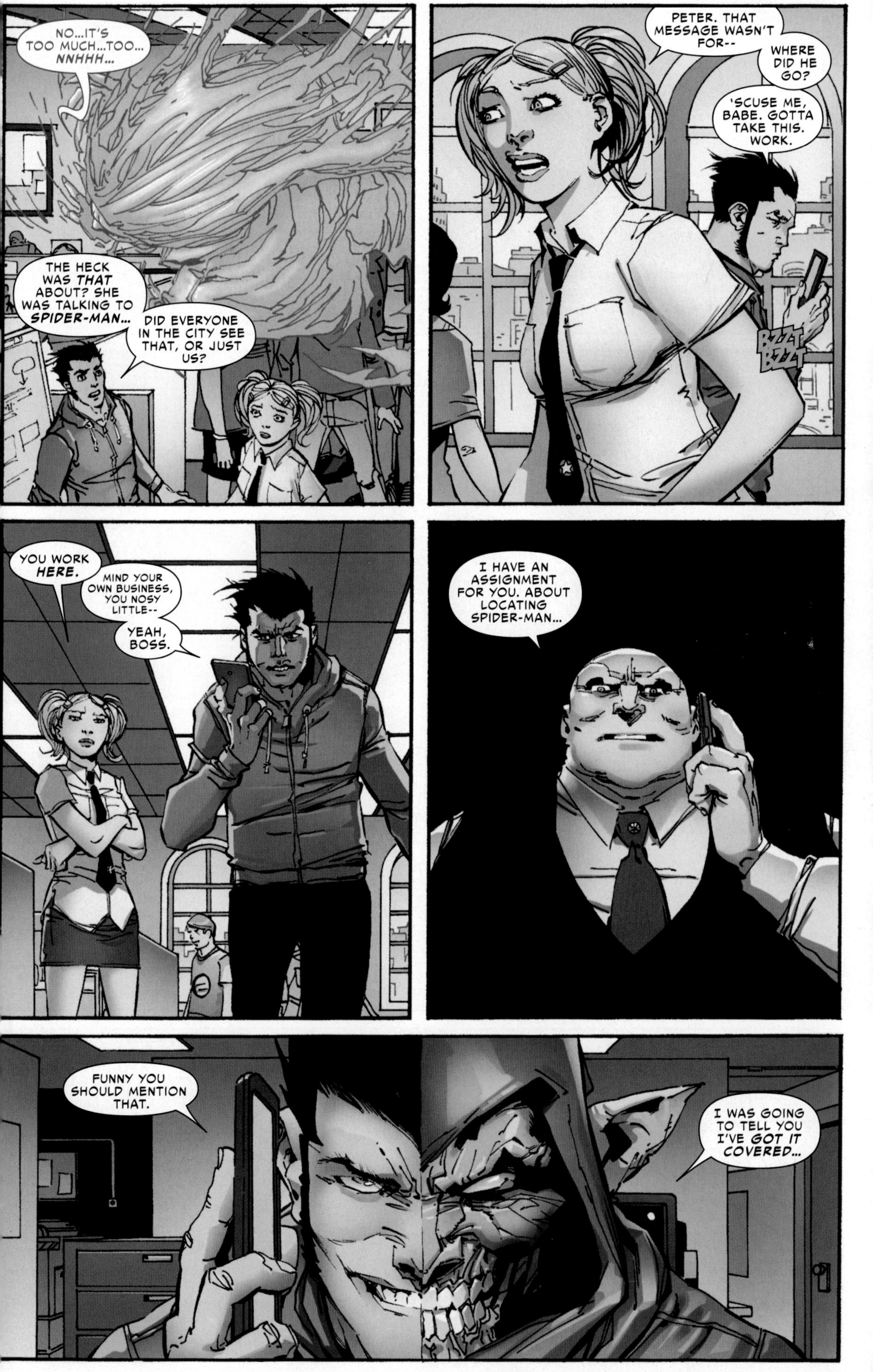
NO...IT'S TOO MUCH...TOO... NNHHH...
PETER. THAT MESSAGE WASN'T FOR--
WHERE DID HE GO?
'SCUSE ME, BABE. GOTTA TAKE THIS. WORK.
BZZT BZZT
THE HECK WAS THAT ABOUT? SHE WAS TALKING TO SPIDER-MAN...
DID EVERYONE IN THE CITY SEE THAT, OR JUST US?
YOU WORK HERE.
MIND YOUR OWN BUSINESS, YOU NOSY LITTLE--
YEAH, BOSS.
I HAVE AN ASSIGNMENT FOR YOU. ABOUT LOCATING SPIDER-MAN...
FUNNY YOU SHOULD MENTION THAT.
I WAS GOING TO TELL YOU I'VE GOT IT COVERED...

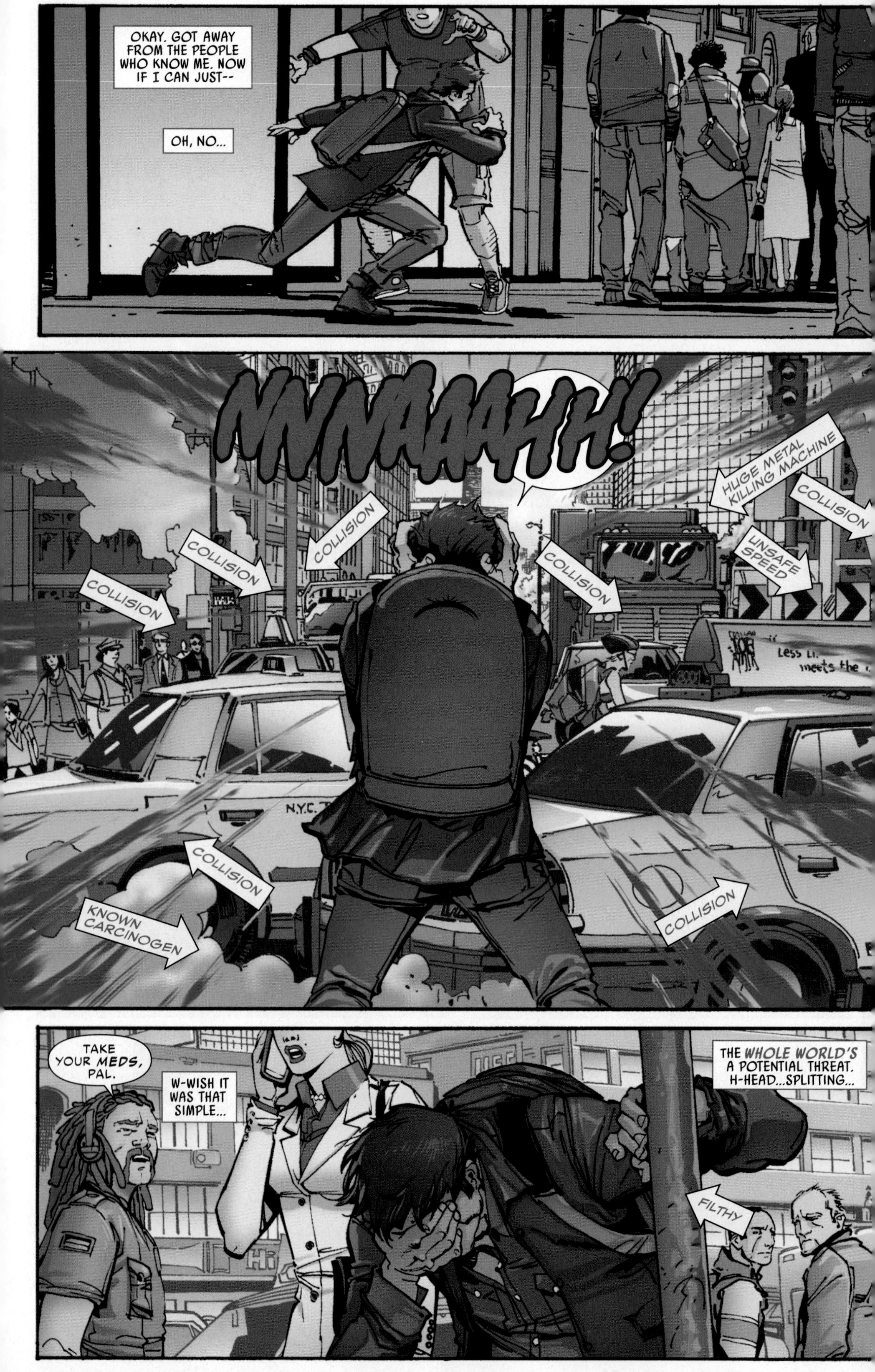

OKAY. GOT AWAY FROM THE PEOPLE WHO KNOW ME. NOW IF I CAN JUST--
OH, NO...
NNNAAAHH!
HUGE METAL KILLING MACHINE
COLLISION
COLLISION
UNSAFE SPEED
COLLISION
COLLISION
COLLISION
COLLISION
COLLISION
KNOWN CARCINOGEN
COLLISION
TAKE YOUR MEDS, PAL.
W-WISH IT WAS THAT SIMPLE...
THE WHOLE WORLD'S A POTENTIAL THREAT. H-HEAD...SPLITTING...
FILTHY

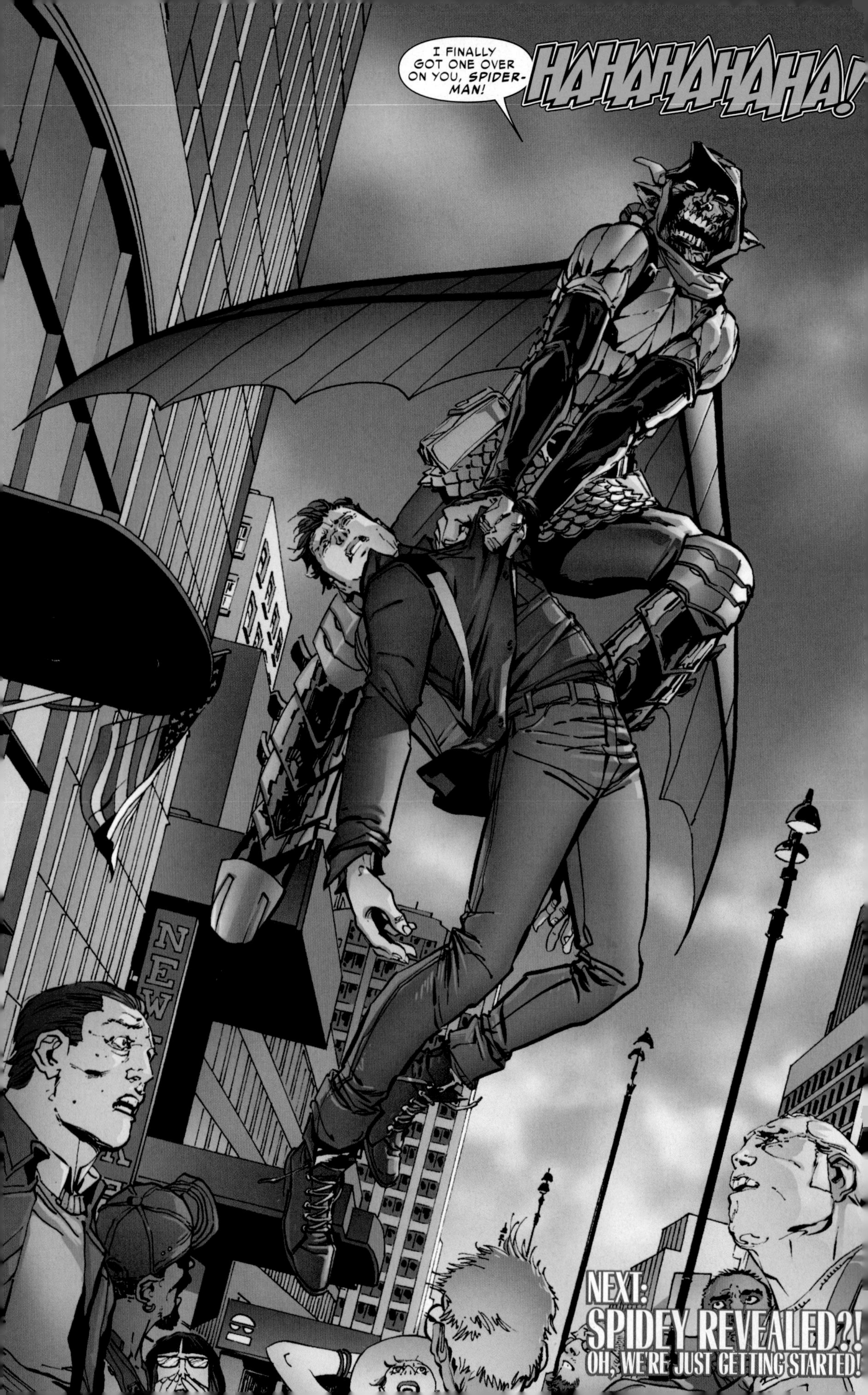
I FINALLY GOT ONE OVER ON YOU, SPIDER-MAN!
HAHAHAHAHAHA!
NEW
NEXT:
SPIDEY REVEALED?!
OH, WE'RE JUST GETTING STARTED!

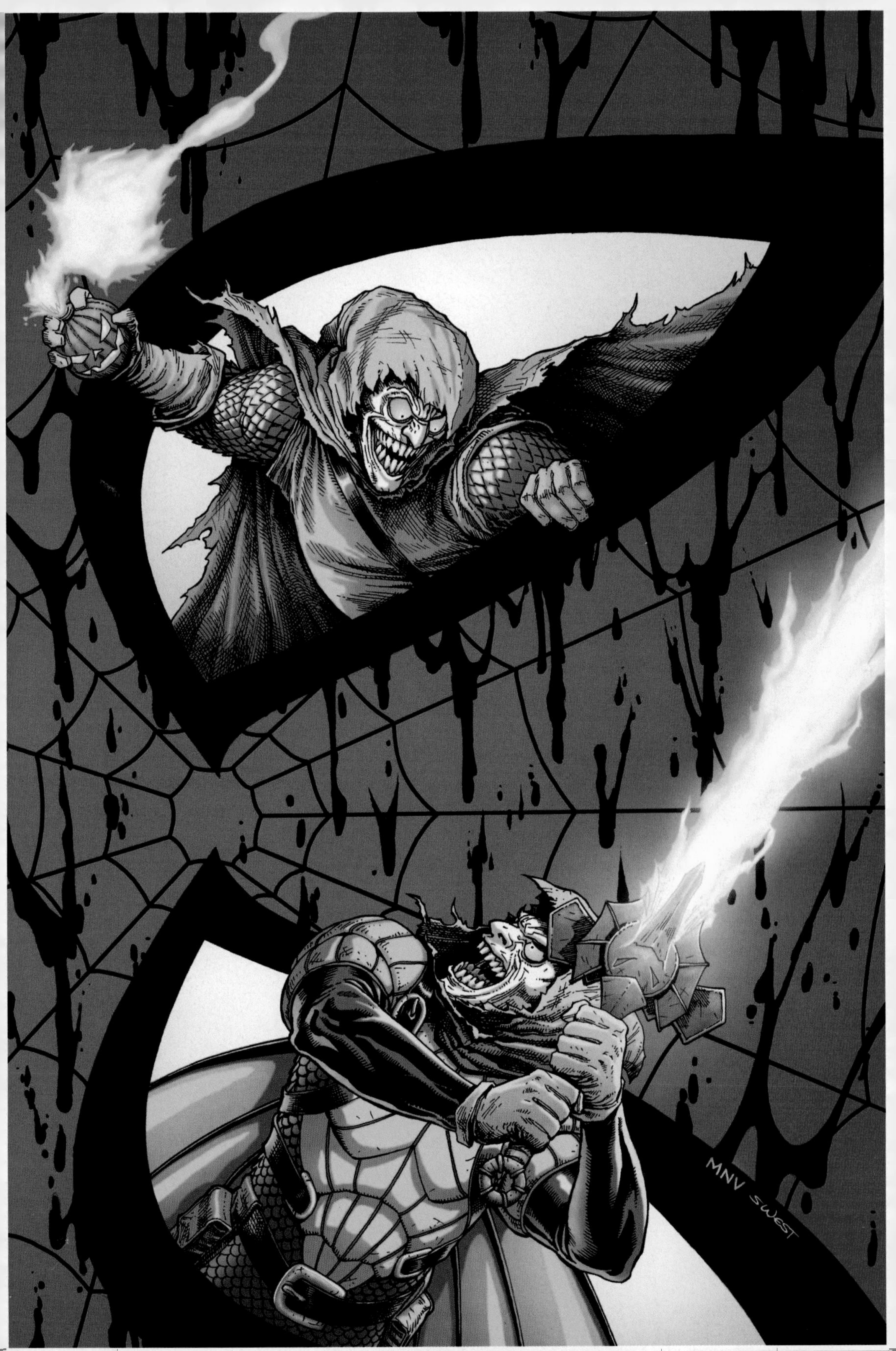
MNV SWEST

PIDER-MAN #696
/EN & SIMON WEST

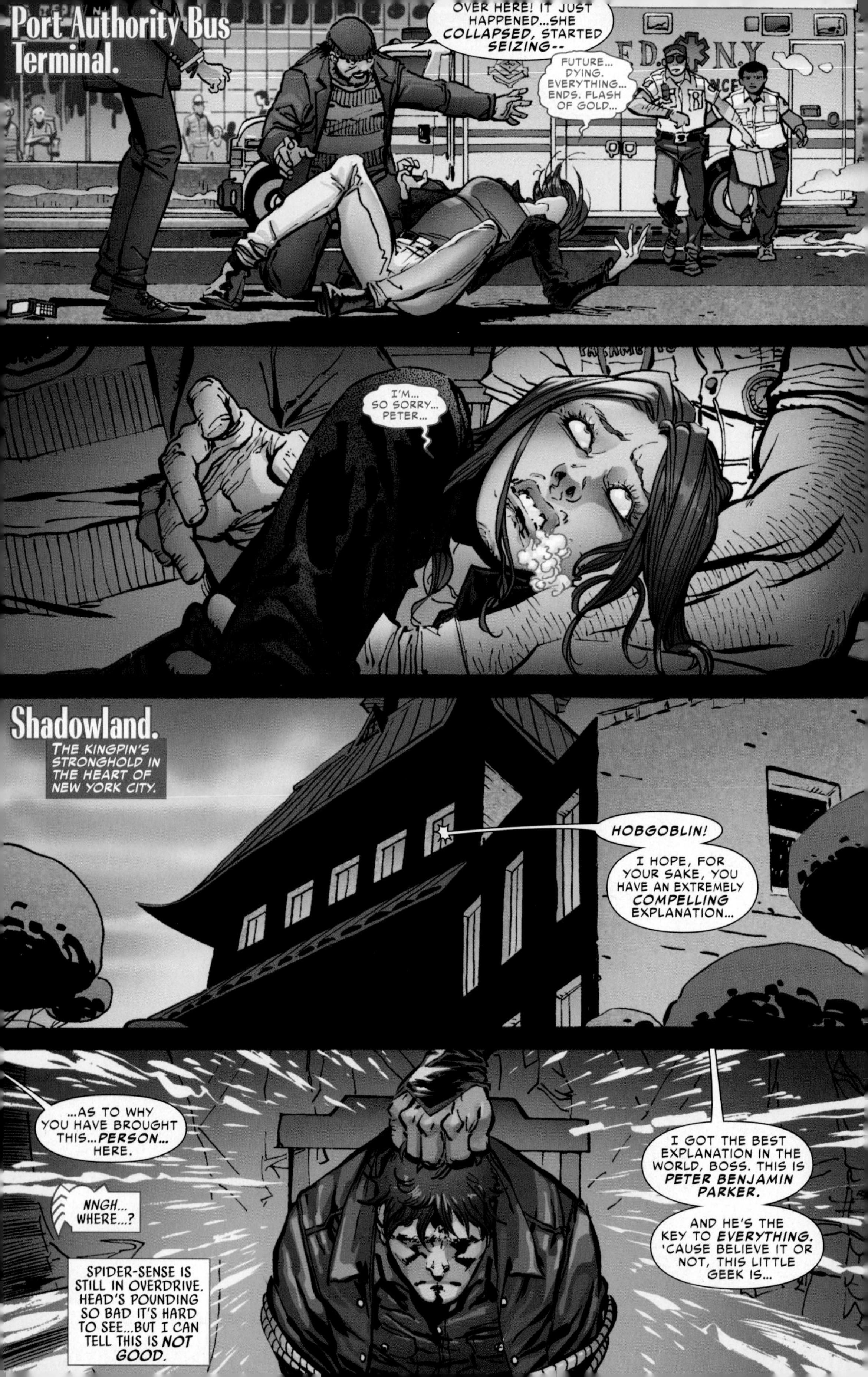
Port Authority Bus Terminal.
OVER HERE! IT JUST HAPPENED...SHE COLLAPSED, STARTED SEIZING--
FUTURE... DYING. EVERYTHING... ENDS. FLASH OF GOLD...
F.D.N.Y.
I'M... SO SORRY... PETER...
Shadowland.
THE KINGPIN'S STRONGHOLD IN THE HEART OF NEW YORK CITY.
HOBGOBLIN!
I HOPE, FOR YOUR SAKE, YOU HAVE AN EXTREMELY COMPELLING EXPLANATION...
...AS TO WHY YOU HAVE BROUGHT THIS...PERSON... HERE.
NNGH... WHERE...?
SPIDER-SENSE IS STILL IN OVERDRIVE. HEAD'S POUNDING SO BAD IT'S HARD TO SEE...BUT I CAN TELL THIS IS NOT GOOD.
I GOT THE BEST EXPLANATION IN THE WORLD, BOSS. THIS IS PETER BENJAMIN PARKER.
AND HE'S THE KEY TO EVERYTHING. 'CAUSE BELIEVE IT OR NOT, THIS LITTLE GEEK IS...

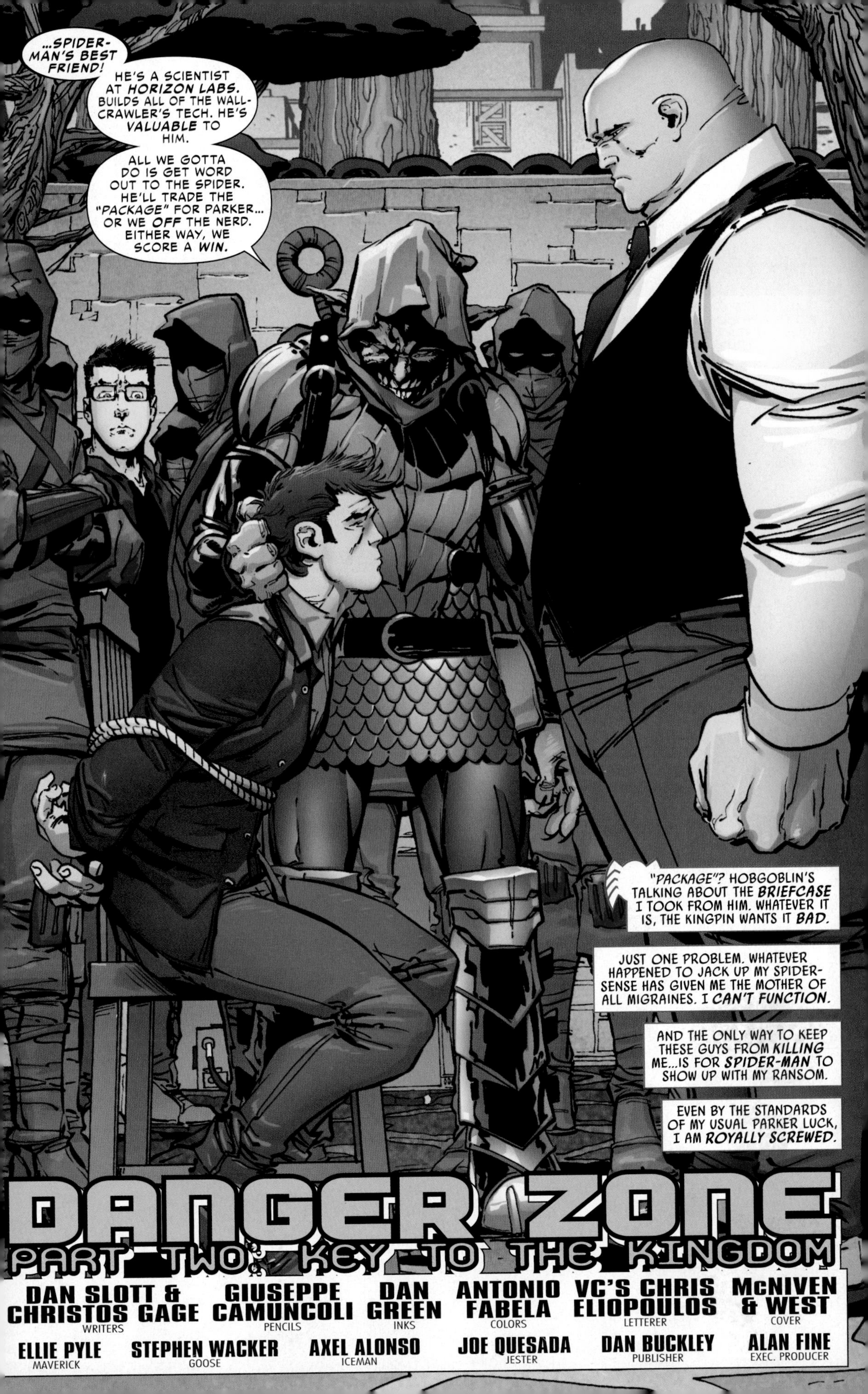
...SPIDER-MAN'S BEST FRIEND!
HE'S A SCIENTIST AT HORIZON LABS. BUILDS ALL OF THE WALL-CRAWLER'S TECH. HE'S VALUABLE TO HIM.
ALL WE GOTTA DO IS GET WORD OUT TO THE SPIDER. HE'LL TRADE THE "PACKAGE" FOR PARKER... OR WE OFF THE NERD. EITHER WAY, WE SCORE A WIN.
"PACKAGE"? HOBGOBLIN'S TALKING ABOUT THE BRIEFCASE I TOOK FROM HIM. WHATEVER IT IS, THE KINGPIN WANTS IT BAD.
JUST ONE PROBLEM. WHATEVER HAPPENED TO JACK UP MY SPIDER-SENSE HAS GIVEN ME THE MOTHER OF ALL MIGRAINES. I CAN'T FUNCTION.
AND THE ONLY WAY TO KEEP THESE GUYS FROM KILLING ME...IS FOR SPIDER-MAN TO SHOW UP WITH MY RANSOM.
EVEN BY THE STANDARDS OF MY USUAL PARKER LUCK, I AM ROYALLY SCREWED.
DANGER ZONE
PART TWO: KEY TO THE KINGDOM
DAN SLOTT & CHRISTOS GAGE WRITERS
GIUSEPPE CAMUNCOLI PENCILS
DAN GREEN INKS
ANTONIO FABELA COLORS
VC'S CHRIS ELIOPOULOS LETTERER
McNIVEN & WEST COVER
ELLIE PYLE MAVERICK
STEPHEN WACKER GOOSE
AXEL ALONSO ICEMAN
JOE QUESADA JESTER
DAN BUCKLEY PUBLISHER
ALAN FINE EXEC. PRODUCER

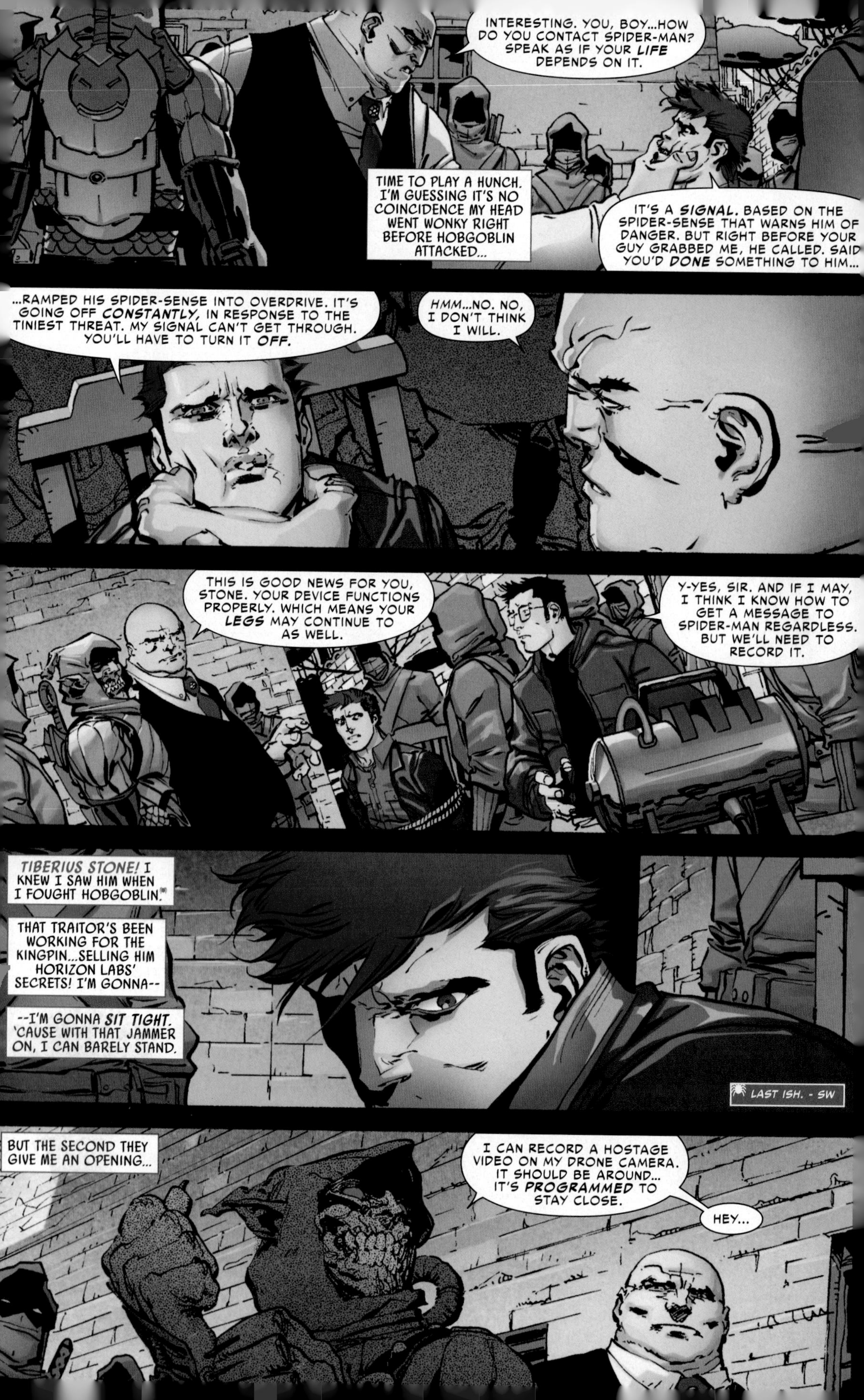
INTERESTING. YOU, BOY...HOW DO YOU CONTACT SPIDER-MAN? SPEAK AS IF YOUR LIFE DEPENDS ON IT.
TIME TO PLAY A HUNCH. I'M GUESSING IT'S NO COINCIDENCE MY HEAD WENT WONKY RIGHT BEFORE HOBGOBLIN ATTACKED...
IT'S A SIGNAL. BASED ON THE SPIDER-SENSE THAT WARNS HIM OF DANGER. BUT RIGHT BEFORE YOUR GUY GRABBED ME, HE CALLED. SAID YOU'D DONE SOMETHING TO HIM...
...RAMPED HIS SPIDER-SENSE INTO OVERDRIVE. IT'S GOING OFF CONSTANTLY, IN RESPONSE TO THE TINIEST THREAT. MY SIGNAL CAN'T GET THROUGH. YOU'LL HAVE TO TURN IT OFF.
HMM...NO. NO, I DON'T THINK I WILL.
THIS IS GOOD NEWS FOR YOU, STONE. YOUR DEVICE FUNCTIONS PROPERLY. WHICH MEANS YOUR LEGS MAY CONTINUE TO AS WELL.
Y-YES, SIR. AND IF I MAY, I THINK I KNOW HOW TO GET A MESSAGE TO SPIDER-MAN REGARDLESS. BUT WE'LL NEED TO RECORD IT.
TIBERIUS STONE! I KNEW I SAW HIM WHEN I FOUGHT HOBGOBLIN.*
THAT TRAITOR'S BEEN WORKING FOR THE KINGPIN...SELLING HIM HORIZON LABS' SECRETS! I'M GONNA--
--I'M GONNA SIT TIGHT. 'CAUSE WITH THAT JAMMER ON, I CAN BARELY STAND.
*LAST ISH. - SW
BUT THE SECOND THEY GIVE ME AN OPENING...
I CAN RECORD A HOSTAGE VIDEO ON MY DRONE CAMERA. IT SHOULD BE AROUND... IT'S PROGRAMMED TO STAY CLOSE.
HEY...

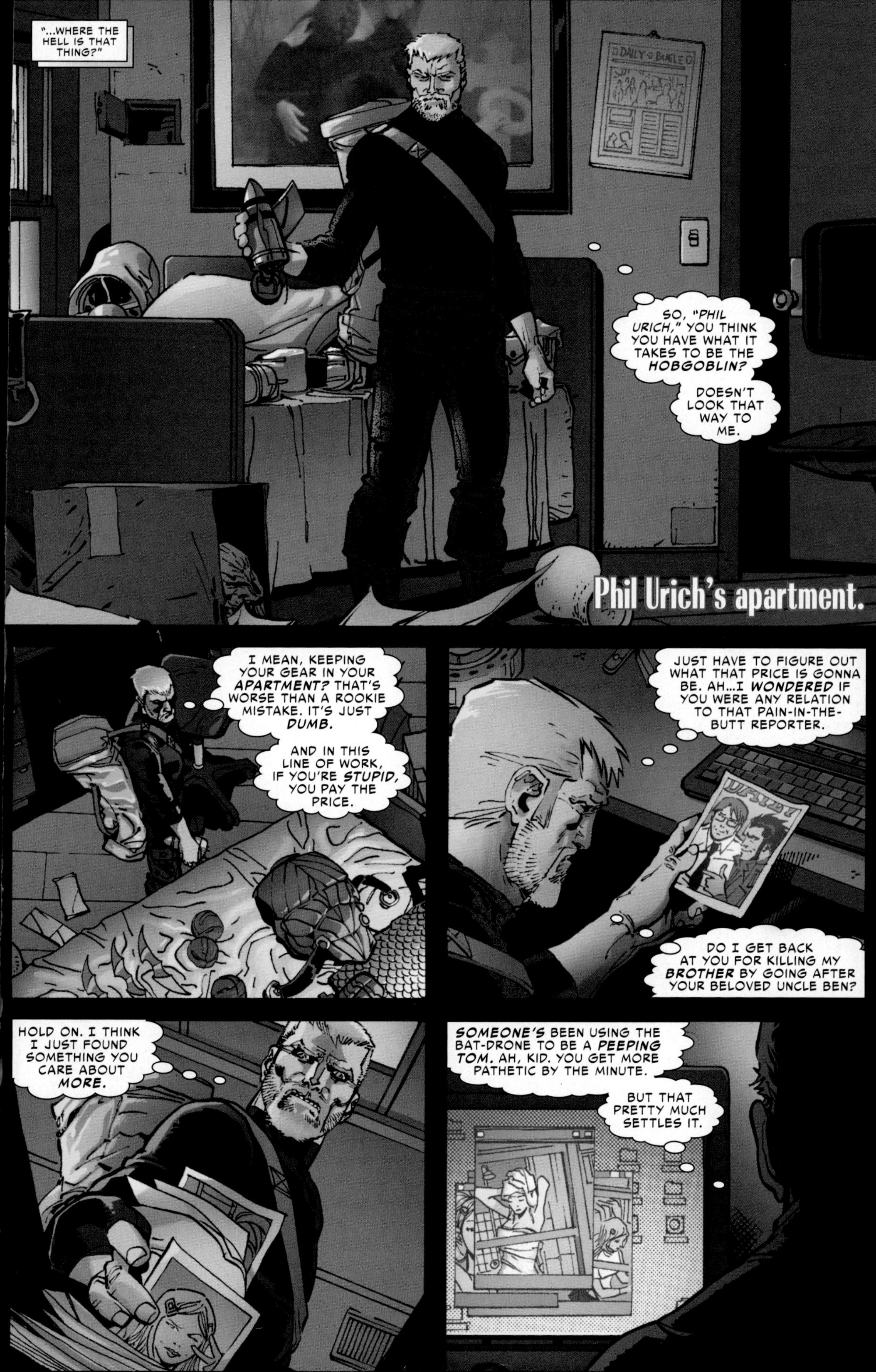
"...WHERE THE HELL IS THAT THING?"
DAILY BUGLE
SO, "PHIL URICH," YOU THINK YOU HAVE WHAT IT TAKES TO BE THE HOBGOBLIN?
DOESN'T LOOK THAT WAY TO ME.
Phil Urich's apartment.
I MEAN, KEEPING YOUR GEAR IN YOUR APARTMENT? THAT'S WORSE THAN A ROOKIE MISTAKE. IT'S JUST DUMB.
AND IN THIS LINE OF WORK, IF YOU'RE STUPID, YOU PAY THE PRICE.
JUST HAVE TO FIGURE OUT WHAT THAT PRICE IS GONNA BE. AH...I WONDERED IF YOU WERE ANY RELATION TO THAT PAIN-IN-THE-BUTT REPORTER.
DO I GET BACK AT YOU FOR KILLING MY BROTHER BY GOING AFTER YOUR BELOVED UNCLE BEN?
HOLD ON. I THINK I JUST FOUND SOMETHING YOU CARE ABOUT MORE.
SOMEONE'S BEEN USING THE BAT-DRONE TO BE A PEEPING TOM. AH, KID. YOU GET MORE PATHETIC BY THE MINUTE.
BUT THAT PRETTY MUCH SETTLES IT.

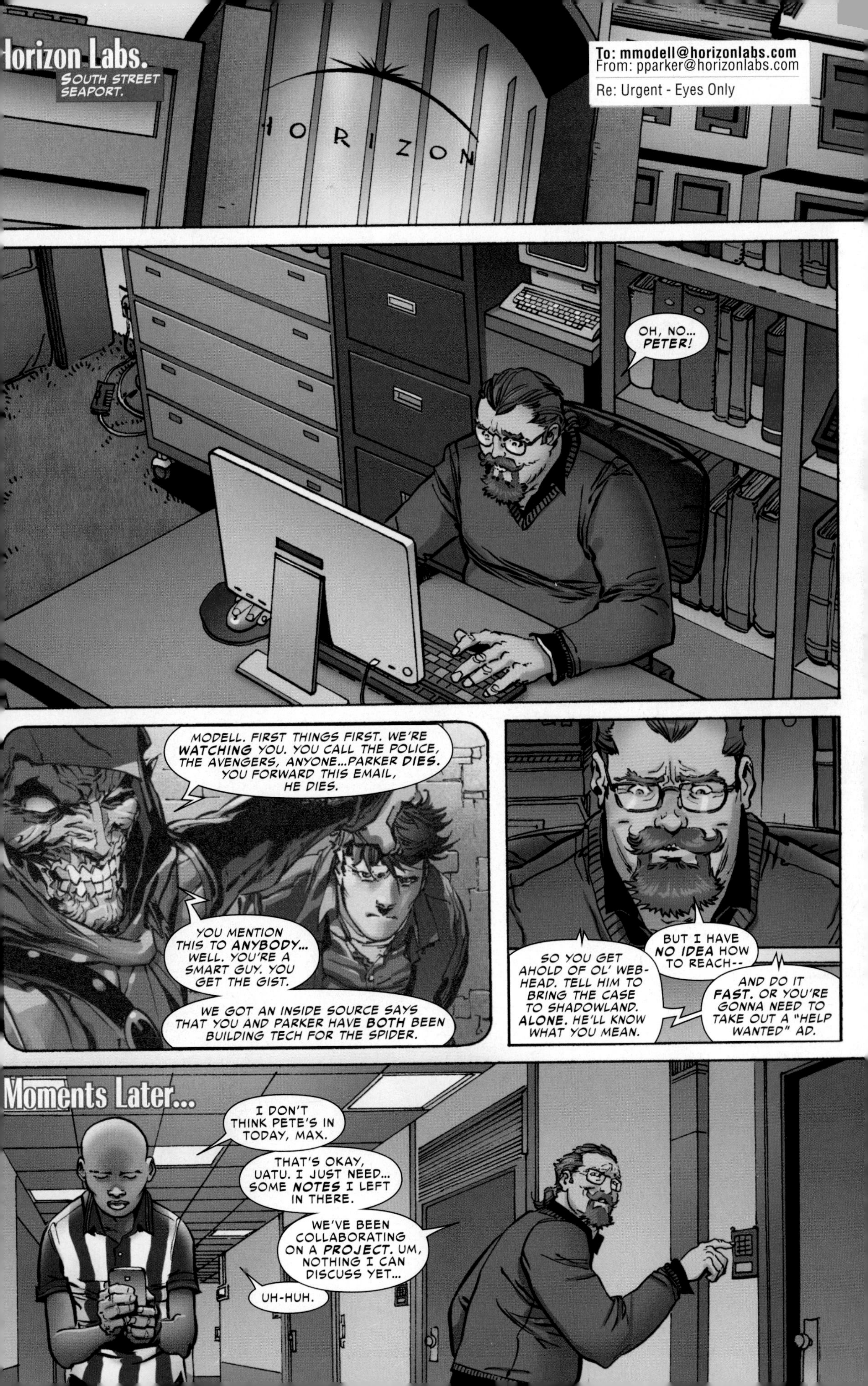
Horizon Labs.
SOUTH STREET SEAPORT.
To: mmodell@horizonlabs.com
From: pparker@horizonlabs.com
Re: Urgent - Eyes Only
HORIZON
OH, NO... PETER!
MODELL. FIRST THINGS FIRST. WE'RE WATCHING YOU. YOU CALL THE POLICE, THE AVENGERS, ANYONE...PARKER DIES. YOU FORWARD THIS EMAIL, HE DIES.
YOU MENTION THIS TO ANYBODY... WELL. YOU'RE A SMART GUY. YOU GET THE GIST.
WE GOT AN INSIDE SOURCE SAYS THAT YOU AND PARKER HAVE BOTH BEEN BUILDING TECH FOR THE SPIDER.
SO YOU GET AHOLD OF OL' WEB-HEAD. TELL HIM TO BRING THE CASE TO SHADOWLAND. ALONE. HE'LL KNOW WHAT YOU MEAN.
BUT I HAVE NO IDEA HOW TO REACH--
AND DO IT FAST. OR YOU'RE GONNA NEED TO TAKE OUT A "HELP WANTED" AD.
Moments Later...
I DON'T THINK PETE'S IN TODAY, MAX.
THAT'S OKAY, UATU. I JUST NEED... SOME NOTES I LEFT IN THERE.
WE'VE BEEN COLLABORATING ON A PROJECT. UM, NOTHING I CAN DISCUSS YET...
UH-HUH.

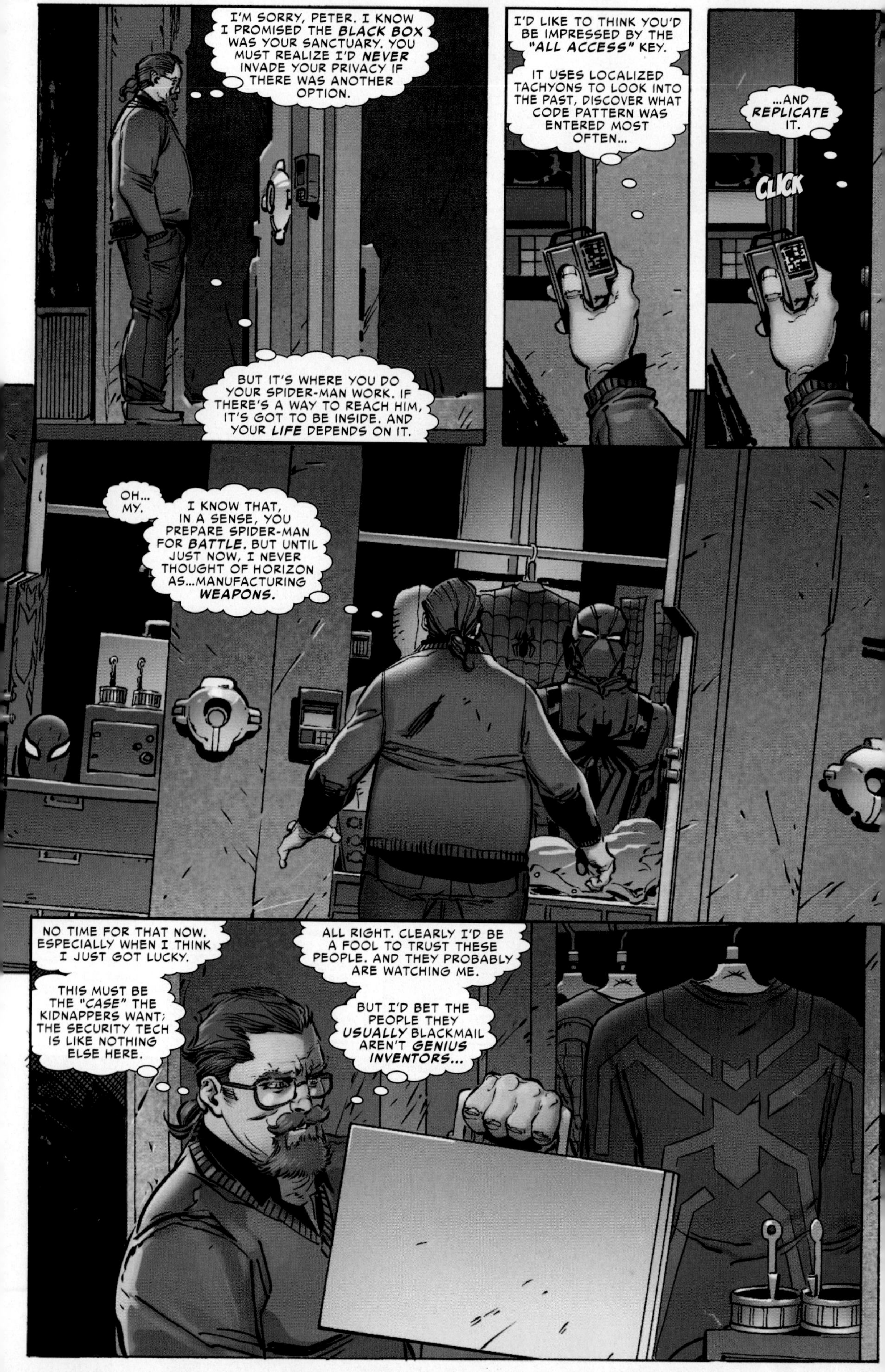
I'M SORRY, PETER. I KNOW I PROMISED THE BLACK BOX WAS YOUR SANCTUARY. YOU MUST REALIZE I'D NEVER INVADE YOUR PRIVACY IF THERE WAS ANOTHER OPTION.
BUT IT'S WHERE YOU DO YOUR SPIDER-MAN WORK. IF THERE'S A WAY TO REACH HIM, IT'S GOT TO BE INSIDE. AND YOUR LIFE DEPENDS ON IT.
I'D LIKE TO THINK YOU'D BE IMPRESSED BY THE "ALL ACCESS" KEY.
IT USES LOCALIZED TACHYONS TO LOOK INTO THE PAST, DISCOVER WHAT CODE PATTERN WAS ENTERED MOST OFTEN...
...AND REPLICATE IT.
CLICK
OH... MY.
I KNOW THAT, IN A SENSE, YOU PREPARE SPIDER-MAN FOR BATTLE. BUT UNTIL JUST NOW, I NEVER THOUGHT OF HORIZON AS...MANUFACTURING WEAPONS.
NO TIME FOR THAT NOW. ESPECIALLY WHEN I THINK I JUST GOT LUCKY.
THIS MUST BE THE "CASE" THE KIDNAPPERS WANT; THE SECURITY TECH IS LIKE NOTHING ELSE HERE.
ALL RIGHT. CLEARLY I'D BE A FOOL TO TRUST THESE PEOPLE. AND THEY PROBABLY ARE WATCHING ME.
BUT I'D BET THE PEOPLE THEY USUALLY BLACKMAIL AREN'T GENIUS INVENTORS...

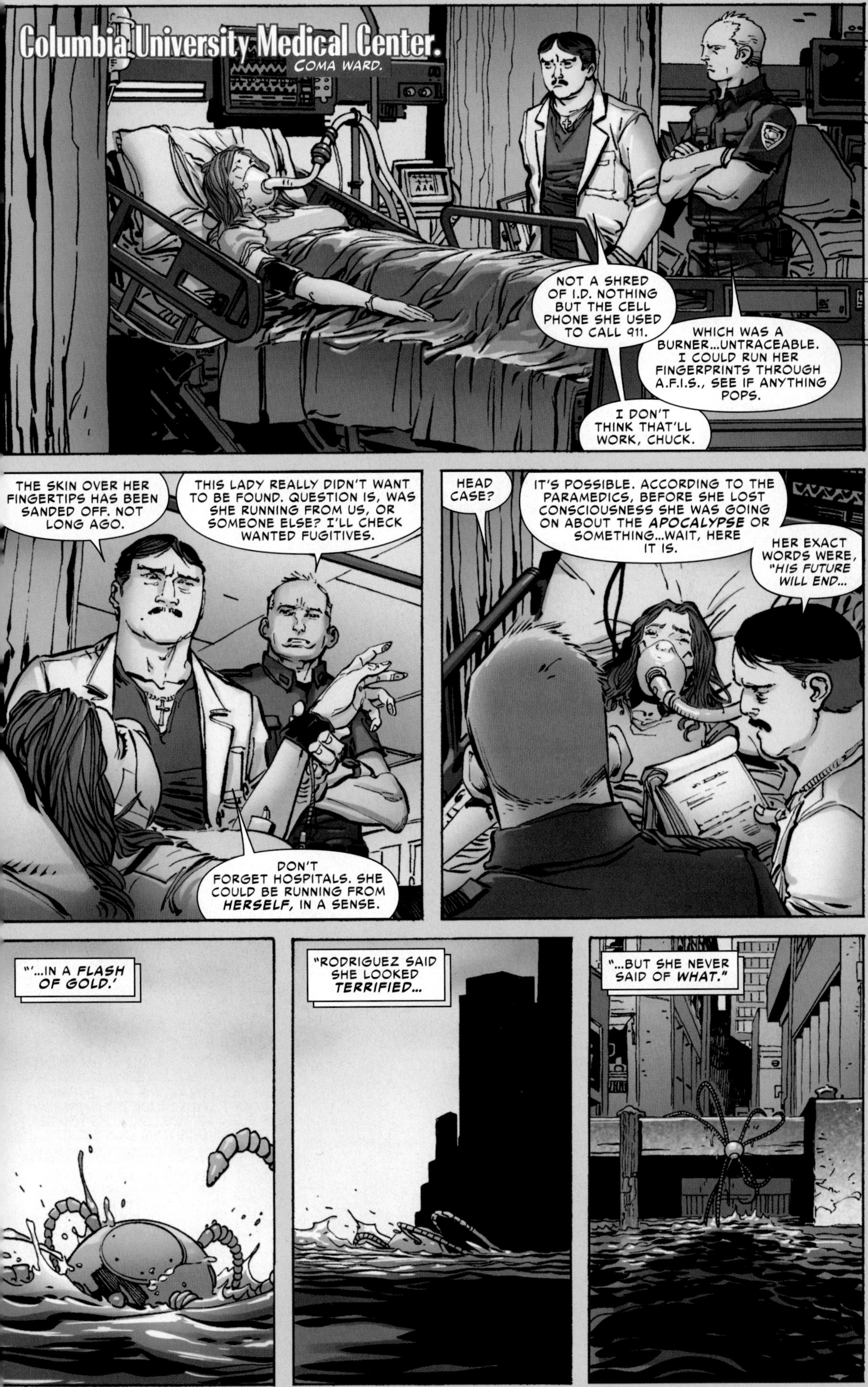
Columbia University Medical Center.
COMA WARD.
NOT A SHRED OF I.D. NOTHING BUT THE CELL PHONE SHE USED TO CALL 911.
WHICH WAS A BURNER...UNTRACEABLE. I COULD RUN HER FINGERPRINTS THROUGH A.F.I.S., SEE IF ANYTHING POPS.
I DON'T THINK THAT'LL WORK, CHUCK.
THE SKIN OVER HER FINGERTIPS HAS BEEN SANDED OFF. NOT LONG AGO.
THIS LADY REALLY DIDN'T WANT TO BE FOUND. QUESTION IS, WAS SHE RUNNING FROM US, OR SOMEONE ELSE? I'LL CHECK WANTED FUGITIVES.
DON'T FORGET HOSPITALS. SHE COULD BE RUNNING FROM HERSELF, IN A SENSE.
HEAD CASE?
IT'S POSSIBLE. ACCORDING TO THE PARAMEDICS, BEFORE SHE LOST CONSCIOUSNESS SHE WAS GOING ON ABOUT THE APOCALYPSE OR SOMETHING...WAIT, HERE IT IS.
HER EXACT WORDS WERE, "HIS FUTURE WILL END...
"'...IN A FLASH OF GOLD.'
"RODRIGUEZ SAID SHE LOOKED TERRIFIED...
"...BUT SHE NEVER SAID OF WHAT."

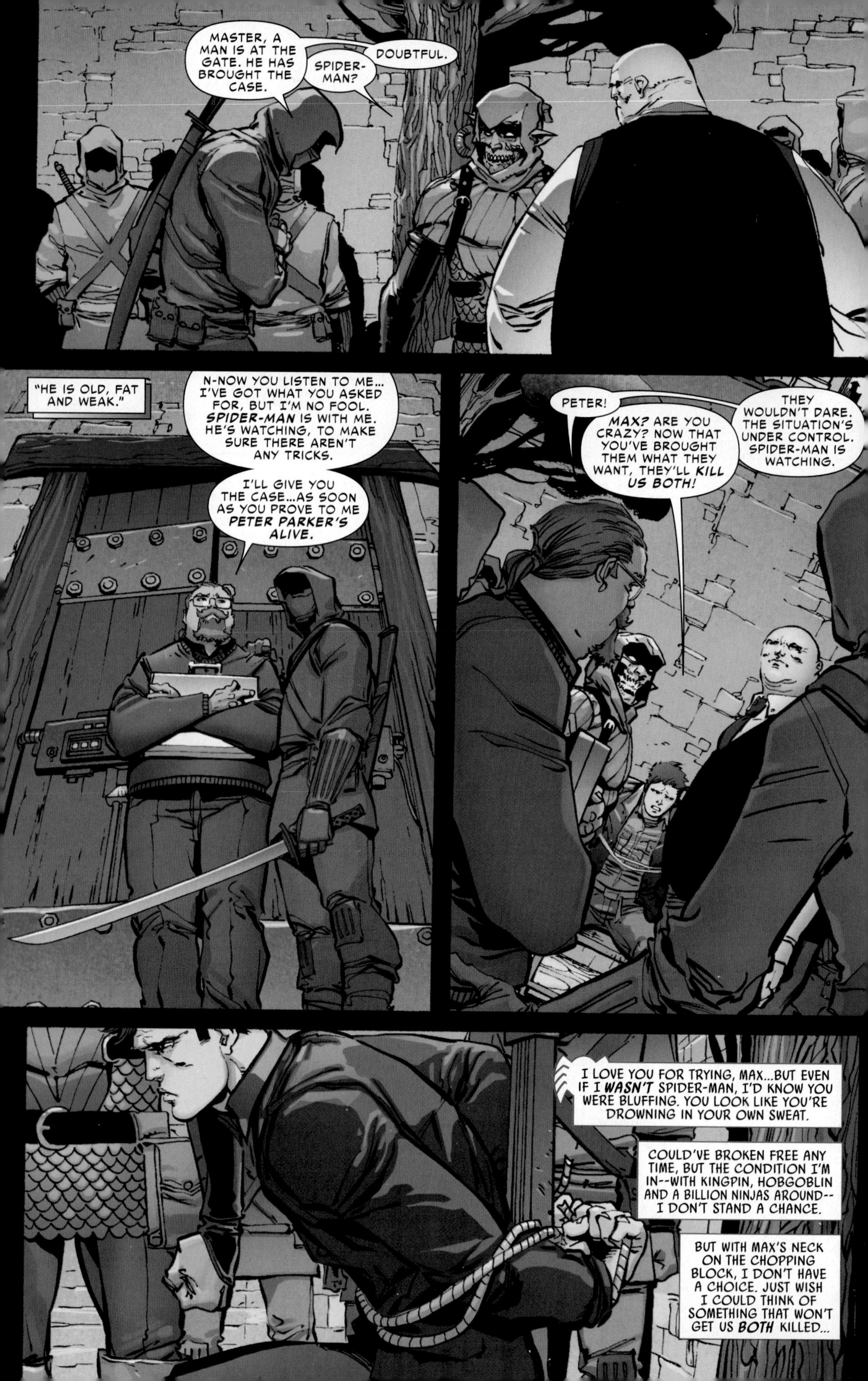
MASTER, A MAN IS AT THE GATE. HE HAS BROUGHT THE CASE.
SPIDER-MAN?
DOUBTFUL.
"HE IS OLD, FAT AND WEAK."
N-NOW YOU LISTEN TO ME... I'VE GOT WHAT YOU ASKED FOR, BUT I'M NO FOOL. SPIDER-MAN IS WITH ME. HE'S WATCHING, TO MAKE SURE THERE AREN'T ANY TRICKS.
I'LL GIVE YOU THE CASE...AS SOON AS YOU PROVE TO ME PETER PARKER'S ALIVE.
PETER!
MAX? ARE YOU CRAZY? NOW THAT YOU'VE BROUGHT THEM WHAT THEY WANT, THEY'LL KILL US BOTH!
THEY WOULDN'T DARE. THE SITUATION'S UNDER CONTROL. SPIDER-MAN IS WATCHING.
I LOVE YOU FOR TRYING, MAX...BUT EVEN IF I WASN'T SPIDER-MAN, I'D KNOW YOU WERE BLUFFING. YOU LOOK LIKE YOU'RE DROWNING IN YOUR OWN SWEAT.
COULD'VE BROKEN FREE ANY TIME, BUT THE CONDITION I'M IN--WITH KINGPIN, HOBGOBLIN AND A BILLION NINJAS AROUND--I DON'T STAND A CHANCE.
BUT WITH MAX'S NECK ON THE CHOPPING BLOCK, I DON'T HAVE A CHOICE. JUST WISH I COULD THINK OF SOMETHING THAT WON'T GET US BOTH KILLED...

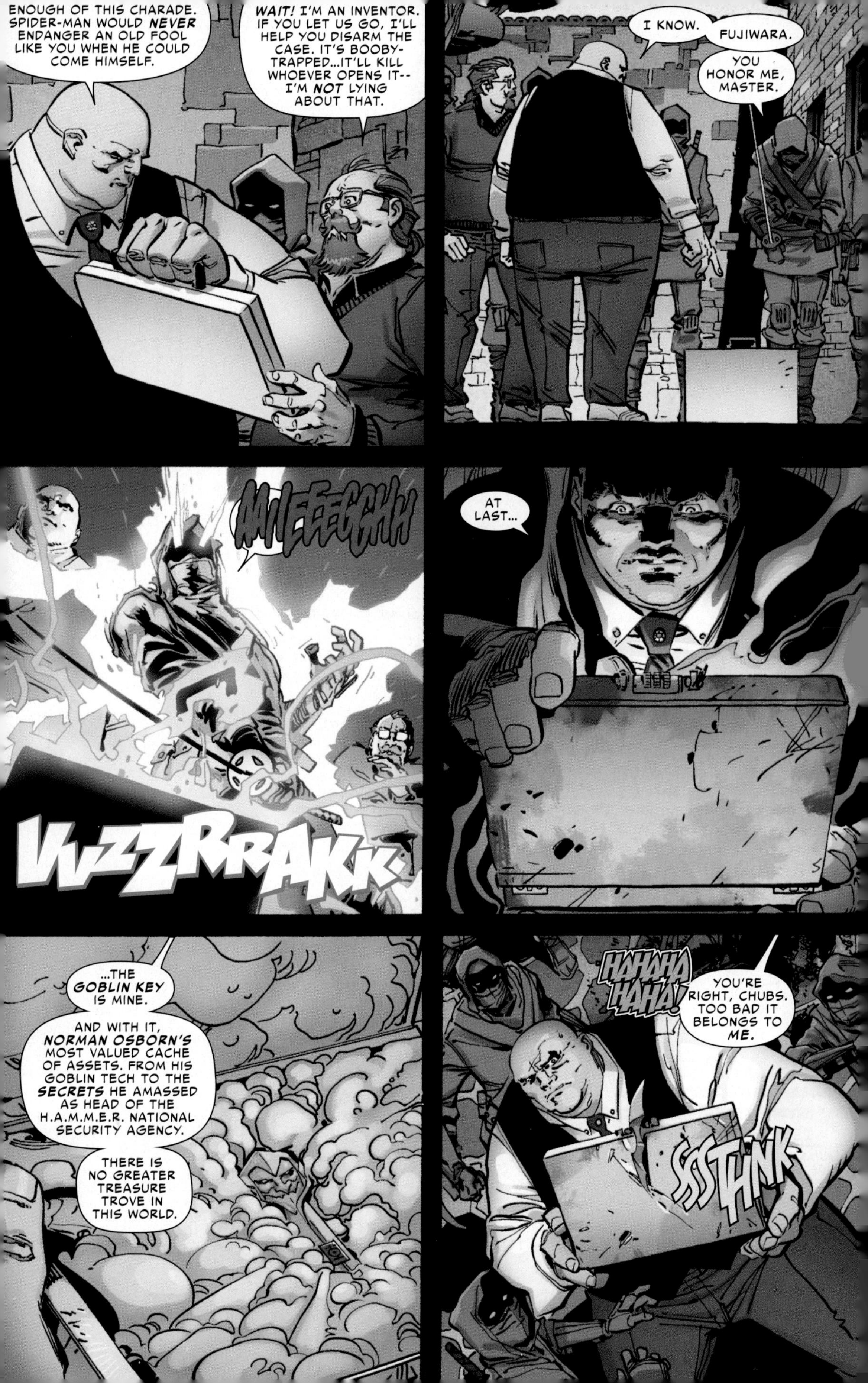
ENOUGH OF THIS CHARADE. SPIDER-MAN WOULD NEVER ENDANGER AN OLD FOOL LIKE YOU WHEN HE COULD COME HIMSELF.
WAIT! I'M AN INVENTOR. IF YOU LET US GO, I'LL HELP YOU DISARM THE CASE. IT'S BOOBY-TRAPPED...IT'LL KILL WHOEVER OPENS IT--I'M NOT LYING ABOUT THAT.
I KNOW.
FUJIWARA.
YOU HONOR ME, MASTER.
AAIIEEEGGHH
VVZZRRRAKK
AT LAST...
...THE GOBLIN KEY IS MINE.
AND WITH IT, NORMAN OSBORN'S MOST VALUED CACHE OF ASSETS. FROM HIS GOBLIN TECH TO THE SECRETS HE AMASSED AS HEAD OF THE H.A.M.M.E.R. NATIONAL SECURITY AGENCY.
THERE IS NO GREATER TREASURE TROVE IN THIS WORLD.
HAHAHA HAHA!
YOU'RE RIGHT, CHUBS. TOO BAD IT BELONGS TO ME.
SSSTHNK

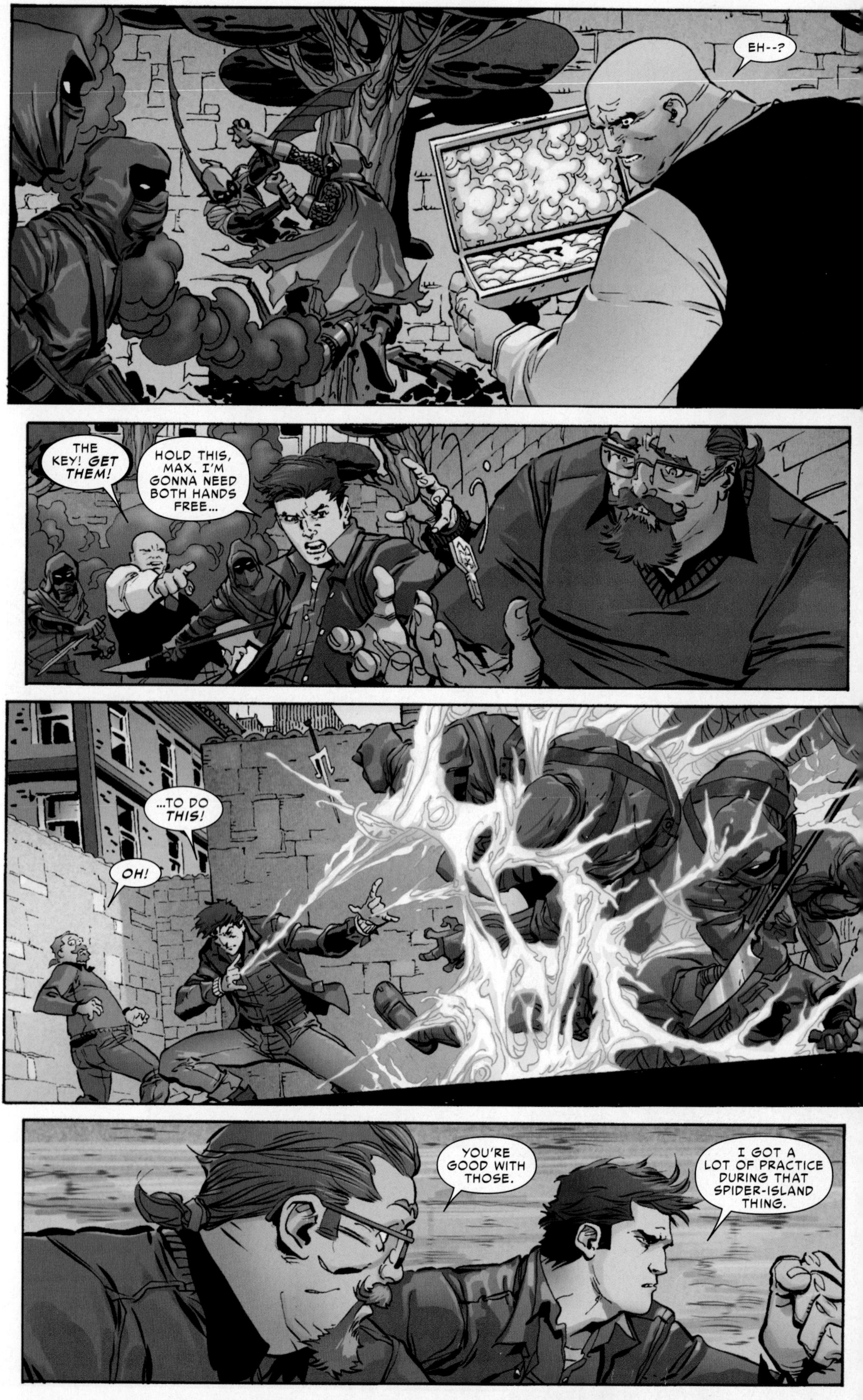
EH--?
THE KEY! GET THEM!
HOLD THIS, MAX. I'M GONNA NEED BOTH HANDS FREE...
...TO DO THIS!
OH!
YOU'RE GOOD WITH THOSE.
I GOT A LOT OF PRACTICE DURING THAT SPIDER-ISLAND THING.

LOCKED. MAYBE I CAN--

LET ME. I HAVE JUST THE THING.

SPIDER-ISLAND... YES. IF I HADN'T SEEN YOU *AND* SPIDER-MAN TOGETHER THEN, I'D ALMOST--

HAAAH--!

--MMFF!

THWIP

THWIP

ALMOST WHAT?

NOTHING. LET'S GO!

NEXT: GET THAT NERD!

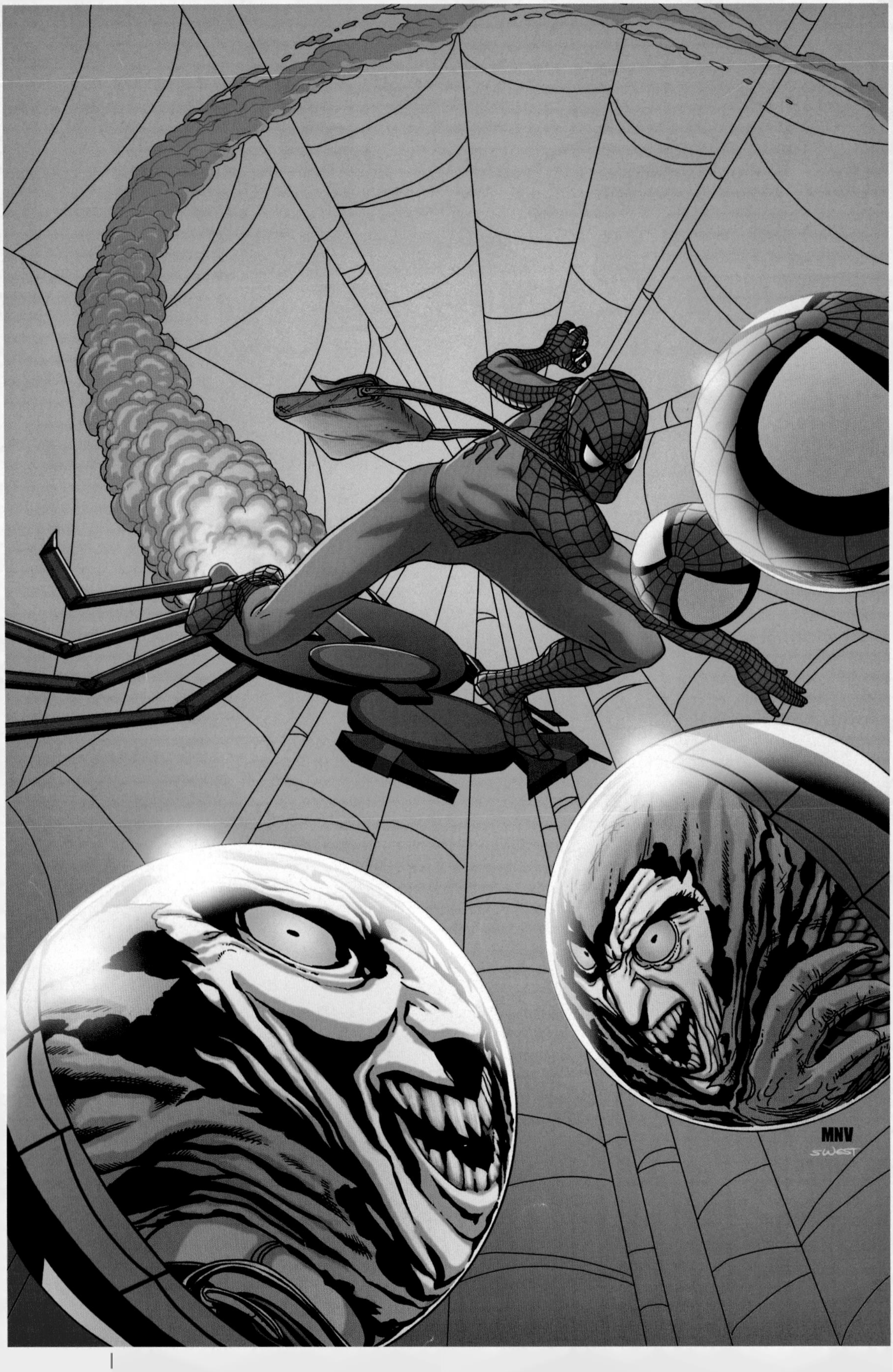
MNV
SWEST

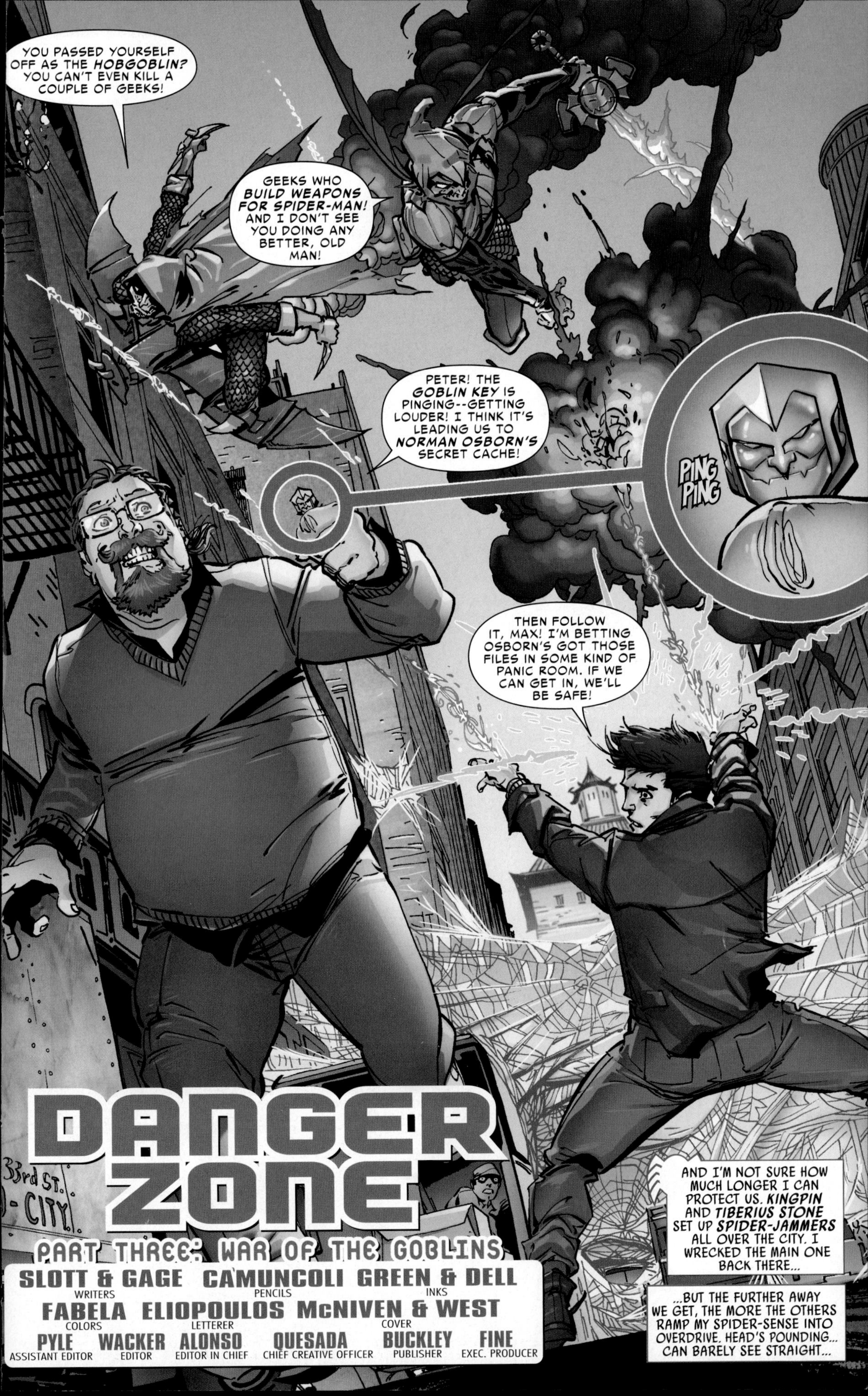
YOU PASSED YOURSELF OFF AS THE HOBGOBLIN? YOU CAN'T EVEN KILL A COUPLE OF GEEKS!
GEEKS WHO BUILD WEAPONS FOR SPIDER-MAN! AND I DON'T SEE YOU DOING ANY BETTER, OLD MAN!
PETER! THE GOBLIN KEY IS PINGING--GETTING LOUDER! I THINK IT'S LEADING US TO NORMAN OSBORN'S SECRET CACHE!
PING PING
THEN FOLLOW IT, MAX! I'M BETTING OSBORN'S GOT THOSE FILES IN SOME KIND OF PANIC ROOM. IF WE CAN GET IN, WE'LL BE SAFE!
33rd ST.
-CITY
DANGER ZONE
PART THREE: WAR OF THE GOBLINS
SLOTT & GAGE WRITERS
CAMUNCOLI PENCILS
GREEN & DELL INKS
FABELA COLORS
ELIOPOULOS LETTERER
McNIVEN & WEST COVER
PYLE ASSISTANT EDITOR
WACKER EDITOR
ALONSO EDITOR IN CHIEF
QUESADA CHIEF CREATIVE OFFICER
BUCKLEY PUBLISHER
FINE EXEC. PRODUCER
AND I'M NOT SURE HOW MUCH LONGER I CAN PROTECT US. KINGPIN AND TIBERIUS STONE SET UP SPIDER-JAMMERS ALL OVER THE CITY. I WRECKED THE MAIN ONE BACK THERE...
...BUT THE FURTHER AWAY WE GET, THE MORE THE OTHERS RAMP MY SPIDER-SENSE INTO OVERDRIVE. HEAD'S POUNDING... CAN BARELY SEE STRAIGHT...

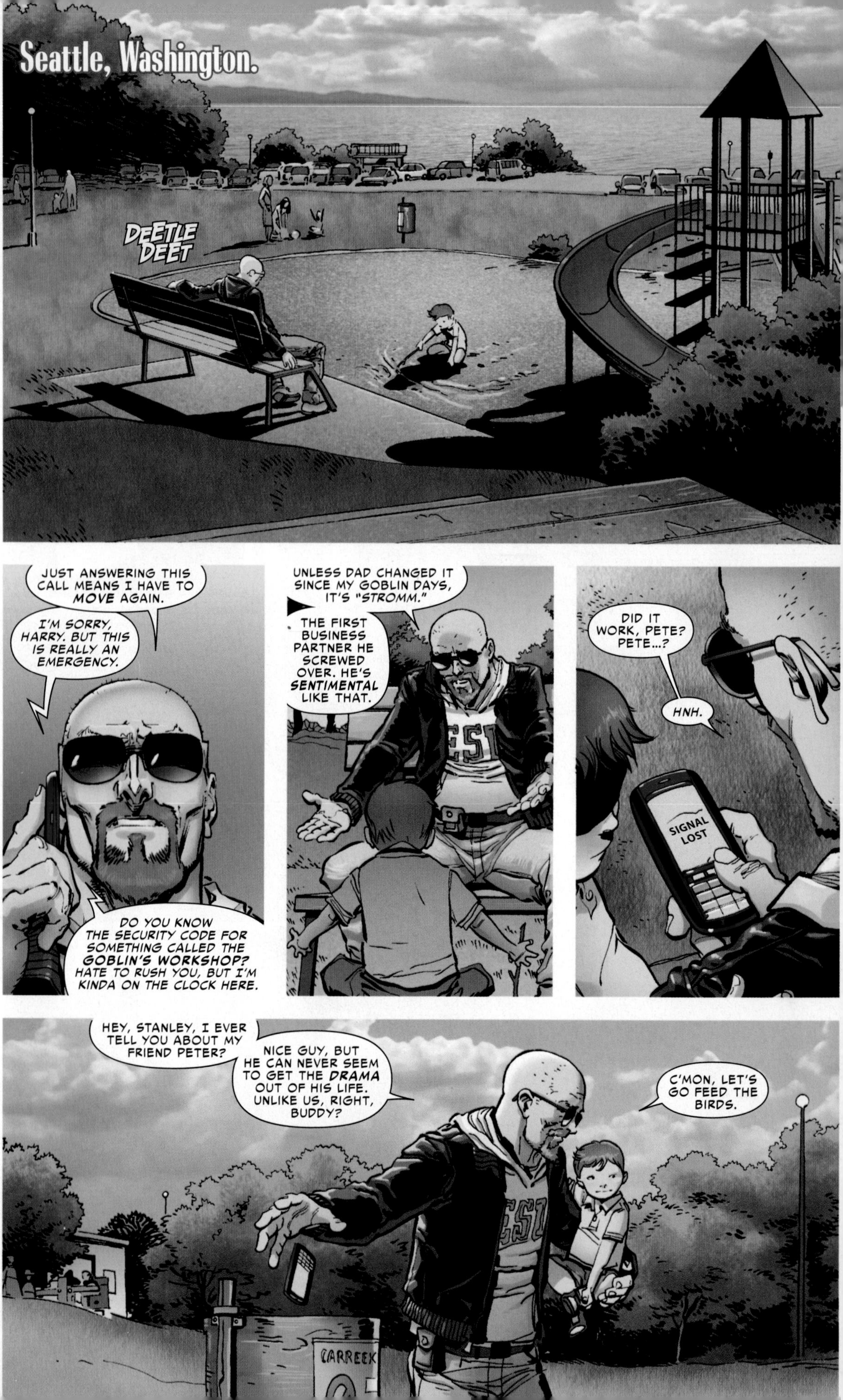
Seattle, Washington.
DEETLE DEET
JUST ANSWERING THIS CALL MEANS I HAVE TO MOVE AGAIN.
I'M SORRY, HARRY. BUT THIS IS REALLY AN EMERGENCY.
DO YOU KNOW THE SECURITY CODE FOR SOMETHING CALLED THE GOBLIN'S WORKSHOP? HATE TO RUSH YOU, BUT I'M KINDA ON THE CLOCK HERE.
UNLESS DAD CHANGED IT SINCE MY GOBLIN DAYS, IT'S "STROMM."
THE FIRST BUSINESS PARTNER HE SCREWED OVER. HE'S SENTIMENTAL LIKE THAT.
ESU
DID IT WORK, PETE? PETE...?
HNH.
SIGNAL LOST
HEY, STANLEY, I EVER TELL YOU ABOUT MY FRIEND PETER?
NICE GUY, BUT HE CAN NEVER SEEM TO GET THE DRAMA OUT OF HIS LIFE. UNLIKE US, RIGHT, BUDDY?
C'MON, LET'S GO FEED THE BIRDS.
ESU
CARREEK

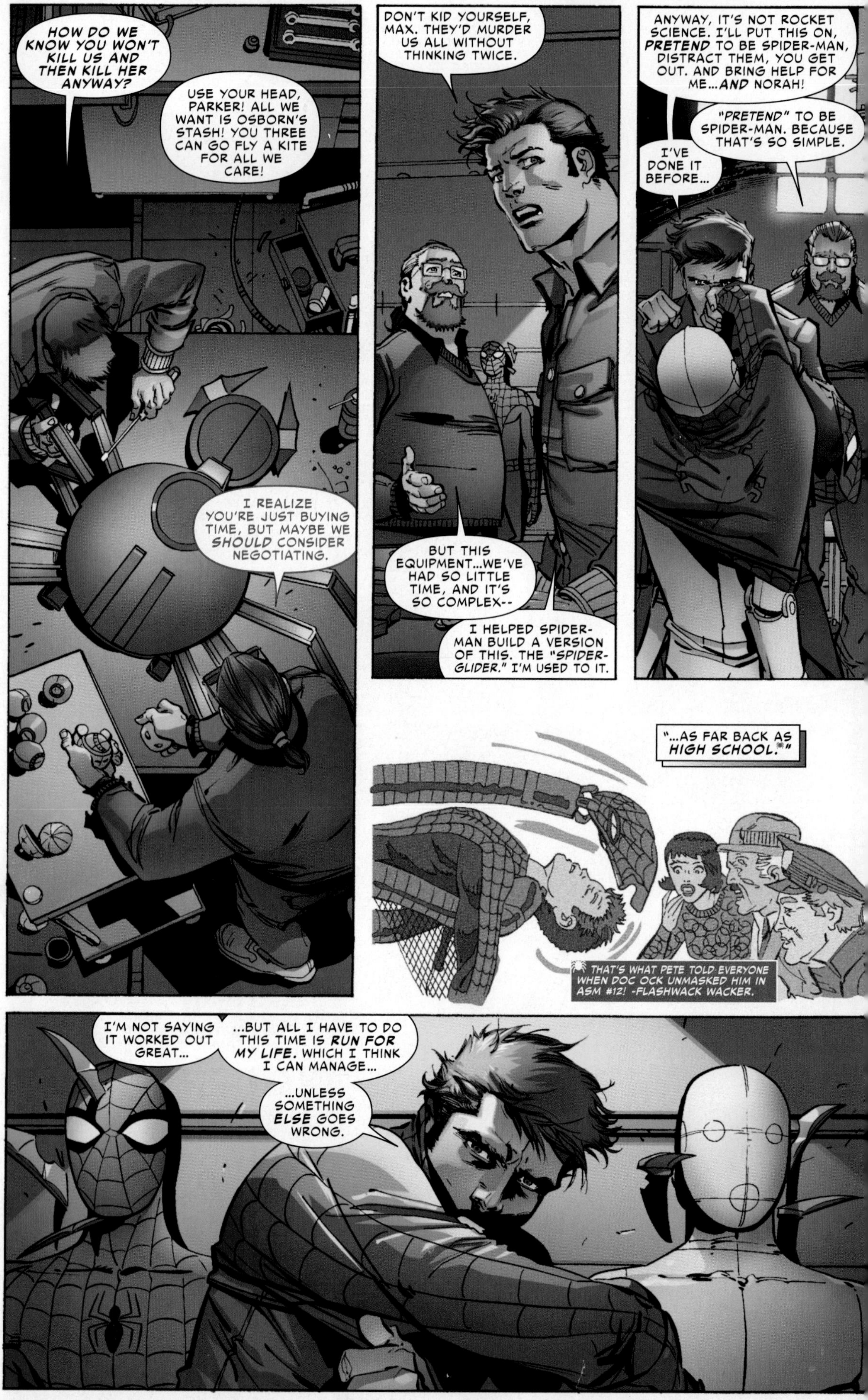
HOW DO WE KNOW YOU WON'T KILL US AND THEN KILL HER ANYWAY?
USE YOUR HEAD, PARKER! ALL WE WANT IS OSBORN'S STASH! YOU THREE CAN GO FLY A KITE FOR ALL WE CARE!
I REALIZE YOU'RE JUST BUYING TIME, BUT MAYBE WE SHOULD CONSIDER NEGOTIATING.
DON'T KID YOURSELF, MAX. THEY'D MURDER US ALL WITHOUT THINKING TWICE.
BUT THIS EQUIPMENT...WE'VE HAD SO LITTLE TIME, AND IT'S SO COMPLEX--
I HELPED SPIDER-MAN BUILD A VERSION OF THIS. THE "SPIDER-GLIDER." I'M USED TO IT.
ANYWAY, IT'S NOT ROCKET SCIENCE. I'LL PUT THIS ON, PRETEND TO BE SPIDER-MAN, DISTRACT THEM, YOU GET OUT. AND BRING HELP FOR ME...AND NORAH!
"PRETEND" TO BE SPIDER-MAN. BECAUSE THAT'S SO SIMPLE.
I'VE DONE IT BEFORE...
"...AS FAR BACK AS HIGH SCHOOL.*"
*THAT'S WHAT PETE TOLD EVERYONE WHEN DOC OCK UNMASKED HIM IN ASM #12! -FLASHWACK WACKER.
I'M NOT SAYING IT WORKED OUT GREAT...
...BUT ALL I HAVE TO DO THIS TIME IS RUN FOR MY LIFE. WHICH I THINK I CAN MANAGE...
...UNLESS SOMETHING ELSE GOES WRONG.

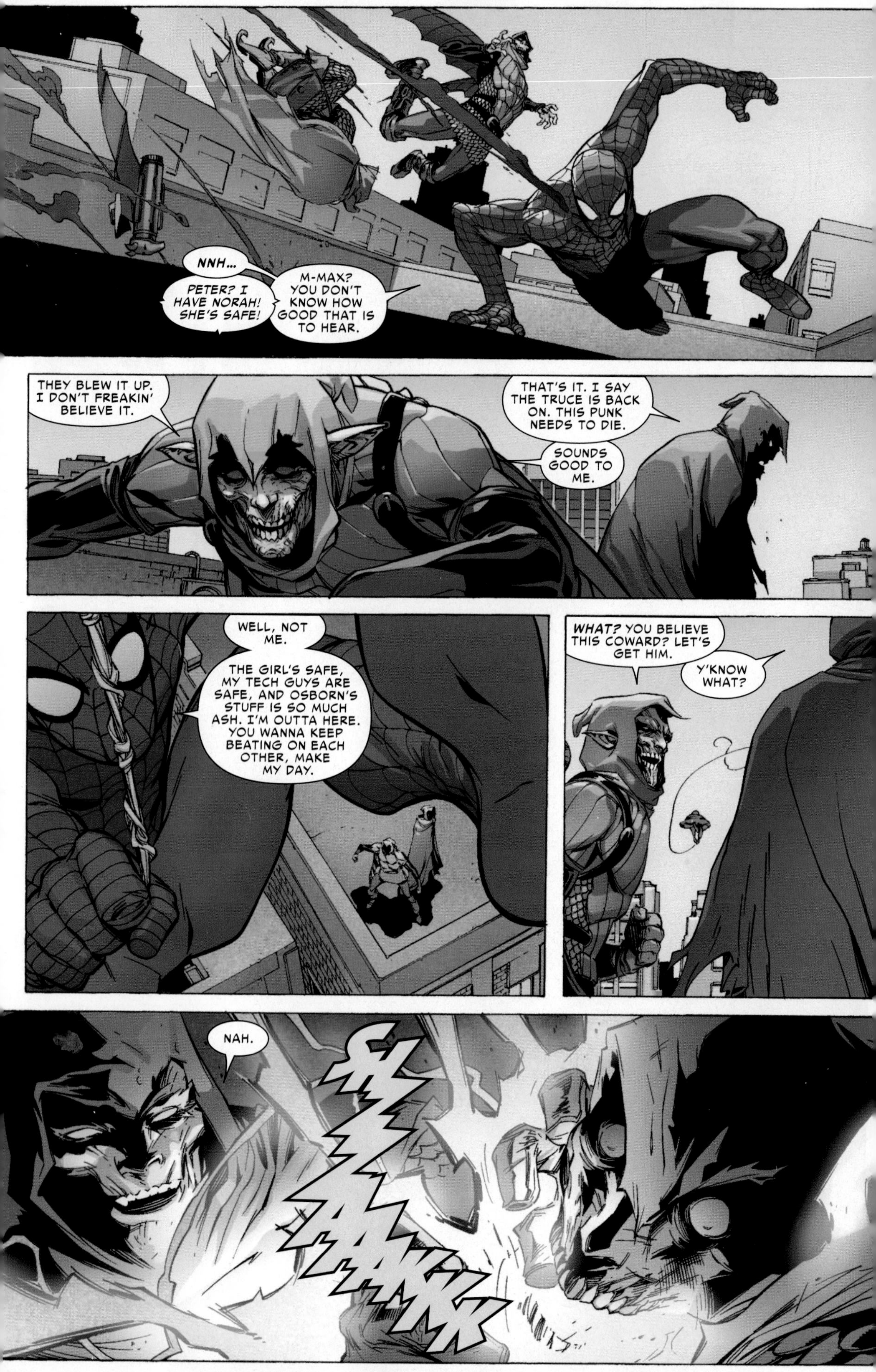
NNH...
PETER? I HAVE NORAH! SHE'S SAFE!
M-MAX? YOU DON'T KNOW HOW GOOD THAT IS TO HEAR.
THEY BLEW IT UP. I DON'T FREAKIN' BELIEVE IT.
THAT'S IT. I SAY THE TRUCE IS BACK ON. THIS PUNK NEEDS TO DIE.
SOUNDS GOOD TO ME.
WELL, NOT ME.
THE GIRL'S SAFE, MY TECH GUYS ARE SAFE, AND OSBORN'S STUFF IS SO MUCH ASH. I'M OUTTA HERE. YOU WANNA KEEP BEATING ON EACH OTHER, MAKE MY DAY.
WHAT? YOU BELIEVE THIS COWARD? LET'S GET HIM.
Y'KNOW WHAT?
NAH.
SHHRAKK

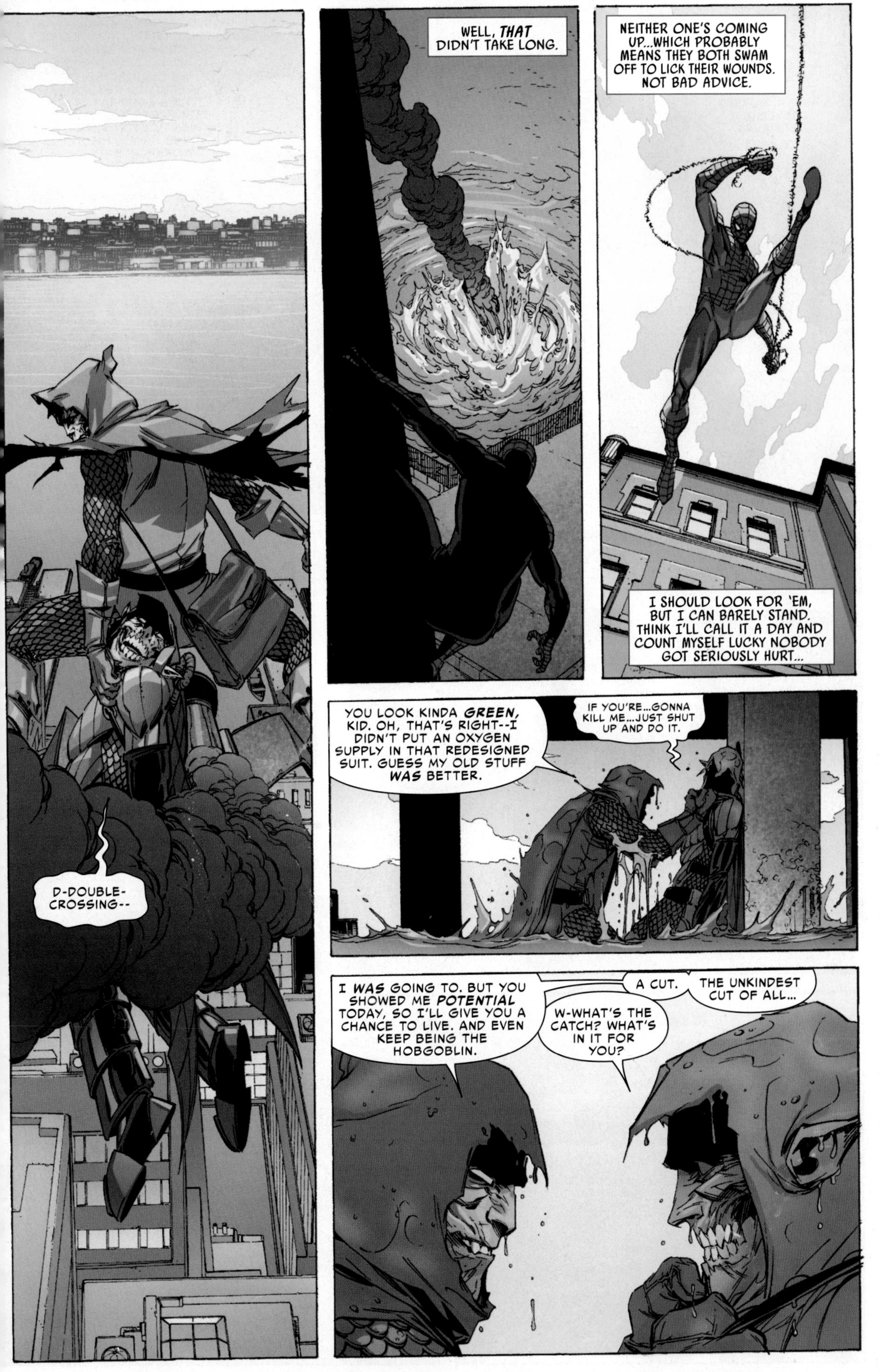
D-DOUBLE-CROSSING--
WELL, THAT DIDN'T TAKE LONG.
NEITHER ONE'S COMING UP...WHICH PROBABLY MEANS THEY BOTH SWAM OFF TO LICK THEIR WOUNDS. NOT BAD ADVICE.
I SHOULD LOOK FOR 'EM, BUT I CAN BARELY STAND. THINK I'LL CALL IT A DAY AND COUNT MYSELF LUCKY NOBODY GOT SERIOUSLY HURT...
YOU LOOK KINDA GREEN, KID. OH, THAT'S RIGHT--I DIDN'T PUT AN OXYGEN SUPPLY IN THAT REDESIGNED SUIT. GUESS MY OLD STUFF WAS BETTER.
IF YOU'RE...GONNA KILL ME...JUST SHUT UP AND DO IT.
I WAS GOING TO. BUT YOU SHOWED ME POTENTIAL TODAY, SO I'LL GIVE YOU A CHANCE TO LIVE. AND EVEN KEEP BEING THE HOBGOBLIN.
W-WHAT'S THE CATCH? WHAT'S IN IT FOR YOU?
A CUT.
THE UNKINDEST CUT OF ALL...

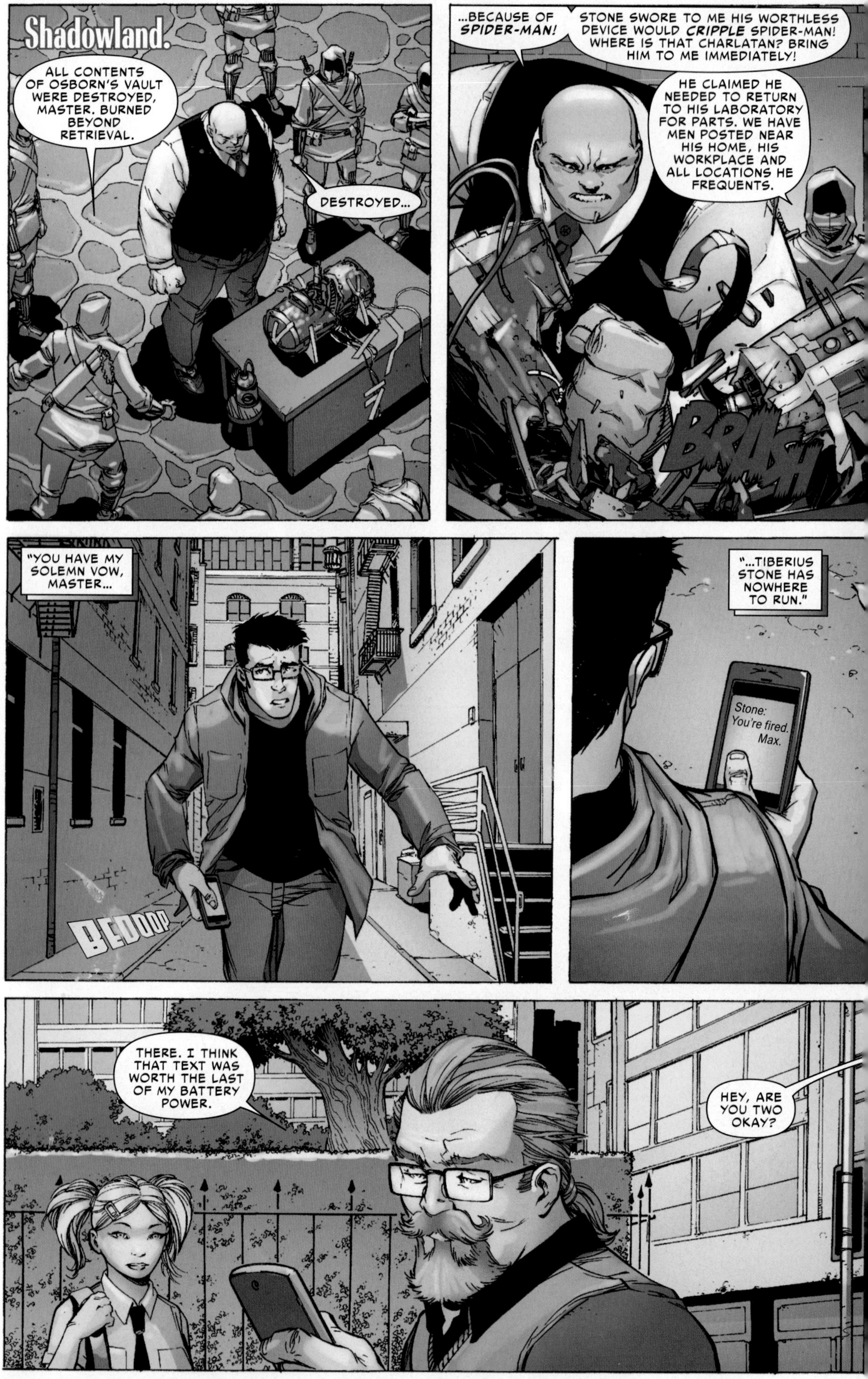
Shadowland.
ALL CONTENTS OF OSBORN'S VAULT WERE DESTROYED, MASTER. BURNED BEYOND RETRIEVAL.
DESTROYED...
...BECAUSE OF SPIDER-MAN!
STONE SWORE TO ME HIS WORTHLESS DEVICE WOULD CRIPPLE SPIDER-MAN! WHERE IS THAT CHARLATAN? BRING HIM TO ME IMMEDIATELY!
HE CLAIMED HE NEEDED TO RETURN TO HIS LABORATORY FOR PARTS. WE HAVE MEN POSTED NEAR HIS HOME, HIS WORKPLACE AND ALL LOCATIONS HE FREQUENTS.
BRUSH
"YOU HAVE MY SOLEMN VOW, MASTER...
BEDOOP
"...TIBERIUS STONE HAS NOWHERE TO RUN."
Stone: You're fired. Max.
THERE. I THINK THAT TEXT WAS WORTH THE LAST OF MY BATTERY POWER.
HEY, ARE YOU TWO OKAY?

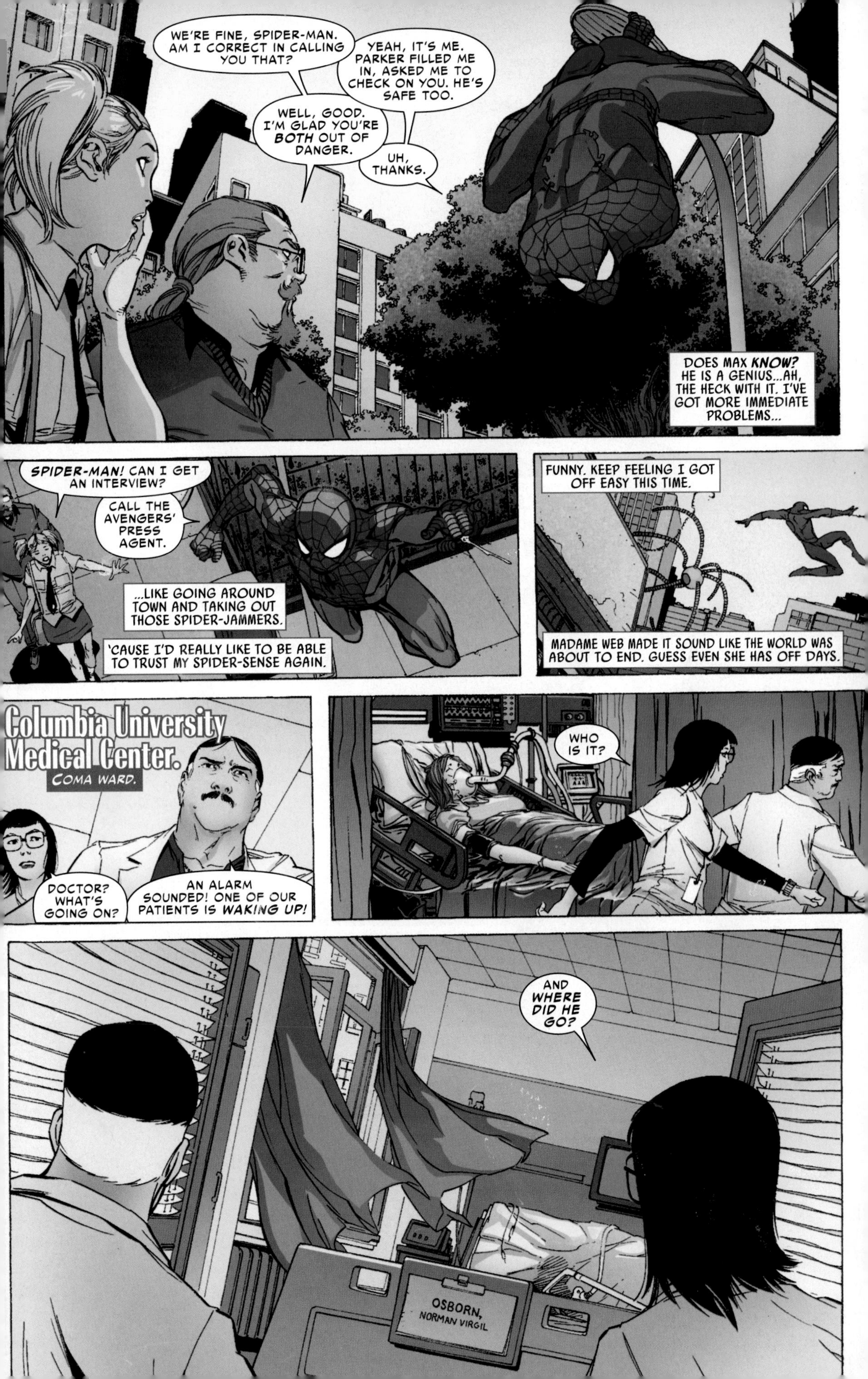

WE'RE FINE, SPIDER-MAN. AM I CORRECT IN CALLING YOU THAT?
YEAH, IT'S ME. PARKER FILLED ME IN, ASKED ME TO CHECK ON YOU. HE'S SAFE TOO.
WELL, GOOD. I'M GLAD YOU'RE BOTH OUT OF DANGER.
UH, THANKS.
DOES MAX KNOW? HE IS A GENIUS...AH, THE HECK WITH IT. I'VE GOT MORE IMMEDIATE PROBLEMS...
SPIDER-MAN! CAN I GET AN INTERVIEW?
CALL THE AVENGERS' PRESS AGENT.
...LIKE GOING AROUND TOWN AND TAKING OUT THOSE SPIDER-JAMMERS.
'CAUSE I'D REALLY LIKE TO BE ABLE TO TRUST MY SPIDER-SENSE AGAIN.
FUNNY. KEEP FEELING I GOT OFF EASY THIS TIME.
MADAME WEB MADE IT SOUND LIKE THE WORLD WAS ABOUT TO END. GUESS EVEN SHE HAS OFF DAYS.
Columbia University Medical Center.
COMA WARD.
DOCTOR? WHAT'S GOING ON?
AN ALARM SOUNDED! ONE OF OUR PATIENTS IS WAKING UP!
WHO IS IT?
AND WHERE DID HE GO?
OSBORN, NORMAN VIRGIL

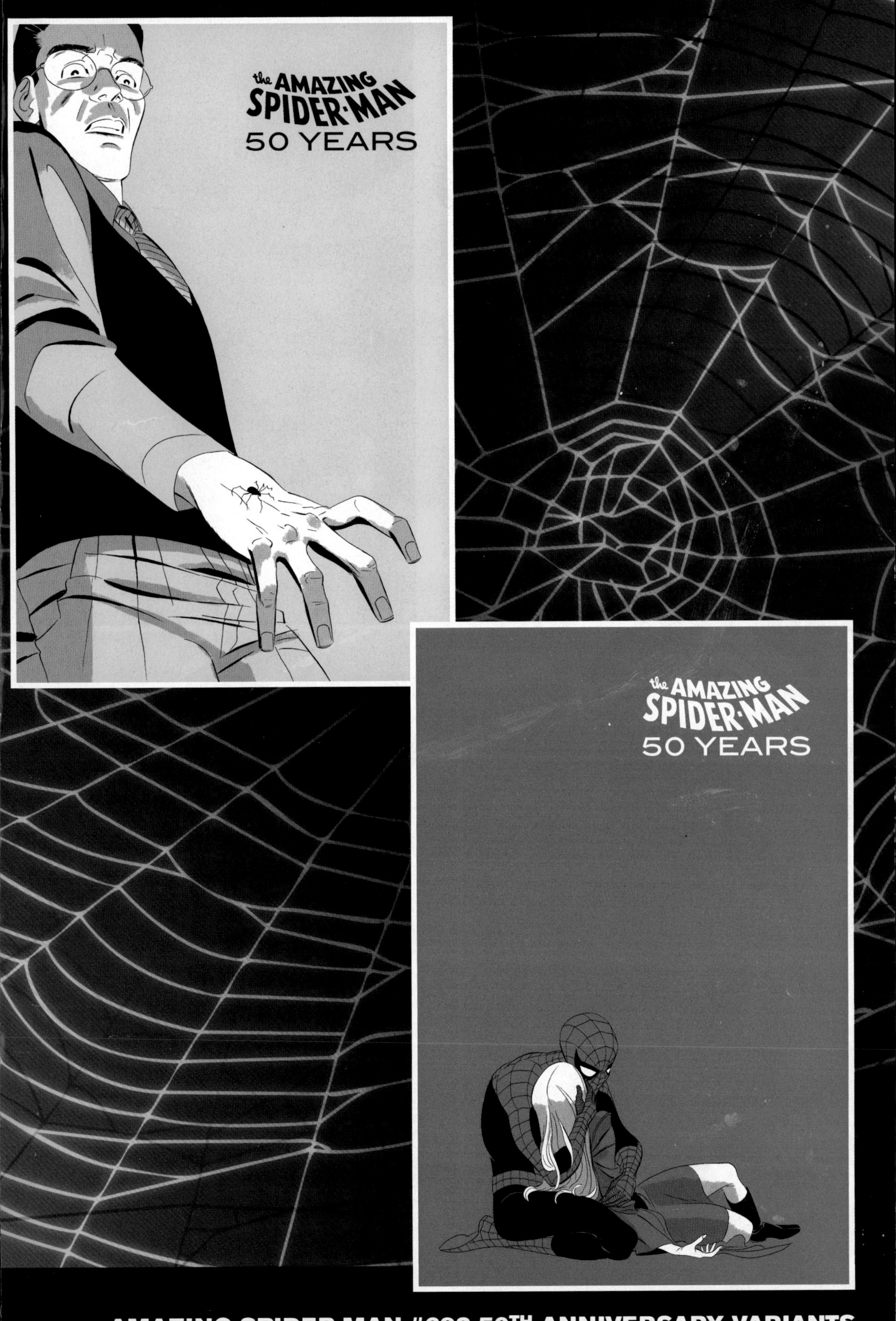
the AMAZING SPIDER-MAN
50 YEARS
the AMAZING SPIDER-MAN
50 YEARS

AMAZING SPIDER-MAN #692 50TH ANNIVERSARY VARIANTS
COVERS BY MARCOS MARTIN

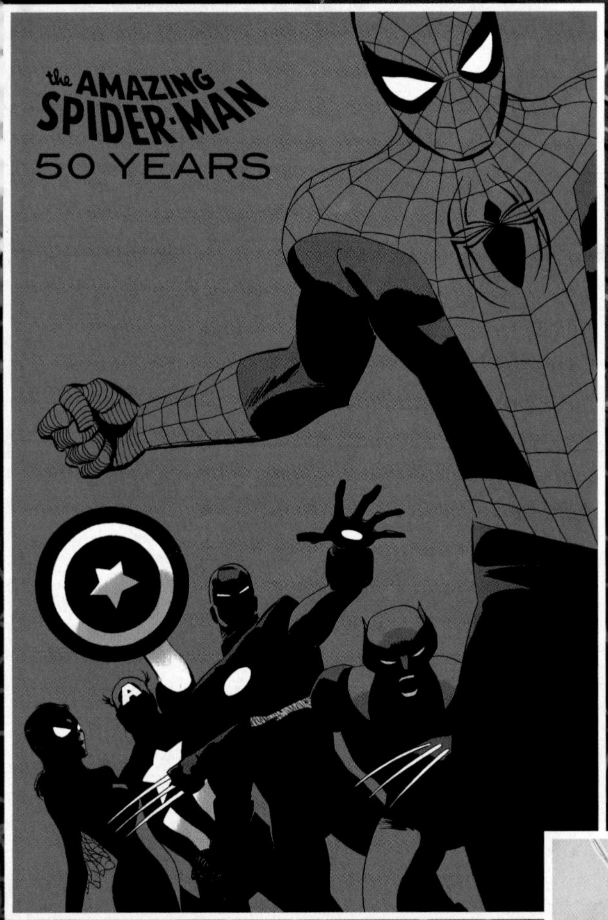
the AMAZING
SPIDER-MAN
50 YEARS

AMAZING SPIDER-MAN #692
50TH ANNIVERSARY VARIANT
COVER BY MARCOS MARTIN

AMAZING SPIDER-MAN #692
FAN EXPO VARIANT
COVER BY J. SCOTT CAMPBELL
& EDGAR DELGADO

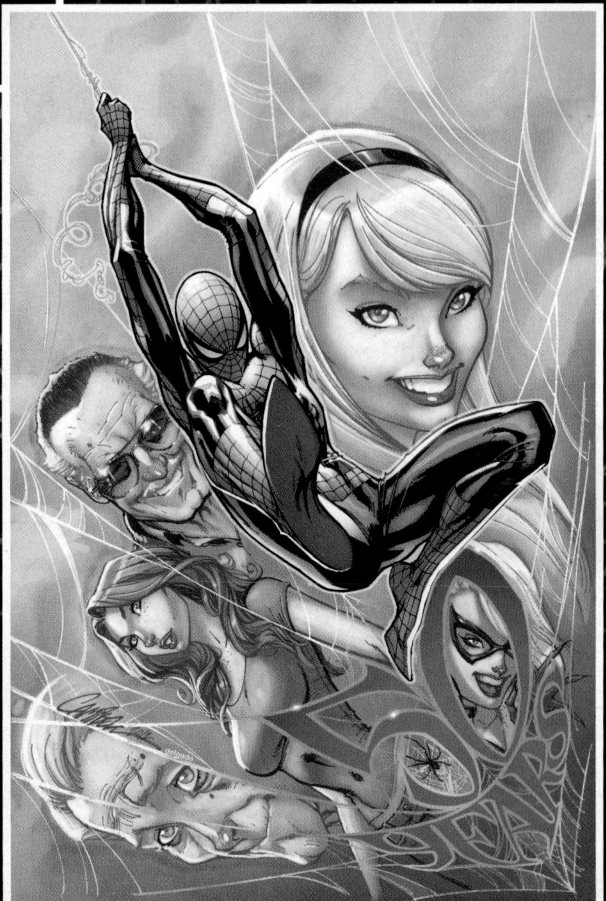

AMAZING SPIDER-MAN #692 LETTER COLUMN

Fifty years ago...John F. Kennedy was President.
Fifty years ago...The Beatles still hadn't released their first hit song.
Fifty years ago...the NY Mets were in the middle of their very first (and very terrible) baseball season.
Fifty years ago...the "quasar" was first identified by John Bolton.
Fifty years ago...the actress Marilyn Monroe died.
Fifty years ago...NASA launched the Mariner 2 probe to explore Venus.
Fifty years ago...the Cuban Missile Crisis terrified the world.

Fifty years ago...the World's Greatest Super Hero was unleashed in the pages of Amazing Fantasy #15.*

*Comic historians will point out that AF #15 was actually "cover-dated" August, so the issue actually went on sale in June most likely, but we've chosen August as the date that most long-time fans recognize as the Anniversary. Besides we had a big Lizard story to get to in June and who has time to be pedantic when the Lizard is chasing after you?!

Although this is the 692nd issue of "Amazing Spider-Man," when you count all the issues of Spidey's various ongoing series (and exclude one-shots, mini-series, stories outside regular Marvel continuity, and odd numbered issues like #0 issues and POINT ONEs), this is — at least by super-intern Devin Lewis' count — the 1,757th comic Marvel has published featuring the ongoing drama of Peter Parker. That's a lot of thwips!

With 1,757 swings at the plate, there've been plenty of great Spidey issues (and, sure, even some lousy ones), but what's been consistent in every issue is the level of talent, heart and dedication that the men and women on this book have brought with them. We started this whole shebang with Stan, Steve, Artie and Jazzy John, but it's continued thanks to many others.

Through the years, the character has been guided by some of the greatest talent in the history of the comic medium. For this Fiftieth Anniversary, I want to just take a moment to say a massive "Thank You" to the giants whose shoulders we stand on (well I do more of a half-sitting/half-kneeling thing) each and every issue.

Truth is, though, there are lots of comics who have had great creative teams guiding the destinies of our favorite heroes. What's made the difference in Spidey's case is, without a doubt, the fans.

From comics to television to novels to newspaper strips to toys to movies to Broadway, Spidey's fans are sensational, spectacular, and downright amazing group.

From kids to adults worldwide, no character in history has ever reached a wider, more diverse audience. You want to waste a day? Try to find someone anywhere who has never at least heard of Spider-Man. They're a rare breed.

So to commemorate the passion of Spidey readers around the world who have supported the wall-crawler for five decades, I've turned to two of the proudest and loudest Spidey fanatics around to share their love and passion. Take it away, boys!

It was 1975, I was an 8-year-old kid riding his bike past the local 7-11, and I saw the sign that would change my life forever:
Spider-Man was coming to town.
That Saturday.
To sign comic books.

I loved Spidey. I raced home every day after school to watch reruns of the old '67 cartoons. And I knew what comics were, because my cousin collected them. But I never owned any. And now I HAD to have one, because I HAD to meet Spider-Man.

That night, the second my dad came home from his long commute, I was all over him. Pleading for a quarter so I could buy a Spider-Man comic. Dad asked if I was old enough to start doing chores around the house. Because if I was, I was old enough to get an allowance. A quarter a week. But he started me out with two — so I could have TWO comics for Spider-Man to sign.

I went back to the store extra early and pored over the spinner rack, looking for the two PERFECT Spider-Man comics. Those were MARVEL TALES #63 and MARVEL TEAM-UP #38. And then I camped out on the stoop, because I wanted to see Spider-Man swing in. I kid you not. I sat on the curb and kept looking up. Over time I got worried, because it was suburban California — there were NO tall buildings — so there was nothing for Spidey to stick a web to. I didn't know HOW he was going to get there.

And then it happened. The moment that sealed my fate and made me a Spidey fan for life. If you can imagine a couple of guys in the 70's who had access to a Spider-Man costume than this will make perfect sense. You could see the freeway and the off ramp from the 7-11, and there was a red pickup racing along, with Spider-Man — standing arms akimbo — in the bed of the truck. People who were stuck in traffic were cheering him on. It was surreal.

And the pickup drove down the exit, rolled into the parking lot, and — for my benefit alone — that crazy 70's guy in his Spider-Man suit, leapt out the back of the truck, landed in a spidery crouch, straightened himself up, and walked into that 7-11 like it was something he did ALL the time.

And I bought it. I believed. And he was great. He stayed in character, signed my books, and that was it for me. Spidey. Fan. For life.

It's 37 years later, and since then I've given tours of the Marvel Offices WITH Spidey (he says "Hi" by the way), written video game dialogue for Stan Lee and four of TV's animated Spider-Men, worked with the talented writers, artists, and editors of the Brand New Day team — and now the Big Time team. And look, we're here, on the 50th Anniversary issue... and it's all 'cause of you guys.

We get the honor and the privilege to be at this very special moment in Spidey history — and Humberto, Victor, Edgar, Chris, Ellie, and Steve, we all want you to know that we're very grateful for your patronage and your support. Thank you for letting us have these dream jobs.

See you in another 50! Thwip thwip!

Dan Slott
High above New York City

Dear ASM crew,

Wow! Fifty years of Spider-Man.

Though I've only been a serious reader of Spidey and comics in general for about a decade, without a doubt Spider-Man was the character that first drew me into the world of super heroes and brought me back after a brief hiatus from reading comics.

Like a lot of people my age, my earliest memories of the web-slinger probably came from the 90's cartoon. Maybe some things like the animation limits don't hold up that well, but for my money it's still a quintessential Spidey adaptation with some of the best storytelling and characterizations. (Some perfect casting as well like Ed Asner as J. Jonah Jameson who is right up there with JK Simmons in my opinion.) Plus it was pretty much the gateway drug that introduced me to the rest of the crazy world of Marvel like Doctor Strange, Blade, and Daredevil.

Over the years, my interest in Spidey started to wane until the release of the Sam Raimi Spider-Man film in 2002. Suddenly my childhood love of the character came flooding back and a renewed interest in comics. I immediately got a Marvel subscription to the Amazing Spider-Man title starting with issue #482 of the JMS/John Romita Jr. run and I have not stopped reading and collecting since.

It's hard to pinpoint precisely what the draw to Spider-Man is out of all the supe heroes, but I think one of the reasons is, like Peter, we all at some point in our lives can't help but feel like a small bug in a big world...especially those of us who have ever been a bit of a social misfit or outsider. Spidey has come a long way since his early days as that the shy introverted kid in Amazing Fantasy #15 and has really come into his own as both a person and a hero in the Marvel Universe.

The costume itself is also probably one of the most iconic outfits in comics that allows practically anyone to project themselves onto Spidey. As great as that original Stan Lee and Steve Ditko costume is, readers can't help but enjoy when a new variant or look does pop for however length of time. I've made it no secret that I have a strong love of the Bombastic Bag-Man costume, going so far as to dress up as Bag-Man for Halloween. But whatever the look may be, the hero inside will always remain true.

There's never been a better time to be a Spidey fan thanks hugely to what all of you guys at "Spidey Sentral" have accomplished in the last few years starting with Brand New Day and the work of the various Web-heads to Dan Slott's solo run as writer with "Big Time." It's all been a seamless and natural progression of everything that's come before.

Villains in particular, both new and old, have really stepped up and offer serious challenges to Spidey. The best villains are usually ones that are dark reflections of the hero and the "Great Power/Responsibility" adage, which is why Phil Urich has quickly become my favorite person to take on the Hobgoblin mantle. Same thing with Flash Thompson as the new Venom. It's funny because when Mac Gargan/Scorpion got the symbiote I kept waiting for Eddie Brock to reclaim it, but now that Flash has it I never want to see anyone BUT Flash be Venom.

You guys have not let up and that's why I can't wait for what's coming up for the end of the year and beyond. As NYC citizens know well, 2013 is a mayoral election year, so I'm eager to see how this plays out within the pages for everyone's favorite skinflint JJJ. (I personally am holding out for the long awaited return of my favorite new Spidey villain: Paper Doll. What's taking so long, Dan!?)

So here's to the first Fifty years of Spidey and — with any luck — Fifty more! You guys at Spidey Sentral keep making 'em, and I'll keep reading 'em!

Taimur Dar
a.k.a. Your Friendly Neighborhood Spidey616

And here's to fans like you, Taimur. Thank you for your almost daily support of the book. We appreciate all the terrific fans out there across the world and across the internet.

Whether people love what we're doing or loathe it with the white hot intensity of Brevoort's pastrami filled beard, there's no doubting or denying the intense passion Spidey brings out in otherwise well-mannered people.

On behalf of Dan, Humberto, Victor, Edgar, Chris, Manny, Stefano, Cammo, Klaus, Frankie, Brennan, Ellie, Brevoort, Axel, Joe Q., and the rest of the folks here in Spidey-land...I can honestly say we love ya all (but not in THAT way!)

And with that, I think we're done. It's back to regular business next issue with part two of our Alpha story and the continuing drama that is going to build all around Spidey culminating in the sure-to-be-disastrous ASM #700 in December.

Fifty years in ... and we're goin' out with a bang!

Viva Flo!
Simperin' Steve